To: Ric

Best Wishes

Jack McCoy

9-20-14

A Tugboat Sailor:

The Life and Times of Billy Jack McCoy

In the Forgotten War

JACK McCOY 3129 MAIL

Contents

Acknowledgements

Joyce Gibson Roach

I wish to acknowledge Joyce Gibson Roach, my *sister*, longtime family friend, and native Texan, who hails from my same home town, Cleburne, Texas, and Texas Christian University. Without her encouragement, patience, her leading and her pushing me with these words, “Jack, you can do better than that,” this book would never have been written. Joyce’s love of the West, her country, and firsthand experience with the 1930’s and WWII aided greatly in the telling of ‘my story’. I have tried to write in a readable and interesting manner - the period of history so few have experienced. I cannot say enough about Joyce and our friendship all these years. As they say, ‘We are family.’ I encourage the reader to go to www.joycegibsonroach.com for a journey and a taste of the Old West.

Andria Bicknell

I also wish to acknowledge Andria Bicknell for the considerable contributions she has made this year toward the editing and publication of this book. Andria is a talented writer and blogger living in Burleson, Texas. She can be found online at:

Website: www.typeAplansB.com
Facebook: Type A Plans B
Twitter: @typeAplansB

Stephanie Wetzel

I would like to thank Stephanie Wetzel, editor with Story Gurus and social media representative for John C. Maxwell, for the comprehensive editing and proofreading that she provided.

Nancy Pendleton

I also wish to thank Nancy Pendleton, president of Woodwind Press, for the invaluable publishing and editing services she provided.

Dedication

A Tugboat Sailor: is dedicated to…

> all those who served on the *Tawakoni* and other tugboats and ships of the Auxiliary Fleet, including minesweepers, rescue and salvage vessels—the unsung sailors of the many auxiliary ships of the Forgotten War;
>
> my brother Dewey, Coxswain aboard LST-474, during World War II, that made numerous landings of troops and equipment on the beaches of the Philippines while under air attack by Japanese Kamikaze aircraft late in the war.

Jack's notes: After the war he had no desire ever to return to Korea. He crossed under the Golden Gate Bridge and left it all behind, or so he thought. In 1983, however, the Korean Government sponsored a revisit program for Korean Veterans. This was an opportunity for Jack and Margie to go to Hong Kong because they had always wanted to go. Korea would be a stopping off place before going to Hong Kong. While in the hotel he met people there who bowed to show respect and say, **"Thank you for my freedom."** All tours and banquets held for the Veterans and seeing the development – Korea *re-born* with a democratic constitutional government – brought a kind of closure; an end had been brought to that part of his life.

Forward

The journey is the oldest literary device known to mankind—from the Odyssey to Cormac McCarthy's The Road. But without laboring the point, Billy Jack McCoy's *The Life and Times of a Tugboat Sailor in the Forgotten War* is the story of a journey—a trip away from the place of his roots and a voyage to another world—worlds, really—geographic, socio-economic, political, and military, even philosophic.

The narrative is one of an innocent, naïve young man with an all but rural background who leaves home to join the Navy because his brother served in World War II, making it sound like a grand adventure —"You can do three years standing on your head." Billy Jack missed the grandeur of World War II and knows that the Navy will change him for the better. And change him, it does. His shipboard life isn't, however, the storybook fantasy he imagined. In fact, it turns out this seafaring life puts him below *Mister Roberts*. While Roberts doesn't get to see any action in World War II and he engages in following ridiculous orders from an idiotic commander, at least he serves aboard one of the Big Ships. Billy Jack doesn't even get close—he serves as storekeeper on what amounts to a tugboat, although it is an ocean tug—but he turns his disappointment into something positive, learning new skills of manipulating and maneuvering the system in order to secure all the best for his crew even if a tugboat gets the short end of every stick. His story is filled with some typical but also atypical stories of enlisting, boot camp, days at sea, shore leave and faraway places with strange sounding names, and strange people. He occasionally gets to carry a sidearm weapon.

But when his discharge is rescinded just at the end of his term and he is sent to Korea when an epic police action begins—it was never called a war—his story becomes more than a rite of passage. He is called on to use the skills and knowledge of both the sea and ships when his vessel, the Tawakoni, is called into action to move supplies, perform minesweeping operations, tow other essential craft, and patrol harbors as a support vessel armed with guns inadequate for their own protection. And the Tawakoni is fully engaged in the evacuation of Hungnam, known as the Korean Dunkirk. Death, destruction, and human suffering play descant to his indoctrination into manhood. As any military man can testify, the rites of passage are different when you are on the battlefield, land or sea. Ask any veteran; ask any man serving in Iraq right now.

Seaman McCoy might have been content to tell good stories, some simple and straightforward, some fraught with terror, but he falls early under the spell of the Korean people, their history, their hardships under Japanese occupation, their value as human beings. And he interlaces his narrative with that information. Untold is the revelation, an epiphany that links his later life with Asia where he has become a force for good. But that, as he says, is another story.

Often self-effacing about his own shortcomings and humorous about his personal naiveté, a reader can only notice that, like Cyrano who stood not high but alone, Billy Jack McCoy is man for all the seasons of the sea and of life. He is *the real McCoy*.

Joyce Gibson Roach

Personal Endorsement:

"Mr. Jack McCoy is a great example of what is good about America and the people of America. He has many years of being a great representative of America to international college students in Oklahoma City, OK. I met Mr. McCoy when I was a graduate student at Oklahoma City University in 1998. He was a great friend, teacher, mentor, and feeder of US culture for all of students from other countries. Whenever international students need help, he was the one to be there for them.

He tried not only to teach practical English, Bible, and American culture, but also to learn foreign cultures and languages to show respect to those students. He had served in the US Navy during the Korean War. He has visited Asia multiple times including South Korea, Taiwan, Hong Kong, and China. To acknowledge and honor Mr. McCoy, The Lint Center established "Jack McCoy Scholarship" to spotlight and transmit his personal diplomacy.

While I have been reading his book, I am amazed by his deep knowledge and research effort to depict the situation in a rigorous manner. His book starts from his personal background and experience, and then moves to the area study of Korea including history, society, and geographic details. I personally praise him for his great work and good heart. Thank you, Jack, I am so fortunate to have met you in 1998!"

Anna Hyonjoo Lint, Ph.D.

Introduction

The Korean War is known as the Forgotten War, and much has now been written to ameliorate what was a national shame. There was also a forgotten Navy, or at least a part of it, identified as the Auxiliary Fleet, representing service ships to the largest ships of the line such as battleships, cruisers, and destroyers – the front line of attack ships. Supply vessels carrying food, clothing, water, and other items needed to sustain daily needs of those both at sea and on shore, fuel and ammunition, rescue, repair, the hospital ships, minesweepers, and the tugboats were among the Auxiliary Fleet. Other than hospital ships, little is known about these armed and trained ships ready to protect and defend our Country.

While Auxiliary Fleets were perhaps overlooked in all major US wars, it is about their role in the Korean War that this book is written. Just as important are the men who served aboard such vessels. But the most important personal consideration is that I was aboard a tugboat, a fleet tug that could tow anything that would float anywhere in the world. Later I had duty on a general stores supply ship. These two tours of duty were during the most critical times of the war. The North Korean port of Hungnam was evacuated on Christmas Day of 1950, and is known but not officially as the Second Dunkirk.

How I came to be there in the first place had not so much to do with the idea of defending my country or patriotic stirrings of any kind at first, but partaking of the slogan, **Join The Navy And See The World**. I joined the Navy in 1948 after my brother, Dewey, who had just returned from World War II, told me there was *nothing to it.* I failed to recognize the grin on his face and not seeing through his deception that belied the terrible circumstances of his service. He later apologized for his flippant advice.

I have written a first hand story to provide the reader a detailed picture of shipboard life—experiencing carefree Navy liberty ashore, the unpredictable sea, duties and dangers in the Pacific, and the making of a sailor from boot camp to sea duty, from peace time to war time, still to this day defined and remembered as a Police Action resulting in a cease-fire agreement, never a victory.

In 1948 after boot camp and Storekeepers' School, I went aboard the USS Tawakoni, ATF-114, at Pearl Harbor June 3, 1949. After about eighteen months of roaming the Pacific, my ship was sent to Korea to join the Korean Conflict, as it was known. Two weeks later we began mine sweeping operations in North and South Korea on both sides of the peninsula. Minesweeping and buoy laying is serious and dangerous business; we were the first in to clear the channels, making the way safe for supply ships and a firing line for heavily armed ships. We had no Destroyer or Destroyer Escort cover at first while the big ships lay off in deep water awaiting our completion of mine eradication.

From island to island, from port to port, there are descriptions with enough emotion and personal revelation to encourage the reader to see through my eyes Navy life both at peace and at war. By the end of November 1950, the Red Chinese entered the fray and War *with a capital W* was on. The same operations became more intense and terrifying with the added burden of extreme cold and rough seas above the 38th Parallel where necessary to expand our operations.

During the same time, the Tawakoni was continually called upon for salvage and rescue, at times under harrowing conditions. Many tugs working close ashore had to return fire when fired upon. My ship experienced shelling, but fortunately the shore batteries' range and accuracy was not that good. Our guns were often used to sink floating mines—still risky business.

It was not until some years later that I was able to go beyond the experience itself at the time it happened—life in the Navy, skills gained, experiences on land and at sea - and go beyond a life in wartime. For me, there was a need to fit the experience into a larger context: Korean history including legend and lore; the effort to conquer or open ports by Europeans and force unfavorable treaties; unfavorable relationships between Japan and Korea, and the later annexation by Japan; productive political intercourse with the United States dating back to the late 1800s; the rise and spread of Communism and the destruction of the nation's infrastructure; the aftermath of the War and restoration, which gave a democratic voice to a once devastated country; with a world view that now recognizes South Korea's place of influence in Asia and the world.

This book marked closure for me, as one might expect, but there is more—an epiphany of sorts. In 1983, I went back to Korea and began a different journey into the Land of Golden Embroidery that continues to this day. But that is another story.

Chapter 1

All Aboard

"You can do three years standing on your head." — the words ignited the embers of adventure in my heart when my brother Dewey spoke them to me. Older and an ex-Navy World War II veteran, he had served aboard LST 474 fighting the Japs and as coxswain on LCI (Landing Craft Infantry) landing troops and equipment for the Australian Construction Battalion Engineers and soldiers of the American 163rd and 156th Regimental Combat Teams at Aitape/Hollandia (Jayapura) and Wewak, Papua, (Northeast) New Guinea. He was awarded the *Presidential Unit Citation* for his efforts. The war had ended in 1945, too soon for me, with the explosion of the Atomic Bomb on Hiroshima and Nagasaki. It had passed me by. I was sixteen at the end of the war, too young to enlist, and felt left out. Not that I did not know how devastating war was, because I had experienced the loneliness of families with a *Blue Star Banner*, known as the *WW II Service Flag—Son in Service Flag*—and witnessed the grief and sorrow of neighbor families, who displayed the *Gold Star Banner* in their front window - for a son or daughter who had paid the ultimate price for our freedom. The Blue Star represented hope and pride; the gold, sacrifice. It was not until 1966 that the Department of Defense revised the specifications for design, manufacture, and display of the Service Flag. Any family with a loved one in service can display either of the two flags.

But I wasn't thinking about service or sacrifice after World War II. I was naive and ready to leave my depressed town and go aboard a gleaming *Man o' War*, a U.S. Navy ship of the line to serve in the peacetime Navy. Surely there would not be another war. Years of doing without would be put behind me, replaced by sea adventures, sailing the wide ocean, and visiting mystical and foreign lands. I could return home with interesting tales to tell - tales of faraway places with strange sounding names.

From the year I was born, in 1929—the year of the Great Depression, the crash of the stock market, bank failures, and the recession of 1937-1938, our family could have been called poor folks, I guess. Only at Christmas did we have fruit—an apple or an orange—a few nuts, and usually a red and white striped stick of sugar candy. There was always one main toy, maybe a cap pistol with a few rolls of caps. The Christmas tree was one we had cut from some man's cow pasture along the side of a dirt road. My dad did see that we had a few fireworks—the popular Roman candle and the loud-stubby Baby Giant firecracker. The powerful little firecracker entertained me and friends by blowing up tin cans, once a pop bottle unwisely, or other objects our imagination took us to. The one toy I remember best was a wind-up tank with rubber tracks that was a good climber. Later I would receive a Daisy air rifle, and when times were better, a red American Flyer wagon. An ulterior motive may have come with the wagon because I had to use it to haul firewood.

Only our garden, two milk cows, two pigs that would become hogs by fall, and a mixed flock of chickens of unknown progenitors supported my dad's meager earnings. He worked hard, long hours in the round house of the Santa Fe Railroad as a machinist keeping the locomotives and trains rolling for the war effort. I suppose we were better off than most city folk though, because we did have butter, fresh raw milk, fresh eggs, ham, bacon, and sausage. The garden provided us with a few fresh table vegetables in the spring and for canning in early summer. The dried lima butter beans and black-eyed peas were gathered, winnowed, and stored in a dry place for winter. The old folk had the superstitious custom - and it is still prevalent today in Texas, Oklahoma, Arkansas, and down south - of eating black-eyed peas on New Years Day for good luck. A new pea crop would be coming off soon, and this was just a way to get rid of the old peas. And too, if kept too long, the peas would get weevils and have to be fed to the hogs. We had a few knobby peach trees and wild pear trees that produced fruit for canning. Wild grapes were down by the creek, and wild berries were found in the ditches alongside the road. The grapes were called *Mustangs,* and I learned their acidity would quickly blister my mouth, but they did make great jelly. Watermelons were always plentiful, and as kids we could usually find a ripe one in some farmer's field. Hard shell and soft shell pecans were plentiful along the creeks and rivers. And there was my favorite – the fig tree. We had a kind of rural farm life, but in many instances so did everybody else. I'm not claiming my life was any different, either better or worse than anyone else's. It was just the way things were. My mother was the quintessential female figure of the times—making do, getting by with what we had or didn't, bowing to the authority of her husband and looking after a family of six children. Her cooking is what I remember most, especially breakfast—dozens of biscuits made from scratch complete with lard for shortening, eggs, bacon, preserves and jams—the works!

There were several of us: Mother – Malda Josephine Cashion McCoy; Father – William Joseph McCoy; Sisters – Dora Mae, Opal Elizabeth and Esther Varnell; Brothers – Everett Jefferson and Dewey Wayland. I was the youngest. All the others had found their places in life, for better or worse, by the time I was out of high school. They had jobs, were married, were well on their way to wherever they were bound. I was left behind and had to endure five years of fussing, quarreling, embarrassment and uncertainty in a house where the father was an alcoholic. By all reasons I too should have been an alcoholic because Falstaff, Southern Select, Pabst Blue Ribbon beer and Four Roses Whiskey was plentiful. My Dad was a very hard worker, a big man of Irish temperament, physical strength and honest character, but weak emotionally because of his selfishness to drink. What a waste. He was very intelligent, personable, likeable and with business acumen. Four years later I reluctantly came home from the Navy with a degree of apprehension. I shouldn't have. He had given up drink and even gone back to church, but with much remorse.

Youth overlooks important facts. The grass is "greener on the other side," and is oblivious to the demands of leaving its roots. That was my attitude and ignorance of wanting to leave not only the family but Cleburne, Texas, a small conservative railroad town we made fun of: Cleburne has two streets – Main and Plum; if you get off of Main, you're "Plum out of town." Or, "this might not be nowhere, but you can see it from here." My desire was just to go anywhere!

I should have known there was more to my town than being small, clean, religious, conservative, patriotic, and friendly, because there were markers a few miles west of town on Highway 67 denoting the Chisholm Trail crossing on the Nolan River, identifying Cleburne as a post for cattle drive provisions. Because of the Indian activity, the Army had established Camp Henderson that became a permanent settlement in 1867. Markers about Indians and Indian raids were strategically located in the county.

A statue of an imposing figure of the Confederate Army that fought in the Civil War is a permanent fixture on the southeast corner of the Court House Square. The honorable town of Cleburne was named after **General Patrick (Pat) Ronayne Cleburne.** He died with a single bullet to the heart, not more than fifty-yards from Union lines at the *Battle of Franklin.* When asked about death one day, he replied, ***"Life has always been a small matter with me when duty points the way."*** His charge at Franklin was larger than Pickett's famous charge at Gettysburg. He was known as the *Stonewall Jackson of the West.* Confederate President Jefferson Davis said in regard to his ability and leadership, he was equal to the South's General Robert E. Lee. His sword, belt, engraved belt buckle with the state seal of Arkansas, and cash were sent upon his death to his fiancée, Sue Tarleton of Mobile, Alabama. Men who had served under General Cleburne named the town in his honor. The town has a good location for a small town, then and now—fifty-five miles southwest of Dallas, or twenty-eight miles south of Ft. Worth. So what? I still wanted to leave.

The *Chisholm Trail* should have been named: ***The McCoy Trail,*** after Joseph G. McCoy, who trailed the first longhorn cattle north, and established the Stockyards and the McCoy Land and Cattle Company at Abilene, Kansas. It was McCoy's idea of trailing cattle from Texas to the railhead that would take the cattle to eastern markets. A marker in his honor is located on East Johnson Street, one and one half miles from downtown Denison, Texas. There is a McCoy Avenue in Cleburne, *three blocks long* located just off North Anglin Street going north. But in spite of the fact that the place reeked of my last name, although no mite of connection, I wanted to leave... Family, local history, good location did not matter – get me out of there!

I knew there was something better than dragging Main and Henderson Streets of Cleburne until they were rolled up at eight o'clock for the night, or circling the County Court House until you became dizzy, and closing down the only two drive-ins in town. I had been working at Sears part time under the DECA program and was now working full time at what I thought was a dead-end job. Too, I did not like getting shocked all the time putting up and taking down light fixtures from the overhead light display. Besides, I could get my job back after I got out of the service if I wanted it.

I began asking around and recruited three unlikely buddies to join up with me. There was the tall, good looking Oscar, who was the oldest and a meat cutter at Bill Gray's grocery store over on the East side of town. He had served a hitch in the U.S. Army and now would enlist in the United States Navy as a cook. He looked slim and handsome in his Navy Dress Blue Uniform.

Oscar's previous military service exempted him from Boot Camp, except for the mandatory shots and the tailoring of uniforms. He was assigned permanent duty on an aircraft carrier, and visited ports in Europe, especially Italy. I did not know it at the time of his enlistment, but ***he walked in his sleep!*** He could have walked off the deck on a pitch-black night, never been missed for hours, lost at sea and never found.

Raymond was rather short,and pudgy, a real *mama's boy.* But he was adventurous, I thought, because he rode his motorcycle recklessly, really fast - even at night. He had hit a stray pig early one morning while delivering newspapers and was thrown over a barbed wire fence into a cow pasture. He was unconscious for a few hours and in recovery for a day or two. Now he was breaking his mother's heart on this cold, *hoar-frosty* early November morning. He was to become an airman - an ***airdale*** on a naval airbase some place in Arizona.

Dwayne was to have enlisted with us, but family matters precluded his doing so. He was later drafted into the Army and served time in Germany watching the Russians during the cold war. He was very tall, maybe too tall for the small hatches and low overheads of a ship. His temperament was not that of a sailor either.

The doors of the blue and white **Central Texas Bus** opened. My Dad was a great hand shaker, but this morning it felt strange shaking his big firm hand. Oscar and his Dad were saying a few indistinguishable last words. I never noticed whether they shook hands or not. Maybe not...his Dad was *cold*, never close to his children. Both parents smiled and told each of us to be careful and that they would see us on our first leave after boot camp. I believed they were proud of us but did not let it show.

Raymond was last to get on because he had to hug all his kin, and his family had to hug him. Oscar and I were afraid he would be delayed and get left behind. His *Navy caree*r lasted one year and four months. He got out on a *hardship* discharge. I never saw him or spoke to him ever again. His family had money!

The sloped-backed late 40's model GMC bus roared away from the curb, and ***we were free,*** heading to the way beyond. The sun was coming up over Dallas. We could just make out the skyline, and see the silhouettes of the tall skyscrapers. The buildings glistened, cast long shadows and changed color as the sun rose higher and brighter. It wasn't Cleburne, and it looked good.

The Southern Pacific Railway locomotive was waiting to take our group of enlistees to Los Angeles. Then a bus would bring us to the receiving station in San Diego, California.

I was completely unaware of the many changes, the hard lessons, the dangers at sea, the Korean War, and President Truman extending my service in the Far East for another year. I was about to find out that someone, somewhere was now pulling the strings of my life and filling in the details of my adventure.

The two long days and one night train ride to California were uneventful, except for my nervous expectation of Navy life, and the one hard lesson—***don't gamble***. Blackjack, the game of twenty-one, began as the silver and orange Southern Pacific streamliner pulled out of the train yard. In quick succession, almost immediately, new decks of playing cards flashed into view. My interest and curiosity grew as the seasoned and unseasoned players grouped together, and the quick, sharp, sound of card shuffling, anteing, and dealing began.

The voices of winners resonated through the passenger car; voices higher, louder, and more boisterous as the game became hotter. I was a beginner, and it was my inclination to just watch and observe the spectacle and maybe learn a little of this man's game. I could see some were winning and some losing, some getting in, some getting out. After one day, I began to wonder why there were more out than in. It was about this same time that I was invited to try my hand at lady luck.

With much encouragement and exuberant instruction as to when to hold and when to fold, I felt confident - ready to play. I could wager a few dollars at least, maybe win a few. After all I was good at *Forty-two, Whist, and Hearts*.

How exciting it was to say, ***I'll stay, Hit me,*** **or** ***Hit me again***. I hardly noticed I was ***taking a beating*****!** I was down to only eleven dollars. Suddenly I felt a jolt, a sinking feeling, an acute awareness that I was an amateur and that I had better take my losses and never play poker again. And I never did. This Cleburne boy was a quick learner.

We alighted from the train in Los Angeles and boarded the awaiting bus that would take us to San Diego. Necks strained at all the windows, even the rear window, to see the many tall buildings and great city sights. One thing I saw, even took a picture of, was the *McCoy Hotel*. I pondered and mused upon my early childhood, the dust bowl, and how Tex, Arkie and Okie made the journey west, only to find hardship and menial labor. I grinned approvingly, knowing the five-story hotel surely belonged to one of my distant relatives who had made good.

For the first time in my life, I was to see the coastline of California and the blue waters of the Pacific Ocean. I wondered if the explorers, Lewis and Clark, were as awe-struck by the beauty, and vastness of this – the largest body of water in the world—the unfathomable, untamable Pacific.

Our group of enlistees struggled stiffly from the bus to a position directly in front of a long wooden building that was open on both ends. There a large sign with four square knots, one in each corner which read:

WELCOME ABOARD

You are now men of the UNITED STATES NAVY.

The tradition of the service demands your utmost effort. Give it cheerfully and willingly.

Coarsely and loudly were we instructed to form a straight line for instruction, and indoctrination into the United States Navy.

We straggled into a large room and were divested of our civvies and cosmetics, even my favorite *Yardley Cologne* that was my very best graduation present. With quick dispatch, we were issued a complete set of *Navy dress blues and undress blues, hats, dungarees, leggings, two pairs of shoes, underwear, socks, belt, P coat and a ditty bag, complete with sewing kit and razor.* We lugged our heavy sea bag across the grinder to well-kept Spanish-styled barracks in Camp Decatur, named after our famous Admiral, Stephen Decatur.

He was captain of the *Enterprise* during the Barbary Wars and is quoted as saying to a hot-headed Spanish official who attempted to see his papers before being allowed ashore at Barcelona, ***"Inform him that Lieutenant Decatur pronounces him a cowardly scoundrel, and if we meet ashore I will cut his ears off."*** Record has it the Spaniard preferred to keep his ears.

Stephen Decatur was felled in a duel with Commodore James Barron, captain of the Chesapeake, one misty morning in 1820. Code and tradition mandated their differences be settled in this fashion, but the death of Admiral Decatur ended dueling in the Navy. I was ready for *full speed ahead,* or so I thought.

"The Sailor's Creed"

I am a United States Sailor.
I will support and defend the Constitution of the United States of America,
And I will obey the orders of those appointed over me.
I represent the fighting spirit of the Navy and all who have gone before me to
Defend freedom and democracy around the world.
I proudly serve my country's Navy combat team with honor, courage and commitment.
I am committed to excellence and the fair treatment of all.

Chapter 2

Boot Camp

There was much confusion and squabbling over who would select and claim an upper, lower, or middle bunk. An important decision had to be made whether to choose an upper bunk with a degree of privacy, the lower bunk that everyone stepped on but you could just roll into, or the middle bunk that was most convenient for everyone to lay things on.

The more assertive decided quickly which they thought was the best bunk; the fainthearted, and those who procrastinated took whatever was left. There continued to be grumbling, but in no time with intimidation, discipline, and exhaustion of daily routine Company #533 shaped-up and came to respect the sanctity of another recruit's bunk and personal belongings.

Each bunk had a long, narrow and not too thick mattress that was known as the *sack.* The mattress cover was actually a sack in which the mattress was fed into, as you would a pillow into a pillowcase. At the open end were a flap and three or four ties that folded over which were tied in a bowknot fashion. The mattress was flipped over with tie side down and placed upon wire mesh springs that were attached to and supported by a steel frame. Often times this arrangement was affectionately referred to as the ***fort sack!***

This was the beginning of and my first introduction into the world of Navy slang, jargon and terminology. One of the fanciest descriptive words the Navy used for classification or designation was the word, *nomenclature.*

In the small town I came from we didn't have any nor did we need any nomenclature. But I was to learn this was a whole different world, where a stair was *a ladder*, a wall *a bulkhead*, a ceiling *an overhead*, a floor *a deck*, the front *the bow* or *fo'c's'le, (foc's' le)*, the back *the aft* or *stern*, the left *the port*, the right *the starboard.* The bathroom was *the head*, and underwear were *skivvies.* Quartermasters were known as *skivvy wavers*, so designated because of their use of semaphore flags when signaling other ships.

The cook was naturally *Cookie*; boatswain mates *bosun's*, and the deck force was either *Deck Hands, Deck Apes* or *Swab Jockeys*; enginemen were *Firemen*, or *Snipes*, and occasionally *Bilge Rats*; electricians went by the name *Sparky*; a gunner's mate was *Gunner*; storekeepers were *Stores*; and the ship's captain was always the *Skipper* or *Old Man.*

Sailors in general have been referred to as *Jack-tars, bluejackets, swabbys, gobs* or *mariners.* And many unfamiliar words like *gunwale, scupper, scullery, lanyard, hawser, cleat, and bollard, windward, leeward; coxswain (cox'n – originally cocksu'n), landlubber, pollywog* or *shell-back* easily became part of Navy life. Even that word, *nomenclature*, fit in with this new vocabulary and was necessary to keep the ship afloat and the crew fed. I felt better educated learning all the new words—words I would never have learned in Cleburne.

Very early the sound of a scratchy needle on a well-worn record, then a loud clear sound of a bugle blasting reveille, was heard. Lights came on ever so bright. We were abruptly wakened by a husky voice and the jar of a nightstick whacking our metal bunks. Little time was wasted in hitting the deck, brushing the teeth, shaving, and falling in for inspection. The rest of the day was consumed with marching—marching, marching, marching – marching for hygiene movies, marching for knot-tying, marching to shoot, marching for fire fighting, marching and trudging on the grinder until the high topped shoes were frayed and the once thick soles worn thin. The *grinder* incidentally was the parade ground.

Learning to march, I realized, was very necessary and was not that hard for me. Actually it was fun. I was the shortest, always the last one in the platoon. When we had a dress parade or competition, I marched most erect in time to the music with pride for my country, for my Company #533, and for myself. Other times I straggled behind until we neared the *gedunk*, (pronounced gee-DUNK) stand, the leatherneck/sailor snack bar, and fell out prematurely to have an ice cream, candy, snack food—pogie bait. (*Pogies* are also bait fish, or inexperienced sailors.) The rest of the company would have to march another ten minutes to the barracks, be dismissed, and then retrace their steps to where I sat enjoying my refreshments. I relished my accomplishment of never getting caught.

Ever since I had enlisted and sworn in with my right hand raised, there was in the back of my mind the ever present thought of the forthcoming Navy physical. This I knew was the most dreaded, embarrassing, humiliating, and often the painful part of Boot Camp.

We were divested of all our clothes where we waited in a line of fifty or sixty stark naked men, all waiting to be checked by the doctors. This is the first time I was to become aware of the term, *short arm inspection,* and I came to know that it was required at various times throughout Navy life.

Next was the blood sample collection and inoculation station. A counter about shoulder high was where you laid your arm for drawing vials of blood. The counter was messy with spilled and strung blood. Full vials filled the accumulation racks. It was hard to make yourself put your arm upon the bloody counter and not know if your blood might be mingled with some other unfortunate's.

With quick dispatch and little compassion the job was done. I was now to step into a line of corpsmen, which we were told gave shots in the ***left testicle with a square needle!*** The needles used back in the late 1940's and early 50's were much larger, and sometimes would bend or break off in an arm muscle. Used needles were often pitched into aluminum like dish pans – dulled even more. I never knew if they were ever sharpened. Nevertheless as you stepped through the door, one corpsman needled you on one side, and two shots were given in the other arm. Last was the smallpox vaccination, which I had never taken before. The place festered, turned red, and formed a kernel in my left armpit. The scabbed sore gave me a low-grade fever and much misery for several days.

I knew some men would pass out and I was afraid I might succumb to the shock of the injections and sight of blood. In front of me was a big, tall sailor who I thought would surely not faint. But no, as I turned I saw him fall onto a waiting couch, placed there for that very purpose. I left him in care of a corpsman, not knowing his outcome. I was proud of myself that day, but I too would later experience the humiliation of fainting.

It was one early morning in Japan, after a night on the town, and only coffee for breakfast. I donated a pint of blood needed for our troops wounded in Korea. A slug of Scotch Whiskey was given to every donor instead of orange juice - why, I do not know. But after one large shot of scotch, the last in the bottle, I was on the floor perspiring, looking up at bright lights and white uniforms. I could tell there was great concern.

I later joined my group and was asked, "Who else fainted?" Very sheepishly I had to admit that I too had passed out. And although weak, I had to pull SP *(shore patrol)* duty with a bunch of Marines that very night. I was delighted when a compassionate Marine duty officer gave me easy duty with a fine Marine from Alabama. I never knew that fainting would leave you so weak, exhausted, and fatigued. Scotch was not the best drink for me after giving blood. I never tasted Scotch again.

After the three injections and required Navy physical, we returned to our barracks with anticipation of some rest and recuperation. We should have known there would be another task, and a strange endeavor it was. With arms now becoming sore and stiff, we were shown how to tightly roll our clothes. The task had to be completed by morning. The act of rolling was very exacting and caused me much frustration for the material had to be pulled very tight, edges smoothly aligned, rolled and tied in a square knot with clothes stops. The use of clothes stops was discontinued in 1973. I was stymied by this complexity and swapped my shoe shining abilities with others for their clothes rolling expertise. All these pieces of clothing had to be carefully placed into the sea bag ready for inspection.

The dreaded clothes inspection required every item of rolled clothing to be displayed in an exact and prescribed manner on top of a clean taut bunk. Loosely rolled,or uneven clothes, or those tied with granny knots had to be redone until they passed the next inspection. Woe to the sailor who did not pass and was assigned extra duty. I understand this tradition is no longer part of Navy life. Even so, when I travel I roll my clothes to save space and prevent wrinkles - but not to pass inspection.

After breakfast and in great succession we were marched over to the base barbershop for one of Uncle Sam's free GI, one-style haircuts. I had never had much hair anyway, so to me a burr was no big deal, except the peeled-onion-head-look of a recruit. Several with full, beautiful, wavy-curly heads of hair, vain about their appearance, were reluctant, truly agonizing over the loss of their manly tufts and tresses. Two or three in our company tried to evade the regulation by reporting in with a short hometown haircut they thought might pass inspection. That was not to be. Electric razors hummed. Hair in all shades, colors and textures fell to the floor and had to be continuously swept up.

The look of shock and disbelief was on the face of the more blessed, who had so quickly lost both their hair and coiffeurs. I determined their loss and what was done to them was little short of sacrilegious! We left the barbershop with exposed scalps waiting to see whose hair would grow back the quickest. In addition to sanitization requirements, the burred heads changed personalities which equalized and molded us into Company #533.

Gleaming heads bobbed in the clear California sunlight as we marched over to an Olympic size pool where we were introduced to the Navy swimming test. A required proficiency was the timed ability to swim the length of the pool, tread water, swim under water, float on your back, and hold the breath under water. Fortunately, I had learned to swim on my own in Buffalo Creek with the use of an empty syrup bucket under my chin some years before.

I had great compassion for those who failed, and even more so for those unfortunates that did not know how to swim at all. The sailors who failed had to drag their tired bodies over to the pool every night after chow for special instruction until they passed. They had to endure no-nonsense instructors who were equipped with long poles they used for encouragement and to rescue the perishing. Those who had passed, when entering the barracks, were given a hearty applause and numerous pats on the back.

We were given extensive instruction and drill on how to safely put on and use the Mae West lifejacket, especially jumping from great heights. Later I learned these canvas-covered, cumbersome kapok keepers of life were tested and found to fill with water. They were later replaced with the compressed-air-filled life preserver, like those in use today on airplanes.

The thick kapok collar and its steel saved one sailor's life. I was second loader on a 3"50 gun that fired prematurely during a training exercise aboard ship. The sudden recoil knocked the number one loader flat on the deck and he lay unconscious for several minutes. We thought he was dead. The helmet saved his head from a fatal concussion, while the oval kapok collar saved him from sustaining a broken neck. He recovered, sore but okay. The gun had an electrical short and continued to have problems which proved to be dangerous. I requested a transfer and was made gunner after being loader on the starboard twin 20mm's, a position I held while in Korea.

The first laundry day in Boot Camp was a day of consternation, uncertainty, and dismay to recruits learning to properly wash their clothes, pillows cases and mattress covers. Each batch had to be hung a certain way, facing a certain way, and tied with only square knots. The system was quite efficient in that the clothes were soaked, soaped, and scrubbed with a stiff bristled KiYi brush.

The white hatband on the hat had to be scrubbed, preferably with a toothbrush to be completely white. The hat was rolled and held tightly, then pressed to the lips and blown hard into. All the soapsuds had to be expelled, else the hat would dry with an ugly dingy yellow tinge.

All the rinsed laundry was hung on lines that were lowered, but not so low as to drag on the concrete. As more clothes and more weight were added, the lines had to be pulled higher and tighter, until all the washing was enjoying the California air and sunshine. The reverse was true when taking the laundry down. The lines were gently lowered a little at a time until all the clean fresh smelling clothes were removed and stowed away.

No clothes or personal belongings were ever left strewn around or left lying on the bunk. *Ship shape* was always the word—a place for everything and everything in its place. I had heard it said that mothers told their daughters to marry a sailor man because they made the best husbands—they were neat and clean and good housekeepers. This thinking might be truer for those who served during the forties and fifties—WWII and the Korean War. I can only speak of sailors of yesteryear and not for the seamen of today. I understand clothes are no longer rolled, laundry is commercially washed, and the uniforms have been modified to have side and back pockets, as well as many other changes.

Navy dress uniforms of my era had no bulges and only two pockets, one in the waistband to hold a small black Navy issue billfold, and a jumper pocket to hold a comb, handkerchief, maybe a pack of cigarettes, matches, or lighter. Some carried their cigarettes in their right inside sock and their handkerchief across the shoulder hidden underneath the jumper.

Every morning after bunks were made and we had all shaved, whether we needed to or not, an order was given for us to muster for a cleaning detail. The entire parade ground/grinder had to be police-swept clean; all debris had to be picked up and placed in trash receptacles strategically located. I quickly realized picking up *butts* was much easier than man-handling a heavy straw broom the length of the marching field.

We were ordered to fall in again and readily marched over to the mess hall - a sparkling clean building, where men in whites or in clean dungarees were waiting to serve us a variety of wholesome food and drink, including my favorite—hot oatmeal with cream and raisins. For many who came off the farm or from families of meager means, this was the first real meal they had ever had. Some had found a home. Three times a day we were fed a sumptuous fare of excess calories, necessary for strenuous basic training. The feeding was by company rotation. The first company fed one day would be the last fed the next day.

My buddy and I decided we would like to be fed first every day. We would fall in with the first or near the first company being fed, until our success came to an abrupt halt. One day we were spotted and taken to the Officer-of-the-Day where we were given a royal chewing out and made to stand at parade rest until the very last sailor in the very last company was fed.

I do not remember how long we stood, but the sun had set and it was getting quite dark. We were admonished once again and set free to go eat cold leftovers. We regretted our misfortune of getting caught, but relished the thought that our punishment was not too severe. And we found solace in remembering the good times and good food, until that one fateful day.

The winter nights in California, especially in San Diego, were cold – the mornings chilly, with warm days. The late mornings and early afternoons from 10:00am to 4:00pm were mild and pleasant, actually shirtsleeve weather. This fluctuation of temperatures and the putting on and taking off of the wool turtleneck sweater caused an outbreak of cat fever. I too was taken with the fever – influenza like symptoms that caused great weakness, exhaustion, and excessive sweating.

One night while in sickbay, I heard a corpsman roughly command *bottoms up.* This was an order to roll over and pull down the skivvies for an injection of penicillin. The night corpsman's behavior was pitiless, bordering on sadistic. I observed him making this one sailor give another an injection. The effort was pathetic. The needle went in only half way, and swayed back and forth in the buttocks. The job was crudely, even mercilessly finished by the deranged petty officer.

I was on a top bunk across the aisle, still sweating, when sneeringly he asked if I wanted an injection. Even though I knew it would make me well, I said no. A compassionate medical officer – a full Commander, if I recall – checked on me every morning and asked how I was feeling.

A week had passed, and I would miss my company if I was not released the next day. My fever had gone down but not enough. I drank ice water and breathed on the thermometer held between my teeth. The thermometer was looked at then and stuck back in my mouth for another reading. The sly glance and sheepish grin told me the morning corpsman knew! Again I sucked air across the thermometer not allowing too much contact under the tongue, and careful not to get the reading too low this time. The results must have been within range of dismissal for I was allowed to return to the barracks to rest. By morning I was not one hundred percent, but continued basic training and graduated with my original company.

The men of Company #533 had completed all the preliminaries required of recruits, and were excited with the thought they were to be issued rifles. The advanced companies had their rifles and marched smartly, and we wanted to be like them. Our egos fell with great disappointment once we saw our guns were wooden pieces. If you dropped your piece or stacked it and it fell, you were in bad trouble. But off we went with wooden rifles on the right shoulder in close order drill. The drills were not close and without any order.

Our new company commander was a Chief Petty Officer with many four-year service stripes on his sleeve nearly ready to retire. He was a good compassionate man, but his voice was too soft and weak, for us to understand his orders clearly. Only about half of the platoons could hear and quickly react to the commands—*forward march, to the rear march, right/left oblique* or *halt*.

For several days our company was disgruntled with the chaos—wood rifles clacking and all the head knocking. We felt sorry for the Chief and asked him to assign a tall amiable fellow from Ft. Worth, TX to be our leader and cadence caller. He had a good rhythm and a strong voice.

His assignment let us finish basic training with a mark of excellence in marching and deportment. After graduation he was assigned to Naval Air as a photographer. He was killed in a Navy plane crash in waters near Corpus Christi. I had met his parents just prior to our enlistment. They were really proud of him. I felt so very sorry for them. He had a smooth mellow voice, and was always singing the "September Song"—*Oh, it's a long, long while from May to December, but the days grow short when they reach November*. The song haunts me even today.

We did finally get our heavy 9.51 (4.31Kg) – 10.21 (4.63Kg) pound M I' WWII rifle. We were thoroughly instructed in its use and safety, how to load and unload it, and the different firing positions. The company was all excited the day we were scheduled to enter Camp Pendleton Marine Base to fire live rounds. The Marines were gruff and had little patience with us sailors - who referred to them as sea going bellhops because of the red vertical stripe on the outside pant leg of their dress uniform. Another fighting word was *jar head* because of their round-short haircuts and the hard, harsh physical Marine training endured in the 1940's and 1950's.

I was left-handed but fired right-handed like everyone else to save myself any berating or worse. I had considerable early experience with rifles and shotguns, so there was little adjustment, and I made a plausible score. *Maggie's Drawers* were waved for those who fired and missed the target completely. The Marines were sure to eat alive the imbecile for not aiming properly, not holding his rifle steady, or worse - flinching. For us who were pulling targets it was great fun to keep score. A clear miss was acknowledged by waving back and forth a bright tell–tale orange flag of embarrassment.

The Navy issue at the time was the large, very heavy, short ranged .45 caliber pistol. I made a dismal score and never mastered firing this gun with any accuracy. Later I would have to carry the .45 as a side arm on quarterdeck watch. I believe I could have done better by just throwing it at the enemy.

We eagerly left the Marine base thoroughly indoctrinated and instructed in gun safety, handling, care, use, and respect for our piece - whether rifle or pistol. I believe the lesson learned was, *"You are to be one with your gun and handle it with affection, for one day it might save your life."*

Life in boot camp had its tomfoolery, antics, and absurdities, but there were sobering moments. I vividly recall the night a young sailor was acting strange and not wanting to go to bed. Lights were out but he still would not listen to reason, but walked back and forth between the bunks. Later that night near midnight, there was a loud ruckus at one end of the barracks between him and several of his shipmates. He had sliced his wrists. Blood was everywhere, and his bunk mates were trying to restrain him. The Duty Officer was called, and the deranged sailor was taken to the hospital. He was later discharged. I learned he had threatened to cut his wrists earlier that night. All razor blades had supposedly been taken from him. But somehow he managed to get another, or he had one hidden away. We had all tried to help him make it to graduation, but I suppose he was not mentally or maybe physically strong enough. Each of us felt very sorry and sad, yet at ease knowing we had adjusted to the rigorous training and Navy life.

Another tragic end came to the comic recruit in our company named Youts. He had not one care in the world and was always on extra duty, mess duty, or working in the wet scullery. Often he would return to the barracks with pastry he had snatched. One night he brought a whole cooked ham to share with everyone. I was appreciative of his courage – or was it recklessness – to procure the best ham I had ever tasted. The sad part was he contracted athlete's foot while working on the wet concrete floor. He hid his condition until his feet became severely swollen. He was placed in sickbay and later discharged.

But I must say he gave us the idea that we too might go on a midnight raiding party. And we did. One night it was very dark and rainy. Three of us slipped into our ponchos and made our way to the rear bakery entrance. There we found dozens of Danishes cooling on metal trays. With a quick dash in and out we made off with a whole tray full of apple Danish pastry. The barracks came alive with elated recruits enjoying our efforts of pillaged booty. My first midnight requisition! Others were to come.

Company #533 had progressed from burr heads to fuzzy heads and was assigned to the advanced Camp Farragut, named for the famous Admiral who is often quoted as saying, **"Damn the torpedoes, full speed ahead."** We know now the torpedoes he damned were early floating mines.

We were given a few light duty days to adjust to a more normal life of payday, liberty, and leave. With this new freedom we had more leisure and more responsible duties. Overseeing the base movie was one, and it provided a Seaman Apprentice with sweet duty. Each sailor was searched as he entered the movie theater for any candy or chewing gum he might have on him. It was our duty to confiscate these items, and see that the theater was free of paper and trash. There was much arguing, grumbling, and bickering, but that was the price to see the movie. There was an antiroom off to one side where we stored our loot of Hershey Bars, Mars Bars, Butterfingers, and Wrigley Chewing Gum. After we had our fill of chocolate treats, we divided what was left among our company. Our two stripes on the left sleeve gave us our first taste of authority from Seaman Recruit to Seaman Apprentice.

While in Camp Farragut I became lax about wearing my hat on the back of my head. Our company was lined up single file waiting for the evening meal, when the bugle blew at sundown. This was the signal to turn, face the flag, and salute. I turned smartly and was saluting the best I knew how with my hat on the back of my head, when I was taken into the Duty Officer's office. I was out of uniform. My hat was not squared about two inches above the eye, when I saluted. This officer was mad! I had to yes-sir him many times and explain in all sincerity I loved my country and the Navy. His temper finally cooled, but he gave me the best chewing out I was ever to get in the Navy. He dismissed me with the warning there would be no next time. I was nervous and felt wrung out. My face was all flushed, and I don't remember anything about my dinner.

San Diego was our first liberty port, a city of smoky bars, cheap pitchers of beer, loud music, rousing games of shuffle-board, tattoo parlors, and crooked games that enticed the raw recruit with bright flashing lights and shiny gizmos. One game in particular led my buddies and me on our first liberty to parlay our money to win the big prize. The prize was never won. Always just out of reach. We were broke and realized we had been taken. One bold enterprising sailor went over to an approaching policeman and explained our predicament and dilemma. The policeman confronted this gamester of dubious character and threatened to close the game down. The operator grudgingly made restitution for his wrongdoing. We were young inexperienced sailors who were grateful to have our money back - and much wiser as to the many come-ons and greedy games of chance.

Homesickness was a malady that had spread throughout our company during the months of physical endurance and mental toughening. To be homesick is a terrible debilitating feeling, a hurt that regularly comes and goes, an obsessive desire that only loved ones and familiar surroundings can cure. But my case was a disillusioment brought on by the stress of boot camp and waning recollections of home and small town life. I had heart-felt compassion, though, for the ones who pined away for their mothers, family, friends, and the former soft, secure, sheltered life. Some cried. Some appeared melancholy and grieving, and some talked constantly of home, always about their dog. I thought a few recruits were about at the breaking point when word came we would have a ten-day leave with new assignments away from San Diego upon our return. That is except for one unlucky sailor who was assigned permanent duty in San Diego.

The good news of going home and a transfer to a new environment stirred everyone's expectations and caused much talk and excitement. The heavy malady of the heart would soon be cured. But to get this many men paid and booked to so many states, towns and cities on such short a notice was a hassle. After about three days waiting, filling out papers, and paying the transportation fare, everyone had an itinerary of when he would leave: either by bus, train, plane, or a few by car. I arrived home after a very long and tiring bus ride from San Diego to Ft. Worth, where I caught a Central Texas Bus south down to my hometown of Cleburne, a distance of about thirty miles. Family and friends greeted me with remarks like, *"How's Navy life?" " You filled out real good." "Looks like they fed you well."* I had gained about fifteen firm pounds and was ready for my leave to be over after three days, ready for Storekeepers School and a permanent duty assignment.

This was the last time I was to be homesick. Later I was to realize that each ship, port, island, and country became my home. Whatever was at home was over for me. I was on my own: my own person, making my way, leaving behind what I might have been, becoming what I might be someday. My wanderlust heart was ready for ever more adventure and to test the promise, *Join the Navy and see the world.* I had heard another saying said in jest, *I joined the Navy to see the world. What did I see? I saw the sea.* For me this was a true saying because the Navy kept its word, and I saw three and one-half years of constant sea duty.

Upon returning from my boot leave, I was transferred to Storekeeper's School in Oakland, California. These were the longest and most boring nine weeks of my Navy life. Only one prank of revenge was perpetrated on a large unsuspecting obnoxious sailor, a loud mouth loner, who invariably returned after lights-out and 'broke wind,' no matter our protests and disgust.

His bunk was a lone top bunk. He would invariably swing from the top rail between my bunk and his and flop himself heavily upon the lanyard laced canvas. My bunk shook, and his banged and rattled on the floor. This unnecessary noise and his aggravating antics both woke and disturbed my and the others' sleep.

Something had to give, and it did. We decided to loosen the lines to his bunk and the bunk beneath his, leaving only the bottom bunk taught and intact. We all waited, playing we were asleep. He came in and did his usual acrobatic swing, but this time he suddenly found himself falling, piled up on the bottom bunk, scared and agitated, but not hurt. We roused as if awakened and gathered to witness the surprise and to lecture the perpetrator. He cautiously and quietly climbed into bed the civil way. Something had to give. Sleep was sweet that night and the barracks quiet and peaceful until graduation.

I never knew the Navy had so many bureaus, regulations, and manuals, and that every typed original had to have numerous carbon copies. I had enough paper skills and knowledge to take on the biggest ship in the fleet, so I thought.

Three days after graduation in June 1949, I was on a Navy four engine Coronado PB2M Mars flying boat headed for Hawaii, TH—the Territory of Hawaii did not become the 50th state until August 21, 1959. The slow, loud, lumbering seaplane made a safe landing in the waters at Hickham Field Air Force Base on the Island of Oahu. Back then planes were not pressurized, and my ears hurt something awful upon landing. I should have gone to sickbay for depressurization. This was my very first time to fly, and I did not know the seriousness or the possibility of a busted ear drum. I yawned and cupped my hands over my ears to make them pop and relieve the pressure. The pressure was equalized after two days while I was in the receiving station at Pearl Harbor anxiously awaiting my ship and permanent assignment.

Pain and all, Pearl Harbor was anchorage for me for a little while, and I looked forward to returning time and again. No, life now sure wasn't like home, but there was a growing affection for this new life...maybe because it wasn't like home.

Chapter 3

What Type of Boat Is This, Anyway?

The Naval Receiving Station at Pearl Harbor, Hawaii, was clean and airy with spacious bunks and not too many sailors waiting transfer. Those who were in transit were mostly seasoned Petty Officers wearing service hash marks, some wearing a few ribbons. Each hash mark stood for four years of service. I once saw a very old and short sailor with eight hash marks. They covered his arm almost up to the shoulder. I thought to myself, *He better retire soon or grow a longer arm.*

I began to ask around, "Do you know what type of ship is an ATF?" By this time, I knew not to call it a boat—after all I was not a landlubber anymore, and although not a real sailor yet, I had mastered some vocabulary. But no one could tell me what an ATF was. On the second day a Petty Officer of long service said he thought my ship might be an auxiliary, a tugboat. My heart fell. I had been promised upon enlistment, and signed up for duty on, a battleship, cruiser, or destroyer. Now I was to spend over two-and-a-half years at sea on a ship with a funny name that was difficult to pronounce, and a type of ship no one had ever heard of. *They will tell you anything to get you in, and have you to say I do.* These words haunted me.

My ex-Navy brother did give me good advice, which was to become a storekeeper. He had observed that storekeepers were in charge of supply and naturally had access to the food on board. I was to have keys to the galley, bread locker, reefers, storerooms, and twenty-four hour access to midnight rations on the small ship.

I stayed about four days in receiving doing nothing but eating in the finest chow hall in the entire Navy—Pearl Harbor. I kept my chow pass and used it occasionally when I wanted a real meal. There were three kinds of meat, large selections of vegetables, fresh tropical fruit, melon, and always fresh milk - fresh coconut pie was among the many desserts. Every item was good and tasty and well prepared. A large sign read, **"Take all you can eat, eat all you take."** The Commissary Officer prided himself in a well-run mess and that controlled waste. You were careful not to take too much lest you were turned back and had to sit and finish your tray. There was a large picture on the wall of an obese sailor that resembled a fat, paunchy, pot-bellied *sailor dog* with the line, **"Don't be a Chow Hound."**

Transportation arrived and I was instructed to throw my sea bag into the back of the pickup. The time was 1549 hours, June 3rd, 1949. I remember it clearly and will always remember how unceremoniously I was taken down to the dock - Baker 21 – and left standing to locate my ship's gangplank. I saw this rusted hulk hidden among the larger ships and moved closer out of curiosity. I looked aft and saw that many lines, cables, and hoses extended across the deck and down to decks below.

Civilian workers were noisily working on the engines with their wrenches and tools. The deafening clatter of chipping hammers resounded through the shipyard. Paint scrapers and wire brushes were being used everywhere. Every spot of rust, every sign of paint failure was being chipped, scraped, prepared, and coated with a specified protective coating.

About then a cloud of fine dust arose around men in thick-hooded suits as they sandblasted the many barnacles from the ship's bottom. The light moist afternoon breeze whiffled and mingled together the strong pungent and acrid smells of red lead and zinc chromate primers, the odors of special toxic-mercury-laden barnacle preventive primers, and the battleship-gray finish coat.

On the bow, near the rusted anchor and anchor chain was the ship's designation – name, type, and number – **U.S.S. Tawakoni ATF-114.** I realized at once this was my ship. I was very hurt, disappointed, and ashamed even. Later pride would replace disappointment upon learning the ship's condition was attributed to long operation helping evacuate Chiang Kai-Shek and his forces from Tsingtao, China to the Island of Formosa—now Taiwan. My thought was this former rust bucket might be my ticket to the quaint and peaceful Orient/Far East that had for centuries been mysteriously fascinating.

I made my way up the gangplank with my over-stuffed sea bag, looked aft and saluted the flag as I had been instructed to do. With the request to come aboard, I presented my orders to the duty officer. I was taken below by the Master-at-Arms, Flaber, to the cramped crew's compartment and obligatorily assigned to a bunk - a top bunk that was next to the GQ (General Quarters) alarm – the ***clanging klaxon***.

My bunk consisted of a brown piece of grommet-laced canvas secured by a line to a metal frame. No matter how tight the line was pulled the sag could not be removed. I found the sag was useful though in riding out very rough weather. The low center of gravity and the *trice-up* bunk strap secured across the chest gave me confidence to sleep, while preventing me from being rolled or tossed out on deck.

The crew naturally viewed me with suspicion and with some disdain because I was new on board, and they had to share their over-crowded living quarters with a Seaman Apprentice SKSA. I too came to view each new crew member with suspicion, wondering if he would be a troublemaker. The ship was their home, now my home. I understood newcomers were a threat to shipboard routine, ship seaworthiness, crew safety and morale. Though the ship was their home, it was to be my home for the next two and a half years.

My clothes locker, though small, was better than living out of the sea bag. The heavy, bulky P coat was stored in the P Coat Locker. (The Navy has a locker for everything.) Some excess clothing had to be placed in the sea bag stowed in the forward hold. Two items of issue were *deep-sixed*—the leggings from boot camp and the blue flat ribbon-banded felt hat. The flat hat was usually worn on the East Coast during winter. It reminded me of the British Tam' O' Shanter, but without the tassel. The Navy abandoned the flat hat fourteen years later in 1963 but one can still be had at a price of twenty-one dollars.

The ship's office was forward and one deck below the officer's quarters. Many were the times I heard the Executive Officer's feet rattling the ladder leading down to the office to urgently speak with the yeoman. The Executive Officer, Nilson, was a Lieutenant JG (junior grade), who was a stickler for detail and very professional in performing his duties. His uniform and attire were always fresh and crisp with sharp creases, tie in place, polished brass and shined shoes. Everything was spit and polished. He strove for exact-ness and perfection, bothering the yeoman unmercifully with questions, requests, and assignments. I determined he was cold and calculating, and could be dangerous to a sailor's career.

I was wary and kept my distance and did not enter into any of their conversations. I was new aboard and was just finding my way, assessing my position and duties. Lucky or unlucky—lucky for us, unlucky for him—he had an emergency while at Midway, Island requiring him to leave the ship abruptly. Rumor was that his wife was being unfaithful back in Honolulu. Wives could call the port authority and know the time and day a ship was due to arrive back in port. He caught an unexpected flight back, and discovered his wife consorting with an enlisted man. Very shortly thereafter he was reassigned, most likely to a shore station.

He was always prim and proper, a loner with lack of expression or feeling. I could understand his wife's need for comfort and why she would fraternize with an enlisted man. I wonder today if her behavior hurt his career. Even so, I was a little sad for him. Not only for losing his wife, but losing her to an NCO, a non-commissioned officer, a Petty Officer, second class. Even at my early age and beginning career, I surmised that men with wives and children should not be in the Navy, because of the long periods of separation – especially on the auxiliary small ship.

Ship's yeoman was a congenial, obliging, intelligent, first class petty officer, and possessed great typing skills. I remember with gratitude how he helped a mere Seaman Apprentice get settled in and prepare his first batch of requisitions. Knap and I became good friends. His wife prepared a nice lunch for me and another shipmate one weekend in Hawaii.

His main daily duty was to record the vast amount of shipboard happenings contained in the ship's log. The report consisted of an original and several carbon *onion skin* copies for CincPac (Commander-in-Chief, Pacific.) A mistake required time-consuming erasing of the original and each carbon, then retyping in the correct letter. To my chagrin, Knap was soon to be assigned shore duty at CincPac, Hawaii.

I wished him well knowing his new duty station would afford him a deserved advancement.

Presently, I realized I was the sole storekeeper in charge of procurement. All I had learned in Storekeepers School was applied to big ships - small ships used different forms and accounting procedures. I recognized my responsibilities and knew I had to learn - and learn fast. With a handful of requisitions, I made my way over to the supply depot and smartly presented my request, like I knew what I was doing. Soon I was riding back and pulled up along the starboard side with a truckload of food and supplies. Made me proud and gave me a sense of confidence, purpose, and significance.

The call of *all hands not actually on watch lay-up to the quarterdeck to handle stores* was broadcast over the loud speaker. The work detail formed a line and soon had all the stores below decks in lockers, reefers, or behind locked cages. I was amazed at the dexterity with which a crate of apples or oranges was quickly broke open and spilled into eager hands. I next ordered and had on board ample food and supplies, not knowing they would be required for our upcoming trip to Kwajalein and have to last until we reached Guam.

A Seaman's Version of the Twenty-Third Psalm:

The Lord is my pilot, I shall not drift.

He lighteth me across the dark waters;

He steereth me in steep channels;

He keepeth my log book.

He guideth me by the star of Holiness

For his name's sake.

Yes, though I sail mid the thunders and tempests of life,

I will dread no danger, for thou art with me.

Thy love and Thy care, they shelter me.

Thou preparest a harbour before me in the homeland of eternity.

Thou anointed the waves with oil – my ship rideth calmly.

Surely sunlight and starlight shall favor me on the journey I take,

And I will rest in the port of my God for ever.

-Anonymous

My journey began in calm seas that were to turn into dark thunderous waters of great danger in a small but safe ship, a tugboat, the *USS Tawakoni ATF-114* - that could tow anything that floats up to six thousand miles, and to anywhere in the world. That is the kind of ship she was; an Auxiliary Fleet Tug.

Chapter 4

Islands and Atolls

It was only two days later that water filled the dry dock. We were afloat and ready for what I thought would be a sea trial. This Central Texas dry land sailor was ready to test the water, but not quite ready to set sail on the briny. ***But sail, we did!***

We sailed out of Pearl Harbor at 1335 hours towing a YOG (yard oiler). I was to discover, for us, this was a light and easy tow. We passed close by Waikiki Beach and rounded Diamond Head before setting a due course towards the International Dateline and Kwajalein, approximately 3,000 miles distant.

I sat on the gunnel (gunwale-gunwhale) close to the water watching the ship's wake, enjoying Diamond Head, the beautiful Hawaiian coastline and the shore lights as they came on. I was now a sailor off to see the world. My world would first be the Island (atoll) of Kwajalein, which is about 78 miles long, in the Ralik Chain, west Marshall Islands and West Pacific anchorage. Later it would be Guam and Saipan in the Marianas; Micronesia and Yap Island in the Caroline

Islands; Midway, Wake and Johnston Island; Panama; Japan; and North and South Korea. But I did not know that then.

Long, dark, eerie shadows swept over the island of Oahu, and the scenery was becoming indistinct, lost to the sudden darkness of a tropical sunset. I discovered sunset at sea is very quick with a short twilight, followed by ultimate darkness. The ocean seamed to swallow the sun and reluctantly release it, only because it was programmed to. The shore lights began to fade. They only twinkled in the distance as night fell upon the land.

I decided my eyes had seen enough for one day, and it was time to go below. I was surprised when I tried to stand. I found my legs were weak, a little wobbly and unsteady. I felt somewhat woozy and staggered a bit with the ship's roll. I was able to keep my balance, get below and experience my first night of rock and roll at sea. The small sea swells and the continuous drone of the diesel engines made for a good night's sleep. I felt better the next day and had my sea legs by the time we reached Kwajalein. I had quickly adapted to blue water sailing, and come to know salt water was in my veins. I loved the sea, the reflection of the bright sun on deep blue water, a color so deep there was a purple cast—wine blue. The marvelous flight of the flying fish did amaze me. How could they glide so effortlessly and so far with fins for wings and with the flip of the tail?

Astern was the ever-present tow, sometimes above, sometimes below the horizon depending on the sea condition. The break on the cable drum had to be continuously applied or released, especially when towing a 500', 5000 ton ARD floating dry dock. We were nearing the Equator. The equator water became completely still and calm. There was no wind. Was this the doldrums of Silas Mariner? In the daytime the ocean glistened like a mirror; at night the untold millions of miniscule phosphorescent sea creatures shone and shimmered in the ship's wake, more especially on moonlit nights. Scientifically this condition is called bioluminescent or bioluminescence, caused by a chemical reaction as the surface water is disturbed. The bow wake also activated light emitting single-cell microscopic organisms called dinoflagellates. This was an unforgettable sight - a sight I long to see. Everyone should see it.

Only an occasional swell caused the ship to rise slowly a bit. I would often go to the bow just to see the it split the mirrored water. Otherwise there was no sensation of movement. Porpoises were a delight as they swam, leaped, and played along the forward bow sides. A whale at a great distance spouted a white fountain of water; at least I was told it was a whale. All of this was so exciting! The sea was alive and offered many surprises, as well as contentment. The slow rolling swells were very conducive to pleasant sailing and sound sleep.

But I had had about all the good time sailing I could stand for one trip and was anxiously looking for some firm footing. What I saw was a low-slung, almost treeless, tiny white sand island shining in the middle of the Pacific Ocean. There were a few trees scattered and still standing. Most had been destroyed during the bombardment in WWII. We slowly approached the anchorage, ever watchful not to run upon the coral. We dropped anchor in shallow water and delivered the yard oiler. My section was given liberty to go ashore—Kwajalein, my first island.

The whaleboat (a whale boat is a light motorized but seaworthy boat used as a life boat and to transport ships' crews, stores, and liberty parties ashore) glided over the multicolored coral reef and through beautiful waters that changed from dark blue-green to light green, then to chartreuse in very shallow water. We tied up to a long, low, shaky wooden pier that extended out over the shallow waters. The pier was made of 2"x12" boards that led to a white sandy beach of nothingness. The beach felt as if it moved when I stepped ashore. I stepped high like the ground was rising up to meet me. At sea I had become sub-consciously aware of the rise and fall, the roll and pitch of the ship. I discovered this high stepping was a common and temporary occurrence of all sailors long at sea. With a little caution this malady is soon gone.

The greeting from permanent duty sailors stationed on the island was cold and indifferent, not pleasant at all. I was to learn they referred to their island as the ***'rock,'*** and those whose thinking and reasoning had became somewhat deranged, after a year or two of ocean, sun, and sand, were described as *rock happy.* Later I learned this condition was remedied by flying and rotating Kwajalein duty personnel to Hawaii about every six months for R & R.

We knew we were not welcome because our home was temporarily anchored, but theirs was permanently anchored on a hot, desolated piece of coral in the middle of the Pacific Ocean. The main entertainment was a meta-roofed beer shed, an outdoor movie, and some sports equipment. Our crew drank a few hot beers, and left near sundown before any fights started. We determined from both glances and hard looks, that fighting was the main and more serious form of entertainment. We were being sized up to take center stage.

The ding-ding-ding of the whaleboat's bell signaled us to form up at the end of the pier to board. We glided slowly through crystalline clear, shallow, blue-green waters and over beautiful coral reefs back to the ship. The silhouette of the Tawakoni and her reflection in the calm-mirrored water awakened me to a new realization and appreciation. This small but tough, safe, rough riding, durable ocean fleet tug might be my answer to see much more of the world. We approached the ship's fresh coating of haze-gray paint gleaming in the tropical sun. For the first time I was proud that I was a tugboat sailor. Little did I know how much the experience on this ship would change me over the next two and a half years. But I knew how it had changed me up to this time. I knew I didn't want to go back home to stay, ever.

I was my own man now, had fallen under the spell of *the mistress of the deep*, had a new course set for me, had learned a new set of valuable skills, found a place where I was in charge, not only of myself, but responsible for those who depended on me. The Tawakoni, such as she was, belonged to me; she was mine.

With the realization that I had successfully made a rite of passage, so to speak, I went back aboard ship feeling good. I listened with a sense of pleasure as the engine crew fired off the main engines to get underway. Black smoke always belched from the stack exhaust, and along the water line that caused some griping. I considered the engine noise and smoke a necessary nuisance to leave this Godforsaken island. I was ready to return to Pearl. And I was naive enough to think we would set a course due West with a slight correction to Northwest that would take us to the International Dateline and on East to Oahu. We could hear the clanking of the anchor chain as the anchor winch retrieved the anchor from the anchorage. Later that evening I learned we had set a course for Guam. I was disappointed, but had mixed emotions. Pearl Harbor would have to wait until I was to see and experience another new island.

Guam is the largest (32 miles long, 4-10 miles wide—approximately 206 sq miles) and the southernmost of the Mariana Islands of the Western Pacific in the Ralik Chain. The deepest water in the world was in the Mariana Trench 35,798’ (6.78 miles deep – until the recent discovery of the Challenge Trench, which is 35,840’. Nearby is another deep trench, the Yap Trench, with a depth of 27,976’ (approximately 5 miles). I looked over the side to see if this extremely deep water was any different from usual ocean water. I tried to tell myself the water looked a little darker, but there was no actual difference.

The United States had a naval station on Guam since 1808, except during the 1941 Japanese occupation of WWII, which ended with the invasion of United States forces in

1944. Many nearby islands that were never a permanent possession had been encroached upon by the Japanese before WWII, including the island of Yap. Japan signed the Treaty of Peace (1952) in San Francisco, that mandated all islands be returned and remain only a trust territory of the Pacific.

We entered Apra Harbor on the west coast of the island. There we saw the rusted hulk of the WWI Battleship, the *U.S.S. Oregon BB-3*. She had been purposely placed at the entrance of the harbor to act as a temporary breakwater. I was later to see a permanent breakwater installed, and the Oregon hulk was sold to the I Wai Sangg Company, of Kawasaki, Japan in 1956. But the ship did not go easy. There was a typhoon on November 11–14, 1948, and the Oregon was blown 500 miles out to sea, and had to be located and returned by tow.

I remember thinking this was an unfit burial for so mighty a war ship, a ship that had seen duty in both the Atlantic and Pacific, a ship that sailed 16,000 miles around the Horn in only 66 days with the outbreak of war with Spain in 1898. Congress quickly approved the building of the Panama Canal because of the delay and expense incurred by the Oregon to traverse this great distance and also for national security.

Another striking sight was a high cliff rising above the water. Japanese propaganda stories insisted that American soldiers would eat their children or worse, and such wild assertions had caused hundreds of Japanese and civilians to jump to their death from this suicide cliff.

Two days later we were underway again. This time to Saipan, towing a barge loaded with trucks, lumber and parts. The wind was blowing strong off the starboard side, as we swung the bow close in to dock. Before the deck crews could get a line over, the ship was blown back away from the dock. After several futile tries, the Chief Boatswain Mate resorted to the .45 caliber throw line pistol to shoot a line over. The small line was attached to a larger line, and then to the large bow hawser, which was played out and secured to a dock cleat. With the bow windlass the ship was reeled in close enough for the stern windlass to slowly wind the ship parallel, and secure us to the dock in Tanapag Harbor, Saipan.

Saipan is an island in the South Central Marianas, Western Pacific, and was formally held by Spain, Germany, and Japan until 1944. Saipan saw its share of fighting and bloodshed in the latter part of WWII. Again, Japanese propaganda had caused many on the island to jump to their deaths from high cliffs. I felt very sorry at seeing these cliffs.

The more I entered the islands and saw evidence of the war in the Pacific, the more aware I was that WWII had ended only four years earlier. The damage to trees, the very absence of trees that had been blown away by our planes and ships, was disconcerting. A feeling of respect, high regard, and esteem welled up in me because this was where so many of our young men had died or had been wounded.

We left Saipan towing two barges with a Navy seaplane on each barge. Apparently one seaplane had landed on a shallow coral reef with the other plane following. Severe fuselage damage was caused to both planes. I thought how ironic those two amphibious fast flying machines had succumbed to the sea and were being towed by a slow ocean tug to the nearest repair base. I must say, looking aft, they did make a pretty picture - bobbing up and down, swaying side to side. I just had to get up early the next morning to see if they were still there. I imagined they might have just *flown off* during the night.

The U.S.S, Tawakoni ATF-114 entered Apra Harbor early, and the first line was secured to the dock at 0815. We had successfully retrieved and towed our prize catch of two twin-engine PBY Catalina seaplanes back to Guam safely. The planes were off- loaded and in three days we were on a return trip to Saipan with a dredge and a barge. The crew was curious as to the purpose of this three-day turn-around. Our conclusion, and rightly so, was that the dredge was to be used to dig up rock and coral to provide for a safer seaplane landing.

The winds were calm this time as we came alongside the dock and tied up in fine style. As soon as in-port duty stations were assigned, some of us were given permission to go ashore. I wandered off by myself and was soon following a narrow road that cut through the small trees and the *tangan-tangan* underbrush. Many trees had been damaged or destroyed by large navy guns. I walked further, exploring the island, trying to understand why so much carnage had taken place. I felt uneasy to walk where so many young men, some no older than myself, had been injured, shed blood, and died. This was surely hallowed ground. I walked softly. The invasion count of the 1944 landing was 3,500 Americans dead and ten times that many of the Japanese forces.

I was surprised when I came upon a lonely white building - a church or meeting house with the inscription: *Native Village of Chalan Kanoa – Garden Island of the Pacific*. I continued to walk down a path away from the meeting hall but soon lost interest to see more. My excitement of shore excursion had been replaced by sadness. I returned to the ship, planning to spend a lackadaisical afternoon reading, and trying to write some letters home.

Suddenly, I heard a great commotion coming from the portside aft. I went topside to see several of the crew shouting, hollering, laughing, and jumping over the side. They were swimming, and using a diving compressor air hose to scuba dive. A well-developed, good-natured sailor from Houston named Crane was deep underwater, viewing the myriad kinds and colors of tropical fish. He had gone too deep, and had been under far too long. We all sensed the danger and were anxiously concerned, fearing what we were to witness. He finally surfaced in excruciating pain and agony. He had the *bends*. We pulled him from the water with great haste and immediately rushed him ashore to a decompression chamber.

I did not think swimming in shark-infested waters was too smart anyway. Many sharks had been seen each evening feeding on our garbage. And at sundown their black dorsal fins formed several close-knit circles near the shore. I was later to learn the natives believed these sharks would not attack. I did not want to stretch my luck and be the exception.

All was well the next day. Crane slowly made it up the gangplank. His muscles were terribly sore; pain curtailed any quick movement. He was given light duty for a few days. We realized a few more minutes, and we could have lost him. We were happy to have our full complement of men aboard and be underway back to Guam again. A favorite saying aboard ship was, *Here today, Guam tomorrow!* There was later to be another telling phrase reduced from *gone to Korea* to *gonna Korea*—gon -or-rhe'a.

We made landfall, entered Apra Harbor, and tied up at 1145 hours. After lowering the flag from the mainmast, raising the flag aft, and the Union Jack forward, shutting down the engines and setting the quarter deck watch, the starboard liberty party was given permission to go into Agana (Hagatna), the capital.

Guam is an unincorporated Territory of the United States, being the largest and southernmost of the Mariana Islands. The Portuguese navigator, Ferdinand Magellan, discovered the island in 1521, and it was later claimed by Spain in 1565. Most Guamanians are of Micronesian/Spanish descent and speak Chamoru. English is the official language, but Chamoru is permitted and accepted as well.

Agana back then was comprised of one government building, the Governor's Mansion, a post office, a grocery store, and local residences. We had been warned by the permanent duty sailors to be leery of the locals. The warning was forgotten as we began walking in high spirits down the highway towards town, a few miles Northwest of Apra Harbor.

We noticed several late model unmarked Chryslers and Desotos cruising up and down the fourteen-mile, two lane stretch of highway that our government Construction Battalion and Engineers had built.

The United States taxpayers had compensated the Guamanians for the destruction of coconut trees and vegetation caused by heavy equipment, tanks, howitzers, and the naval and air bombardment in the fierce three-week battle for Guam during WWII. I realized, and am quite sure, this money was used to buy these big automobiles being used as unsolicited taxis.

We were pleasantly surprised and happy when one large Chrysler slowly came to a stop. The driver in broken English asked if we wanted a ride. "Sure," we said. He motioned for us to get in. We flopped down in the back seat of the finest car I had ever ridden in. Our immature thinking was that this was a token of the driver's appreciation for the sacrifices made to liberate his island from the Japanese. We had not considered or remembered the previous warning until we rolled to a stop at the drop off place, a small remote wooden structure on the edge of town. There were several muscular natives to aid in the collection of the fare, which was exorbitant. We learned of their wicked ways. After that we went in large groups, accepted their rides, and paid nothing! We had heard of one serviceman, an airman I believe, who had wandered into a Guam housing area and been fatally stabbed. We learned fast to watch out for each other and protect ourselves, even though most of the islanders were friendly.

Another time a group of us sailors stumbled upon a tavern that was occupied by members of the United States Air Force. When we opened the rickety frame door to the screened-in tap room, we could feel the tension in the air.

Their looks told us we were invading their turf, and it was off limits to sailors. First there was a word or two followed by hard looks, then *yaw-yawing* back and forth increasing the tension. I knew two or three of the more inebriated in our group, brave by drink and short on reason, were going to involve us in a fight. I did not want to get a Captain's Mast, or Court Marshal. I was thinking my Good Conduct Medal was about to be put in jeopardy.

But just then two soldiers wheeled up on a motorcycle with an extra loud muffler and twin tail pipes. One soldier hurried in to buy the beer; the other sat on his machine. He revved up the engine, irritating everyone with his continuous very loud *varooming*! There was mutual but unspoken consent among the troops that such blatant noise had to be dealt with. And sure enough, the driver purposely *varoomed* the loudest when taking off. Airmen and sailors alike made a dash for the door. Beer cans were flung after the perpetrators until one open can splashed on the seat of the rear rider. There was a roar of laughter and hearty congratulations. It was to everyone's satisfaction that the nuisance had been dealt with – abated in fine style. The air had cleared; I still had my *Good Conduct Medal,* and we were all fighting on the same side again.

One day I left the ship mid-morning to find a shortcut through the flora and fauna to the supply depot. I did not find a shortcut, but I did find a most unusual sight by following the music. I heard this real country *hurting* tune wafting its way through the boondocks —"Why don't you haul off and love me one more time, and squeeze me until I'm turning blind" -by Wayne Raney and L. Glosson. I had never heard such a song like that before. I listened closely and followed the faint *whanging* and *twanging* of the guitar and the *whining* of the French harp (harmonica) until I knew the approach I had taken was leading me in the right direction. I came upon a small one-lane dirt road, a wide path really, and followed it some distance, until around a bend and over a small knoll there was the quaintest out-of-the-way shack/tavern. It was thatched together and covered with native materials. I went inside for a refreshment or two and to be out of the hot morning sun. The place was sparse, dark, with a dirt floor, and reeked with cigarette smoke and the smell of stale beer. There was a stubby bearded Caucasian barkeep and one unsavory-looking character whiling away the morning. I thought about taking a seat at the bar and having a cool one, when I heard the question, "What do you want?" I was jolted out of complacency remembering the earlier warnings. My reply was, "I'm just looking for a buddy." I made my exit and my way back to the safety of the ship and the ship's company. Some of the crew asked, "Where you been?" I murmured some nonchalant, feeble response that apparently satisfied their inquisitiveness. This was not the excitement I had joined the Navy for, and I have kept the tale of this misadventure to myself until now. Only recently, was I to find on YouTube this hillbilly, country, western song that had reached *number one*, and was listed in the top 40's with recordings by Porter Wagoner and Dolly Parton.

For many weeks, Skyler, our radioman, played our only record each day at noon. It was the most pleasing operatic instrumentation, accompanied by an Italian singing group. Very pretty, but after listening so many times, it became monotonous. The title was "Come Back to Sorrento", later successfully record by Luciano (Lucian) Pavarotti. If our one record was not playing at the noon meal, it was the baseball game - usually between the Yankees and the Dodgers. I was greatly aggravated by all the noise and chaos. Baseball was never my cup of tea. I went to see only one ball game – that was the Fort Worth Cats in Fort Worth, Texas. I have always regretted that I did not bring the "Come Back to Sorrento" record with me when I was transferred to the *USS Castor AKS-1.* But I do have Pavarotti's recording as a lasting memory.

Western Pacific Atoll

Somewhere on a Western Atoll where the sun is like a curse,
And each long day is followed by another slightly worse,
Where the coral dust blows thicker than the desert's shifting sands,
And the white men dream of finer, cooler, cleaner, green lands.
Somewhere in the Western Pacific, where a woman's never seen,
Where the sky is never cloudy and the grass is never green,
Where the gooney birds scream nightly, robbing man of blessed sleep,
Where there isn't any whisky. Just two cans of beer a week.
Somewhere in the blue Pacific, where the mail is always late,
Where Christmas cards in April are considered up to date,
Where we always sign the payroll and never draw a cent,
Where we never miss the money, 'cause there's no place to get it spent.
Somewhere in a Western Ocean, where the nooneys groan and cry,
And the lumbering deep sea turtles come up on the beach to die,
Oh, take me back to ______________the place I love so well,
For this God forsaken island is awful close to hell.

(Written in 1944- By Unknown Author at Ulithi-Roi-Namur Atolls near Yap, Island)

Chapter 5

The Island of Stone Money

Yap Island, called **The Island of Stone Money,** lies just north of the equator approximately 536 to 640 miles southwest of Guam; 280 miles north of Palau Island, Western Caroline Group, Western Pacific Ocean; 1,000 miles from Manila in the Philippines. Melanesia lies south of the Equator, except for the islands and atolls of the Federated States of Micronesia, which lies north of the Equator. It includes the islands of Guam, Saipan, Kwajalein and other small islands in the Marshall Group and Northern Marianas. Polynesia covers a huge area in the Central Pacific. Islands included are New Zealand, the Hawaiian Islands, Samoa, French Oceania, Cook Island and other small groups.

Now, you may think that you don't need to know all this, but I did because Yap isn't the only place that matters in this sea story of my telling. But truth to tell, I didn't know where I was half the time—less than half in the vast Pacific.

Yap State is comprised of four islands – *Gagil-Tomil, Map, Rumung* and *Yap (Wa'ab).* The other three states are – *Kosrae, Pohnpei (Ponape),* and *Chuuk* (formerly Truk), each with its own small islands and atolls. These four islands are now grouped together as the **Federated States of Micronesia (FSM),** of which Yap is a leading member.

Early Yap history is one of Portuguese discovery in 1520, coming under Spanish, German, and later Japanese rule. Spain (1874) sold the island(s) to the Germans in 1889, and then Germany lost the island(s) in their defeat in WWI.

Japan began encroaching and fortifying the island(s) in 1914, occupying them in 1917. A mandate in 1919 was given to the Japanese with the treaty of Versailles. Japan annexed the island(s) in 1935. They were under Japan's control for these many years, until their liberation in 1944 during WWII.

Americans occupied Yap in 1945, and in 1947 the island(s) north of the Equator became a United States Protectorate, known as a **Trust Territory of the Pacific Islands (TTPI).** Yap was assigned a *United States Administrator* with complete authority, until recently when the Federated States of Micronesia (FSM) agreement was signed. Also signed was a **Compact of Free Association** for the purpose of encouraging the islands to achieve self-sufficiency.

The island's slogan is, "Where America's Day Begins." Actually Guam claims this title, but Yap lies farther west of the International Dateline and is justified in its claim.

The people of Yap are known as the *Canoe People.* A ship's captain of long ago, motioning with his hand, asked a young native boy the name of the island. The boy understood the Captian to be motioning toward an oar and said, "Yap," which meant "oar" in his language. The name stuck, although the original name of the island was *Wa'ab*.

Yap was an unexpected assignment. We were to take thirteen Seabees, tow a barge, and deliver 101 cases of beer – not *99 Bottles of Beer on the Wall***,** as the repetitive song goes. Why the extra case I do not know, unless it was for the only Marine on the island. The Marine had power to arrest and decide local disputes. The brig consisted of a very small office and either one or two cells, I can't remember. I believe there was one "prisoner" detained for some minor infraction. I understood the detainee ran loose all day helping the Marine and returned to claim his cell each night. The Seabees' job was to restore the bombed-out landing field that had sustained heavy damage from our carrier-based aircraft. Yap was never invaded in WWII, only bombed and strafed.

The engine crew fired off number one and number three engines. We were underway with our first complement of Navy Seabees, and a strange cargo to a strange island. The trip from Guam to Yap was a very short three days. The water was very smooth and like glass, *a glass sea of tranquility* – beautiful navy blue water with a tinge of purple, then shallow crystalline waters. We anchored outside the coral reef but close ashore, close enough to feel the pull of the primitive, remote, but enticing island. This was the exact island I had imagined, had read about, mainly in the books by Nordhoff and Hall.

I believe fate had it that I was to ride the only whaleboat allowed in to the landing that day. I was anxious to experience this fascinating tropical isle with an unusually short name of only three letters – Y-A-P. Dolphins were playing around our ship's bow as the whaleboat was lowered. We plowed through the small incoming white-capped waves. The clear azure blue water sparkled like diamonds, and glistened in the hot equatorial sun. Colorful reef fish as well as manta rays were seen in the aquamarine shallow depths. Yap is known for its excellent scuba diving - the second best in the world. I jumped ashore on this quaint but mysterious island lying only eight to ten degrees above the equator, and made my way from the small quay to a well-traveled pathway, along the water's edge.

Our shore party gathered and began to walk and gawk, when a well-built Yapese, wearing only a bright red loincloth or *thuus-thu* and carrying a large machete, confronted us. The sight was unnerving, and we would have considered the situation dangerous if we had not been in a group at the time. There was little if any eye contact as we cautiously passed.

Again we met another native—and later three or four more—whose mouth was all red and whose teeth were all black from chewing a quid of betel nut. Chewing betel nut is an addictive male and female ritual of the island. It gives the chewer a short "buzz," a feeling of well being, euphoria, and a hot sensation in the body - when the stimulant is wrapped in a pepper leaf. The juice of the nut turns red with pounding and is usually mixed with tobacco, lime (citrus), flowers, and plant parts native to the island. The "palm nut," **Areca catechu,** contains alkaloids that are addictive.

I was expecting the unexpected on the island, but I did not expect to see, in all innocence, the surprising sight of bare-breasted, lovely brown-skinned, barefooted women wearing the ankle length *Lava-Lava* grass skirt. My timidity, and the fact that I was innocent of ever seeing a naked woman, let alone a bunch of them, made me momentarily look away. They would *swish* quietly by, and I pondered upon what I had just seen. Before the day was over I was initiated to both young and old alike, wearing skirts made from a combination of betel nut, fragrant ginger, fern, banana, shredded Ti or other leaves. I thought civilization was coming to the island when one of the younger women went back into her thatched hut and came out wearing a bright white new bra. We took her picture. She seemed pleased showing off her new attire, and without any show of embarrassment or reservation.

After many smiles, warm farewells, and gifts of cigarettes, we continued on around the island. I veered off to explore a grove of palm trees. There I saw a shocking, unbelievable sight. Standing under a tree, barely visible, was the smallest, oldest person I had ever seen. Every inch of her sun baked skin was dark and wrinkled; her hair was thin, graying and frizzled. Most of the black teeth in her red mouth were missing. I looked into her big dark eyes and wondered at the sights she had seen, how many typhoons she had endured, how many sad stories of Japanese occupation she could tell. I knew long ago she must have been a beautiful, but fragile young girl, and now she was entering the final days of her life. It had never occurred to me until now, to think about women back home aging, especially while enduring the stresses of WWII.

It was getting late, the sun was very hot, and I was quite thirsty. I motioned to her as if I wanted a drink of coconut milk - *even though there were no coconuts in sight*. But soon she understood. Near her foot, and under several coconut fronds, not two feet away was a large pile of coconuts. She rolled and held one coconut with her big toe, and *swish* - she made a slash with a broad blade machete. Then she rolled the coconut the other way, with the same big toe, very close to where she was going to cut. Quickly and expertly without hesitation she made another whack, a perfect *V*. With alacrity and quick motion she bent down and handed me this rare treat, my first taste of fresh coconut milk. She and I both were smiling. I was grateful for her kindness and generosity. I was grateful she had not cut off her big toe. I presented her with some change and trinkets, and all my cigarettes as a show of gratitude.

She anxiously lit one cigarette and began to take a very long drag - the tip burning red hot. The dense shade made it possible to see the red fire move about halfway up the cigarette, before she began to exhale. A profuse cloud of smoke came from her mouth and both nostrils. Momentarily hidden from view were her upper features. A smile of immense pleasure and a look of complete satisfaction from the taste and effects of an American cigarette was on her face. I still remember as if yesterday. I suppose Yap is the most traditional island all sailors dream about, where spotlessness is common and socially acceptable, even today, where brown native girls clad only in grass skirts hanging below the navel go swaggering along narrow trodden paths. Where strong robust native men wear the traditional red G-string breechcloth supported by a cord with an eight inch flap in front - carry a menacing bolo knife, chew betel nut in red mouths of black teeth that flash amidst lush foliage of banana trees and coconut palms. And all this surrounded by sparkling crystal clear blue water in the remote vastness of the Carolines in Melanesia, Western Pacific Ocean. But even on Yap a strict custom and rule of decency is observed - *the woman's thigh is never to be exposed.* Yes, we all did a lot of gawking and looking, but an exposed female thigh was never in evidence—not once.

I located some of our crew, and we proceeded to look for the Japanese airfield the Seabees were to repair. We came across a sign made of large pieces of what I believe was white coral imbedded in the side of a mound, which read – **YAP.** Straight up behind this sign was a steep rise, the highest point on the island. We made the climb with some effort and were rewarded to see several damaged or destroyed Japanese aircraft - we believed to be *zeroes, zekes, and bettys* – Zeroes with the *red meatball* on each wing...The red circled *meat ball* denoted the emperor—*the sun god,* but for these planes Emperor Hiro Hito's sun had set.

I did wonder about the fate of the Japanese pilots whose planes were all shot up. They were left on an island with hostile natives, whose language they could not speak or barley understood. The Japanese had cruelly treated, threatened, intimidated, and compelled the Yapese into forced labor, building the airstrip, and working the phosphorous and bauxite mines prior to war's end.

We met a White Russian boy very unexpectedly walking down one of the main paths. He told us his mother was a nurse at the small white-framed hospital. The family had leap-frogged from island to island until the Japanese captured them. His father had become separated from the family, captured, and killed on another island. The Russian lad of fifteen or so spoke in broken, but understandable, English and became our tour guide.

He showed us around the island, stopping to explain the difference between *eating* bananas and *cooking* bananas - showed us taro, sweet potato-yams, pepper plants, breadfruit and mango trees, and plants used for building and shelter. We noticed pigs rooting around. He explained fruit, pork, fish, taro, and some crustaceans made up their diet of subsistence living.

The native men, women, and children looked healthy, and in good physical shape. But the Russian boy was concerned, feared the rains would not come to the taro patches. Without rain it would be disastrous. Taro is the main staple and must have an abundant supply of water, lest the patch dry up and die. To replant and grow another crop would take three years, and even then the crop would not be a fully matured. Coming from Texas, I understood the worry about not getting enough rain.

The Yapese aragonite crystalline gray limestone—quartz-like aggregate, and coral limestone, used as money is called **Ray (Rai),** the short form of the word, *rayningochol.* Depicted on the government seal and flag is the Ray, a large gray round stone with a hole in the center. The first Ray was quarried on the island of Palau, 280 miles southwest, and is referred to as *full moons.*

There are five types of money: *Mmbu,* from Yap; *Gaw* from Ganat (near Pohnpei); *Ray* from Palau; *Yar (shell)* from New Guinea; and *Reng* from Yap.

Before 1860, the finished stones were placed on a bamboo raft, secured to a canoe, floated and towed great distances over open waters. Many stones and lives were lost at sea during typhoons, storms, heavy squalls, and rough seas. The difficulty of the voyage, personal risk, lives lost, age, type, shape, quality, color, workmanship, texture, and whether previously owned by royalty helped determine the value of each piece.

Some pieces are preferred over others. Weight and size alone does not determine their value. Stones may be very small, 10" in diameter or so, or be 10' – 12' in diameter, and weigh several tons. A small stone cut with sea shells and formerly owned by royalty may be worth much more than a larger stone. *Old* money is worth much more than the *new* money. The carving of the first money is credited to a mariner named Fathaan of Rull, with his discovery of limestone caves on the island of Palau, about 2,000 years ago.

The stone money that came later by David Dean O'Keefe's ship around 1878 was later known as O'Keefe's money. O'Keefe was a sailor of Irish-American descent on a merchant ship that was shipwrecked on the Island of Yap. He was nursed back to health and made his way to Hong Kong on the German ship Belvedere. Later he became a trader and exchanged his service of hauling the finished Ray from Palau in exchange for *copra* - the dried meat of the cocoanut. His thirty-year lucrative trade was also in sea cucumbers and all things Chinese. O'Keefe money, island products, and Far East trade ended in July 1901, when his Chinese junk disappeared at sea in a storm. The 1954 movie, "His Majesty O'Keefe" staring Burt Lancaster, written by Laurence Lingman and Gerald Green (1952), is based on and portrays the adventures of David O'Keefe.

But great preference was given to the stone discs with a considerable thickness, a symmetrical round hole and a gradual uniform slant from the hole to the rim. The hole in the center was for practical purposes. Several men using long poles could carry the heavy stones, while the extra heavy stones could be rolled along the ground, and down to the dock for loading.

Each stone on the island has an owner, but most stones are kept in a *stone money bank.* The large grayish donut shaped stones, medium and small, stones of every size, each with its hole in the center, were are all piled upon the ground in no certain order, but denoted the *bank.* The money is seldom moved and believed to be under the control of the chief or his controlling council. Most stone money is used in ceremonies, exchange of land, marriage, a dowry, to make amends, to honor, or as a present for a good deed.

The Ray is legal tender, and you might say it's *a hard currency.* American currency is used as well. All goods and services must be paid for with the US dollar. A few houses will have a stone out front to show their wealth or affluence. Should someone take or steal a stone, they will have to make two or three times' the value in restitution. And no longer can the stones be taken from the island.

It is regrettable that the Japanese forced the people to work during WWII by threatening to crush their stone disks (money) to build roads and airstrips. Many stones were crushed for this purpose. The number has been reduced from a little over 13,000 down to maybe 7,000 Ray today. The people of the island are very proud of their unique money, as well as their recognition as the island with two legal tenders. They are comfortable with their two currencies and system of exchange.

We wandered back down to the dock at the appointed time to catch the whaleboat and end this most memorable liberty. The whaleboat was coming, but so too was a heavy evening rain squall, common that time of year. We made a dash for an American road-grader left over from WWII. We stayed in the shelter of the cab until the very last minute. The downpour drenched us to the skin. We were able to see the whaleboat, but the boat crew could not determine exactly where we were. We could faintly hear the Coxswain's bell ding-dinging. We yelled our loudest over the noise of the rain, fearing we might be left on the island. After two or three tries, a very wet and unhappy boat crew located us. Much effort was expended to hold the boat steady, and there was much difficulty getting into the rocking boat. We almost floundered in the choppy waters on our way back to the ship. The less fortunate that did not get to go ashore that day were treated to a bunch of stalk-ripened bananas. The bananas, and seeing us soaking wet, seemed to soften their regret and disappointment of having to stay aboard.

We sailed that night back to Guam and returned to Yap three weeks later with a barge of materials and supplies. I did not get to go ashore again and missed the traditional dance, *the mitmits*. I could see the fires and hear the excitement, and so wanted to experience the island and the people once more. But it was not to be. We sailed that night back to Guam, where we remained in port for the next long weeks chipping paint and making repairs to the engine, awaiting our next assignment.

I had plenty of time to ponder again about casualties of war, native men and women - old, young, misplaced, mistreated people of war – on islands so far from the rest of the world, so far from Hawaii, so far from the United States mainland.

Fair Winds & Following Seas

May the Lord fill our sails with fair wind,

Support our hulls in inviting seas,

Guide our hands upon the tiller toward

Pleasant places,

And bring us home, O Lord, to a safe and

Loving harbor.

The United States Navy
Memorial

2010 Blessing of the Fleet

Chapter 6

Polynesian Paralysis

We had been on the go ever since we left Pearl. I believe the engines never got cold, except for the time in dry dock at Guam. Our two- and three-day stays in port were just enough time for me to draw emergency stores from the only supply depot in the Marshall, Caroline, and Mariana Islands. Ship's rations were always low, the menu repetitive, and the crew was complaining about their chow. I was exceedingly happy to stay in port to replenish our cold storage reefers, dry stores provisions, and stock the bread locker with sugar, coffee, spices and everyday-use items.

Guam's supply warehouse was one of limited quantity and variety back in the late forties and early fifties. Each time I submitted a stack of requisitions half would come back NA, not available, or NIS, not in stock. Time and chance played a big part in whether I would return with a large load of food and supplies. If a supply ship from the states had just re-supplied the depot, and a larger ship had not slipped in ahead of us and pulled a huge order, we could restock with necessary quantities of fresh, frozen, and dry stores.

Just to get to the supply depot was a challenge, especially my first two times to Guam. Dutifully I hit the dock not knowing the right direction to take or how to get there. Transportation was not readily available, so I started out walking, asking for a ride from military drivers – getting a ride whenever I could.

Twice I was caught in a tropical shower, found protection under thick palm leaves, but still got soaked. This is when I found the black topsoil and red clay sub-soil on Guam would permanently stain my clothes, especially the whites. I learned to save my white uniforms for Honolulu inspection. There was no commercial laundry in Guam in 1949, not for ships anyway. These two experiences taught me to manage a ride or wait on transportation. I never got caught in the rain again. The first time I submitted requisitions, I approached the supply office with some hesitation and a little trepidation. Expressionless upturned eyes told me I was considered a necessary nuisance. I had on the right general issue (GI) uniform of the day, right designation of storekeeper on the sleeve, and a white hat that showed I was a genuine United States sailor. But I still felt I was the strangest sight they had ever seen!

I introduced myself, "I'm off the U.S.S. Tawakoni ATF-114." I was to find out a tugboat carried little weight. "I need to get these requisitions filled. We are about out of food and scheduled to leave tomorrow. And, I will need transportation, a truck, to take me back to the ship." The storekeepers continued to look at me, size me up, without expression. One of lesser rate slowly moved toward the counter and flipped through my stack of requests. He told me, "Sit over there." He pointed to the well-worn wooden chair and then said, "We will call you when your load is ready." I waited and waited, knowing and resolved that everything moved slowly in the islands. But finally I told myself, "This is no good," and walked through the warehouse nosing around until I found my truck and the driver. I chatted him up real good and soon was riding in the front seat, headed back to the ship. The truck was an old Reo, the make I considered the sorriest ever made. It would sputter, backfire, slow down, and have to be coaxed up the hill.

The driver only stopped cursing his vehicle when we flew down one steep hill, and swung around a sharp curve. Suddenly I looked to my right and saw both oxygen and acetylene bottles flying off the starboard side of the truck bed through the air, and landing hard on the rocky roadside. I turned away quickly covering my face, thinking the bottles would clash together and explode. Miraculously they didn't.

I yelled loudly over the engine noise and motioned until he understood to stop. With much grinding he found reverse gear and backed up to where the bottles had landed. He and I retrieved the wayward iron bottles, threw them back on the truck, and continued now down hill toward the dock. I was still a little worried about the sputtering and coughing, until we caught sight of the ship at dockside.

But the Tawakoni was not at dockside. She had backed a distance away from the dock, and was being held by only one line - an extended hawser draped over a bollard – ready to be thrown off. A chill of fright came over me at the sight of my home, my bed, my ship leaving without me. I urged the driver to go faster; cursing him and his *snorting beast* under my breath, until the truck finally came to a stop.

It was late afternoon and the ship had received orders to get underway at a certain hour. The deck crew used the forward windlass (capstan) to reel the ship in close and provide a temporary tie up. An all hands working party had the truck unloaded in record time. I leaped aboard as the lines were again being thrown off to get underway. There was a small YW – yard water auxiliary ship tied up right behind us. That would have been my temporary home until the Tawakoni returned, or I might have been reassigned off my ship. It was close.

By and by I befriended a number of warehouse storekeepers and was able to avail myself of stores that were either in short supply, not on the stores available list, or a few that were reserved for the big ships. I was proud of myself riding back to the ship, knowing I had learned how to manage to get groceries, even groceries that belonged to a man-o-war. Some supply officer would be cursing that his requests had been shorted, and he would have to revise the ship's menu. I did have to do some tall talking to get them to take pity on me and prevail upon their good nature to give the little ship with a funny Indian name these extra stores. I had become tired of typing and requesting items not available or not in stock. I obtained a list of what was on hand and what the now friendly supply workers told me was available. I filled my order with only those items. Man, I was working the system. I was learning.

We had been in the Western Pacific for four months, and had not had a drop of milk except for very thin powdered milk – so thin you could almost see the bottom of your cereal bowl through its warm blue cast. I had noticed alongside the road, and in the supply depot trash bin, two or three orange/red quart-size milk cartons. While my truck was being loaded, I asked around about the fresh milk and the origin of the cartons. Everyone played ignorant, dumb, not knowing, but I persisted until I found a young storekeeper striker apprentice who told me there was a reconstituted milk plant, but milk was in limited supply. He told me the name of the man I should see because he was in charge. I found out that the milk was not only for the island, but that a few ships were getting it as well. I thought to myself, "If they can have milk, we can have milk." My argument again was that I was on a small tugboat, that big ships were always getting the good stuff, we had to take what was left, and we had been at sea for four months without a single drop of fresh milk. I said, "We do not need much, only a few quarts for our cereal, but I would appreciate whatever you can let me have."

I pulled away form the warehouse with a big smile and eighteen quarts, enough for each crewmember to have cold fresh milk on his cereal the next morning. I was in the crew's good graces once again. The milk was reconstituted, but tasted like real fresh milk. I never dreamed that all the experience gained in *finagling* supplies and stores would be so useful in the near future, or that I would have to fight even harder for scarce provisions.

With great jubilation we were informed we were returning to Honolulu, the best liberty port a sailor could ask for. The exception of course, being that of Captain Cook in 1779 near Kona on the big island of Hawaii, where he met his demise at the hands of distraught natives over a handful of nails.

I was anxious to get underway and experience once more that strange but wonderful tropical malady of Hawaii—***Polynesian Paralysis.*** It is a sluggish, lethargic, languid, inert condition that manifests itself first by a detached sense of leisure, followed by an overwhelming sense of well-being, and topped with an ***"I just don't care"*** attitude.

I remember the laid-back, lackadaisical feeling brought on by the slow pace of the islands and its gentle natured people; the bright tropical sunshine on white sand beaches continuously and evenly washed by slow incoming tides, the soft trade winds that swayed the palms with gentle puffs at just the right time to cool and refresh, the afternoon mist from the mountains, known as *liquid sunshine*, vivid rainbows hanging over the mountains, and melodious Hawaiian music that soothes the spirit, and calms the nerves. Added to that was an abundant variety of fresh tropical fruits, juices, jams, and jellies, and the fragrant smell of Plumeria, Jasmine, Frangipani, and Orchid leis.

The only two hotels on Waikiki Beach were the readily recognizable Royal Hawaiian, known as the Pink Palace of the Pacific, and the old white framed Moana, which is now the Sheraton Moana Surfrider – *the First Lady of Waikiki*, located on Kalakaua Avenue. These first-class hotels catered to the more affluent and elite – to the military until the late '40s - then to those who could afford to fly on Pan American Airlines, or come across on Cunard's SS Lurline luxury ocean liner.

For tugboat sailors all this was out of our class. Most often after being a long time at sea the more rowdy crew members were down on Hotel or King Streets, insensitive to the tropical magic - finding their own way to enjoy paradise paralysis by getting stoned. The lush greenery and abundant foliage should have reminded them to stop and smell the roses, but roses never did well in the Hawaiian climate anyway.

We were not told that we would be escorting a YW (yard water) and towing ARD-13 (floating dry dock), which was huge and heavy, 488' long with a weight of 5,000 tons. Neither did we expect to spend a month at sea and encounter the outer edge of a typhoon, and endure extremely rough weather. The many dangers and unexpected events experienced on this return trip to Hawaii changed me from a sightseeing pollywog to the makings of one salty sailor.

We caught the outer edge of the typhoon three days out of Guam. The flat-bottomed dry dock was dipping, rolling and pitching, causing a tremendous strain on the towline. It registered way beyond the allowed margin of safety. The strain gauge safety limit was exceeded several times. There was a loud bang of steel on steel, as the heavy metal safety hit bottom. The strain gauge in the towline unit was of little use in seas so rough and with a tow so big. The ship had to slow to lessen the tension. I only hoped the ship could maintain pull (way), and be far enough ahead to keep the monstrous tow from running over us. I went to the bridge and into the chart room to check our progress. We had averaged only 1.3 knots in twenty-four hours. Ships' speed is measured in knots; one knot equals 6,080.20 feet per hour, or 1.1516 statute miles, or 1.85 km per hour. For example, when a ship goes eight nautical miles per hour, her speed is eight knots.

Walking was almost impossible because you were either walking up or down, bracing to port or to starboard, expecting a sudden rise or fall. You felt your stomach in your throat when the bow rode up on an extra-large wave and suddenly dropped into the depths, to be engulfed by tons of water. The ship was awash from stem to stern, water was coming in the gunnels, and at times over the gunnels (gunwales). Fear—absolute terror was more like it—enveloped me once when the bow plunged into the sea, and mountains of water slapped the glass portholes on the bridge. Would the glass crack or shatter – letting water flood the wheel house and chart room?

I believe the ocean's fury seemed to cause it to become confused, not knowing which direction to come from. At least it seemed to me that the ocean was a person, had become personified – the angry, fickle and unpredictable *She.* The water boiled as massive waves curled and rolled. White water foam spread and bubbled with the turbulence. Strong winds blew the salt spray until it stung and hurt the skin – made it burn. Looking aft the waves were sometimes higher than the stern, and we expected they would inundate the ship at any time. The ship was taking on so much water that it was partially submerged at times. Sometimes the ship rolled over to starboard until only the sky could be seen, and then rolled to port until the mast almost lay flat on the water.

We were tossed skyward, then likely to plunge to the ocean deep. The whole ship shuddered. I felt like the ship's four huge engines and oversize towing propeller were trying to help the sea in its effort to put us skyward and at times downward. I knew I was at the sea's mercy – resigned to my fate should the storm get worse. When the bow went down, the ship's screw (propeller) came out of the water and whirred, raced, at full speed. When the stern went down and the bow rose up, our powerful screw running on all four engines bit deep into the water and bogged down vigorously shaking the ship.

I determined that if the storm continued or increased any more in its ferocity, we would soon be another insignificant ripple in Mother Nature's plan. I felt helpless and finite at experiencing this raging force. It was then that I remembered what my ex-navy brother had told me, ***The Sea is always hungry. Remember you have to respect the sea, so be careful. You get careless and it will eat you.*** How many dangers there were and how careful you had to be. I wasn't careless, and held on tightly, riding out the storm to save my life.

Safety lines had been strung along the sides, and the length of both gunnels. This was to prevent anyone from getting washed overboard. All watertight hatches were battened down, exterior bulkhead doors were dogged down, everything that might move was secured and a ***heavy seas*** watch was set.

Every hour as safety watch, I made a complete tour of the ship to check for spills and anything banging or dangling. Any secured item that was now loose, sliding, rattling, or clanging had to be re-secured. Special attention was given to our heavy boom and wire cables lest they break loose, swing out of control, and cause great damage or severe injury.

Food and liquids had to be limited to prevent messy spills and falls. Toast and coffee was the mainstay until the weather calmed and the seas subsided. Special care had to be taken when making coffee after the sea had calmed down, lest the ship make a quick lurch or sharp roll and coffee grounds spill into the large coffee urn. But there was little complaint, just as long as there was some coffee to be had.

The mess tables had rubberized tabletops to prevent the aluminum food trays and heavy glass coffee mugs from sliding, but to little avail if not firmly held. An extra big wave and a deep roll would cause a coffee cup to defy gravity and fly off the table and hit the bulkhead. Shoelaces were tied to the bunk frame to keep the shoes from all sliding across the deck and down into a hole. Bunk straps were often used to keep those trying to sleep from rolling out of bed.

Sleep was shallow, not sound, but fitful. The constant roll and pitch, unusual creaking and banging, waves slapping, and engines either speeding up or lugging down was not conducive to sleep at all. It is amazing we could even sleep a little, with our bodies rolling back and forth in our bunks.

The ship's office was closed, and typewriters, adding machines, filing cabinets and calculators were braced and secured. It was impossible to do any typing in this weather. Even in fairly rough seas the rolls were too great to keep the carriage from sticking and caused over-striking. My typewriter was standard size and even more difficult to use because the tension spring was weaker. At times when rolling to port, there was fear the carriage would break off and keep going. With such force it would crash against the bulkhead. Another problem was when experiencing a large roll you could feel your chair begin to slide across the steel deck, away from your desk. It was several days before the yeoman and I could restore the office and get caught up on our backlog of work.

Eight days out was when we rendezvoused with the U.S.S. Mitchell AP–114, and high lined off three crew-members in still rough, choppy seas, and at night. High lining is an exacting, closely coordinated, dangerous task that is not easy even in daylight and calm seas. When the ships roll together, the lines have to be quickly taken up; when they roll apart, the lines have to be slackened, *played out* to prevent parting. Danger is always present. The two ships close side by side could crash together causing great damage and loss of life. The three were transferred safely without even getting the seat of their pants wet. A job well done!

Underway against high seas and low on fuel, the decision was made to try and refuel our ship from the ARD we were towing. The attempts failed, and worse the towline fouled our screw. A diver was sent over the side to make inspection and see if there was any damage. There was damage to the screw, but not great damage. We continued on course with our tow and maintained our heading toward Hawaii.

The U.S.S. Bolster met us near Wake Island and brought fuel and mail, but no provisions. We refueled from 1530 to 2230 hours and arrived in Hawaii nine days later – a total of thirty hard days at sea.

As we entered port, I went below decks and checked the cold storage lockers. We were down to one case of fresh cabbage and two cases of ground beef. Dry stores consisted of kidney beans, tomato sauce/paste, rice, dehydrated potatoes, powdered eggs, powdered milk, a few cans of coffee, Jell-O, and small amounts of other items. The Chief Commissary Officer, Supply Officer, and I were worried and discussed the fact that the food might all be gone, except for rice and beans, before we reached port. The lockers and storage rooms on ocean tugs barely hold enough food to feed fifty or sixty men three meals a day for thirty days. But we need not have worried; the best supply depot in the world would reward us with an abundant variety of food.

And then there was Dayman - Dayman Finn, a real swinger, and the ship's favorite cook. He could cook and dance – dance while frying eggs sunny side up, over easy, over medium, or well done with six or eight pans going at the same time - sweating profusely over a very hot oil-burning stove near the Equator. He was meticulously clean. He showered three times a day – once before cooking breakfast, once after lunch and once before going ashore.

McConnell, our other cook, was just the opposite. He would seldom take a bath or change his yellowed bedding. I spoke to the corpsman about the crew's health; he spoke to the disheveled cook. It did no good. I told several of the deck crew - they told McConnell! I logged in the date and time of his bath in the ship's log, and soon observed the whiteness of his mattress cover. I recall the saying, *either shape up or ship out.* The threat of being given a bath with a rough-rigged bristled KiYi brush and strong saltwater laundry soap improved the cook's physical hygiene and laundry habit, if not his disposition. He was on the ship only a short time before being transferred. I was glad; we were all glad to see him go. I wondered how he got into the Navy, and why he was a cook, of all things.

One payday, back in the small but safe aft hold and on a stretched blanket, Dayman won all the money shooting dice, *craps*. With his ill-gotten gain, crisp white uniform and white hat just so, about one inch above the eye brow, he bounded down the gangplank on a three day pass.

Late that evening there was a great commotion on the dock. Dayman caused all the excitement by arriving with three good-looking women sitting on top of the white leather seats of a bright red Cadillac convertible. Everyone went topside to see the spectacle. Dayman rushed up the gangplank and down to his locker in the crew's compartment for more of his winnings. He logged in late on the night of his allotted and extended liberty.

For a month he was broke, but happy. He tried to sell his expensive Shaffer Pen and Pencil Set and his gold Gruen watch he had just recently purchased with previous winnings. Ship cooks have an inglorious and demanding job and receive little recognition of their hard but important work. But Dayman was held in high esteem, praised for his daring, and now had endeared himself to the crew in fine style.

Every week I had to ***cut a stencil*** and mimeograph copies of the menu on an antiquated mimeograph machine, left over from WWII. The machine was located in a heavy wire enclosure down in a hole, located just below the ship's office. I kept the precious machine tightly secured and under lock and key lest it be damaged, and we be without a menu. The hold was hot and the machine was very messy, especially in rough weather.

I often came up out of the hold with violet blue hands. This was the one job I detested, but it was necessary to appease the crew, and often times surprise the crew with repetitive fare, or maybe an original dish. I could hear the moans and groans, and many times made a quick exit after posting the menu. I understood their plight, but with limited stores in the islands, they had to endure until we had access to the abundant stores held in the Naval Supply Warehouse at Pearl Harbor.

If you've seen the movie, "Mr. Roberts," you're bound to recognize that even he had it good compared to a storekeeper on a tugboat. But then, I knew the Tawakoni was MY ship and the entire ship couldn't have done without ME, and it made all the difference.

Chapter 7

Flying Boat Home

A clean shiny white pick-up truck and a military jeep were waiting on the pier in Pearl for the ship's private use. The Captain always had first claim to the vehicle of his choice, and rightly so. A priority of urgency had to be set for the Executive Officer, Engineering Officer, mail, movies and supply. We never expected to be in port for more than a few days, maybe one or two weeks.

I would usually be in the first group, but sometimes I would have to hang around the quarterdeck, or on the dock with my tall stack of requisitions exposed, until someone would say, "McCoy needs to be dropped off at the Supply Depot." If I could not be included in the first trip, I knew transportation would be available later in the day to take me expectantly to the famous Naval Supply Depot at Pearl Harbor, Oahu, Hawaii.

I was pleased there were so many items to choose from, like local fresh fruits, fresh vegetables, a large selection of meats, fish and poultry, fresh eggs, and alas, milk - cold fresh milk. The warehouse furnished as well a special *in season* list I could pull from. And best of all, requisitions seldom came back NA (Not Available) or NIS (Not In Stock), as they had on Guam, or later when we would replenish at sea.

We had returned to Pearl Harbor in June nearing the end of our fiscal year. Each crewmember was allotted so much per day (per diem) for breakfast, lunch, and dinner rations. Our extended time in the Gilbert, Mariana and Caroline Islands had allowed us to accumulate an excess of funds that would be lost, if not spent before the end of the fiscal year that ended in July. It was now time to reward the crew for five months of doing without, and traipsing between islands and atolls.

I made several trips to the supply warehouse and brought back stores until every dry stores compartment, every cold storage unit, every locker was filled to the overhead, and even the galley refrigerator was loaded. Chief Sullivan (Sully) and I spent every cent – every taxpayer dollar of our budget until the new fiscal year. We were held in high regard. I believe there was never a happier tugboat crew with so varied and proportioned menu.

Hawaii was a territory of the United States at the time, Hawaii TH. The mainland was referred to as *The States* until the islands became our 50th state. It is now improper and not appropriate, as it was back then, to speak of the US as *The States.* Hawaii's star is on our flag – the last state to come into the Union, 1950.

The ship stayed in port and we were enjoying our good fortune of food, fun, and weather, awaiting our next assignment. Unexpectedly I received a telegram from the Red Cross informing me my older sister was critically ill. My middle sister was a leader in the Community Chest at the time and had to bring pressure on the Red Cross. The Red Cross was very reluctant to send the telegram telling of my sister's grave illness. A third of our crew would later have an unfavorable experience with the Red Cross in Japan. I took emergency leave and flew back to the mainland.

I was transferred to Hickham Air Force Base, and spent two nights in a United States Air Force barracks, awaiting my flight. The airmen were hospitable and helpful, issued me clean sheets, a pillow, and pillowcase - saw that I got settled. How wonderful it was to get to sleep in a real bed on a real mattress, not the customary canvas *sack* in cramped quarters.

The next afternoon I was to fly on a Constellation, the same type of plane as President Eisenhower's Air Force One - the *Columbine.* I waited and waited for my ride to the airfield, until finally a heavy-duty pick up truck drove up. I threw my sea bag in the back, jumped in, and headed for the airfield, not over a mile away. Suddenly the pickup began to sputter and cough, and then died. **Out of gas!** I was really mad because I wanted to hurry and get home to see my sister, and too, I wanted to ride on the '*president's'* plane. As I waited, the new sleek twin rudder Constellation rolled down the runway, rising gracefully into the sky. The driver and I exchanged a *few choice words* until his countenance fell. He never did apologize. If not for the previous good treatment, the incompetence of this airman would have tainted my good view of the United States Air Force.

Another ride came by after a long wait and took me back to the same barracks. I slept another night in the nice bed, and again had breakfast and lunch in a fine dining room - with white tablecloths and cloth napkins, no less. I still remember and appreciate the United States Air Force's (Army Air Force until 1949-1950) hospitality. That afternoon I was taken down to a loading dock, where a large four-engine PB2Y seaplane was loading. I reasoned this was the same four-engine seaplane I had come to Hawaii on, only six-seven months before.

Oh how I hated to ride this slow, lumbering, loud, unpressurized monster another 2,000 miles. I remembered how terribly my ears had hurt the on the flight over and feared the same thing would happen again. I cussed that

airman pick-up driver, and still do. He should have known to put gas in the tank! A water take off at sea is an unforgettable experience. You have to step down into the seaplane, because the boat fuselage part of the plane is under water, and water covers every porthole.

The take off required the plane to taxi a very long way down wind and out into choppy waters. Once turned into the wind, the engines were revved until the plane experienced extreme shudder. We finally began to move with engines at maximum roar, and slowly rose from the water. Water swished by and began to drain from the portholes. The bottom bounced jarringly as it slapped against the waves. The rough ride continued until the plane finally sucked itself from the watery vacuum, and was now airborne. I knew to sit on the starboard side leaving Hawaii, because that is where I could see the Royal Hawaiian, Moana Hotel, and Waikiki Beach and say, ***Aloha.*** Slowly Diamond Head vanished. I said a fond *farewell* to the islands, not knowing if I ever would return. I remembered being told never to say*, Goodbye,* but *Aloha* to assure your return. After a long uncomfortable trip, we made a safe but bumpy landing at Alameda, California. I was given transportation to the Los Angeles airport for my first commercial plane ride - a silver and red American Airlines plane. I told the lady at the ticket counter I was on emergency leave, did not have a ticket, but would greatly appreciate it if she could get me on the next flight. She placed me on standby and asked me to wait. The plane kept loading until there were only three of us standing near the loading gate.

One was a civilian, the other an Army or maybe an Air Force officer whom I perceived to be *spit and polish*, stiff, straight laced. Whatever, I could tell he looked upon me with a snobbish disdain. I could feel his cold feeling of superiority and his certainty of getting the last seat on the plane. The civilian’s name was called out. Only the two of us were standing there, each ready to step forward. I knew he was thinking that being an officer, he deserved to be chosen. The scratchy loudspeaker clicked on; we both waited, anticipating. My first name was mostly indistinct, but my last name was very audible. He was left standing with an astonished look oh his red face. I gloated at my good fortune, but did wish there had been one more empty seat. I was able to have a good visit with my sister, but she died a few months later while I was at sea, on our way back from Kwajalein, about four days out of Pearl.

While I was away on emergency leave, my ship had been assigned to her new homeport at San Diego, California. I was to report back aboard by 2400 hours, December 18, 1949. It was now past midnight and pitch dark along the docks. I was tired, lost, and late. Everything was so quiet except the whine of electric generators, and water slightly slapping the dock. I did not know if I would find my ship. It was really eerie, somewhat spooky. Many ships were tied up side-by-side, and hundreds of shining red mast lights and running lights of different heights and intensities were all scrambled together.

I had been told I should find my ship at Baker 4. I continued walking in the direction I assumed was correct, until I saw a big faint white letter B. I turned and walked cautiously the length of three ships to berth B4. There was a tug tied up, but ATF-114 was not on the hull. Three sister ships of the Abnaki class - the Tawasa, Tawakoni and Tekelma - were tied up together. I inquired at the quarterdeck if one of the tugs might be the Tawakoni, and was told mine was the middle ship. I stepped aboard at 0215 (a little late), but the quarterdeck watch logged me in as being on time. It was good to be home.

The supply depot in San Diego was right downtown at the end of a wide main street that ran past the famous Coronado Hotel. The uniform of the day to draw stores was undress blues. I never liked the loose fitting, plain blue, stripped down light wool jumper. There were no white stripes on the collar, only a thin white band around the left shoulder. The light wool fabric was too light for San Diego's chilly winter mornings. But I soon found undress blues did have an advantage.

After I had submitted my requisitions and arranged for truck transportation, I was off to mix with the civilian population. I knew I was out of uniform to be in public, but as long as I buttoned up my P-coat and was careful not to be spotted by the Shore Patrol (SP's), I was safe.

Being the only storekeeper was good duty with many perks and a sense of satisfaction, but with great responsibility. Every time I brought back a load of stores, I would hear the work detail ask, "What did you bring us?" "Anything good?" "Did you get any milk?" "Where's the fruit?"

Often times I would break open a case of apples or a crate of oranges to share with the men. It was good to know the crew would be well fed. And I relished my storekeeper privileges. Whether I was away from the ship a short time or gone a long time, it mattered little. I was seldom questioned as to where I had been or why it took so long. I had the pat answer, if asked, "I was ashore getting stores and had to wait on transportation." The answer was well received because jeeps, pickups and supply trucks were not a high priority assignment for small ships – auxiliary vessels.

Chapter 8

Stateside Liberty and Panama Pain

Orders came for us to head to Long Beach, harness two YO's (yard oilers) in tandem to our towline, and proceed to the Panama Canal Zone. I received the news with mixed emotion because I was nearing my twenty-first birthday, and looked forward to a night of celebration in downtown San Diego. Now I was to miss out on smoky bars, cheap pitchers of beer, loud music, and rousing shuffleboard games. The legal age to drink, vote, and become a man in 1949 was the long awaited twenty-one. I was disappointed; no party, no celebration, not a present unless sailing along the coast of Guatemala could be considered one. Eighteen days later we arrived at Balboa, a district and small town adjacent to Panama City, and at the Pacific entrance to the Panama Canal. We safely delivered the two small ships dockside. I felt some disgust that our government gave these small ships and later several larger auxiliary ships to the Panamanian government.

Sunday afternoon was the right time, I thought, to apply my storekeeper skills to inspect and salvage some *goodies* from one of the ships. We walked along the *camel* - the large timber in the water that protected the dock. We boarded the port side of one of the YO's where we sliced open the mothballed foam seal and entered the hatch. There we discovered signal flags, paint, electronic equipment, and to our surprise - wire spring bunks. We took the wire bunks back, and traded them for our old swag canvas bunks. These wire bunks were considered a real luxury.

Encouraged, our group on our second trip carried several cans of paint, some electronic equipment and *choice items* back to our ship. I had a heavy, shiny electronic device to take to Broghan, our Electronics Technician. I accidentally dropped it in the *drink* and watched it sink - over a hundred, maybe one hundred-fifty feet in the ultra clear water, until it was out of sight. Accidentally deep-sixed.

The duty watch was set, and the port liberty section was given permission to go ashore to explore the sights and sounds of this new port in Central America. Panama was beautiful with lush green vegetation and clear tropical water - so clear you could see to a depth of many feet. But I was disappointed because of the excessive heat. *Tropical Routine* was from 0500 hours, early morning, until around 1400 in the afternoon.

Ashore there was a lack of safe food, drinking water, and little spoken English. The music was mostly calypso and mambo. Continuously played was the loud, heavy, irritating rhythm of *Mambo Jumbo, More More Mambo* -by Prez Prado and his orchestra. The Yeoman and I had a radio in the ship's office, which told us when we were nearing port or we had distanced ourselves from port. The range was about a day and a half out. How wonderful to hear beautiful Hawaiian music, or the latest popular American songs, but not the constant pounding, repetitive, and monotonous limited selections of Latin American music.

In many stores and office buildings were pictures of President Franklin D. Roosevelt, who had died four years earlier, at the end of WWII. He had protected the Panama Canal during WWII and was much beloved by the Panamanian people.

The people of Panama were warm and friendly with sub-standard living conditions, but apparently happy. Like our people during The Depression, they were poor but didn't know it, because everybody was poor. As for happiness, Will Rogers once said, "People are as about as happy as they want to be." I could relate to their condition since I was born during The Depression and the collapse of the stock market in 1929.

We had been warned by the Corpsman not to drink the water or eat the food ashore, especially from the street vendors. Some of the food smelled so good. I was very tempted to try a small bit. But I remembered the caution of extreme dysentery, referred to as *Montezuma's Revenge.* Some of the liberty party did purchase food from vending carts and would say, "Come try some; it's real good." I wondered if it would be good later that night, or the next morning.

We were somewhat apprehensive though because of the political unrest in this banana republic. The afternoon of our first liberty we heard the popping-cracking sounds of gunfire. The local people scattered into doorways and places of safety. We hurriedly hid behind a thick walled building that would stop bullets. After all was quiet and considered safe, we ventured out, turned the corner, and made off in the opposite direction. The 50's were a time of little political stability in Central and South American Countries lying on either side of the Equator.

The excessive heat kept the Pharmacist Mate busy removing warts, issuing talcum powder for rash, and treating several cases of bad jock itch. I overheard the remark, "*I'll be glad to get back to Long Beach and civilization.*" This was my first visit to a third world underdeveloped foreign country, except one obligatory trip to Tijuana while in San Diego.

A ***rite of passage*** to manhood for me and a few buddies was the obligatory trip to Tijuana, Mexico, only a short ride from our home port of San Diego. The afternoon was very hot and sultry. We had walked the dusty streets, had seen the city's drabness and visited *Tijuana's* - the longest bar in the world. Fireman Sipe, a tall, slow, slim, unenthusiastic crew member from the Engineering Department, was anxious to get back to base and so was I. Unwisely we decided to head back to the ship early with a ride offered by two Navy Shore Patrolmen. Across the room we saw a local shake his head slightly – twice, *No!* Sipe was not the *sharpest* sailor in the Navy. I was leery of his judgment, and I should not have gone with him.

But boredom, the unsanitary conditions, and my naïveté discounted good advice, and we were on our way with what we thought was a *free ride.* The patrol car rolled to a stop in a dim spot, somewhat past the main gate. I wondered why. We got out, so did both Shore Patrols. It was a *shakedown.* They wanted our money. One of them said something like, “This is not a free ride. Give us your money.” This *ole farm boy* was not about to give them his hard earned money without a fight. I was terribly afraid at first, but told them, "No, you are not getting my money. I don't make very much, and I don't have much on me." I said, "Come on Sipe, they are not taking our money”, and *square*d *off.* I could see Sipe would not fight and had moved a ways behind me. He was *chicken.*

I knew the SP's had to be distracted from their dastardly intentions. Remembering how I had cajoled supply clerks, I knew I needed to wheedle my self out of this predicament. I told them I was off the USS Tawakoni ATF-114 and that we had been a long time at sea. Tugboats had small crews, often had to do without, and did not have much of anything. I could see the perplexed look on their face now that I had touched the better nature of the larger SP. At that same time I glanced back at Sipe. He had moved farther away. While they were in a state of indecision, I too turned and walked briskly away, into the light and towards the main gate, where there were a group of sailors. I smiled with a glow of relief and much satisfaction knowing I was free, and had *outfoxed the foxes*. I made a report of the incident to CINPAC the next day. I avoided Sipe like the plague – never spoke to him again.

Slowly and surely I was losing my good nature and becoming hardened with scrounging stores, standing many four hours on and only eight hours off sea watches, lengthy and rough sea voyages, and coping with shipboard routine. The uncertainty of the next destination, and an assignment to carry out the whims of some top Navy brass was disconcerting and took its toll. I was becoming tough and experienced *tugger* – tugboat sailor. But I thought to myself, "Isn't this the price I have to pay to see the world – the 'I do' of enlistment? It is better than staying at home, and too my enlistment will be up in less than two years." I had the resolve and expectation of our upcoming assignments to be better and a determination to perform the duties of my three-year enlistment.

Islands and Atolls in the Marianas, Marshalls and Carolinas were viewed according to size and location, number of trees, water shades of light blue, turquoise, and light green/yellow chartreuse, and whether one was a new Isle never visited ever. But back of my initial inquisitiveness and sightseeing at seeing these islands was always the desire to get underway, underway to a new destination, a better, or a more exciting port – Pearl Harbor, Honolulu, Hawaii.

Just as the *old salts* on the ship before me, it was expedient to absorb the sights and sounds, participate in exciting liberties, and make lasting memories ashore, enough to last for many days at sea. Time was of an essence to release the pent up emotions of spending long days at sea. For tugs, port liberty was only temporary, of short duration – a day, a few days, maybe a week or two. The consensus was that we always had a long ways to go and a short time to get there, even though our ship was a slow plodding tug.

Finding a girl in every port, mischievousness, and minor infractions of *NavRegs,* and getting logged in on time, were basics of a good liberty. Liberation and libation down on Hotel Street or at the Waikiki Tavern were considered necessary for a proper shove off. There was an urgency to make it happen, or let it happen. Happen it did, more to some than others.

I noticed Petty Officers with their additional pay and experience attracted more girls, had more solid fun than young Seamen and Seaman Apprentices. The seasoned sailors had serious fun with memories that would last the whole trip; the young seamen's experience and excitement ashore lasted a few days, yet their experiences were many – and to them the ultimate. By the time I had advanced to Petty Officer I could see I noticed the innocence and ignorance of the young sailor, and felt an obligation to warn and protect. I believe this perceived extra-duty often cut into my and the other Petty Officers' fun. Many a time we admonished a half drunken sailor to shape up or ship out, return to his ship.

We stayed only three days in Panama, returning to Long Beach in the company of two other Ocean Fleet Tugs, the U.S.S. Tawasa ATF –92, and her sister ship the U.S.S. Takesta ATF – 93. The ground swells off the coast of Acapulco, Mexico were a real nuisance for several hours. They caused the ship to roll, wallow, and pitch as if in a storm. Hatches had to be battened down, watertight doors dogged down, and everything secured. We had to remember to tie the shoes to the bunk each time we passed this coastline.

Our running unencumbered without a tow allowed us to make the return trip in record time—three thousand miles in eight days. At one point we were running near flank speed for a short distance. It was good to see the prow splitting the water and making huge wakes. The churning of the large screw bubbled and boiled the water with trapped air, until it turned a foaming white, then a greenish white. I believe the three Captains wanted to race, and were as anxious as we were to get back to Long Beach.

Twenty hundred hours found us back in Long Beach ready for liberty. On my first night ashore a Long Beach policeman gave my buddy and me free tickets to hear Les Brown and his Band of Renown. There was a large ballroom near a broad wooden pier where we observed his orchestra play his top two hits, *"I've Got My Love to Keep Me Warm",* and *"Leap Frog".* Les Brown and his orchestra traveled with Bob Hope to entertain GI's both ashore and on ships during WWII, the Korean War, and the Vietnam War. Les Brown, Woody Herman and the Thundering Herd, and Bob Wills and the Texas Playboys, were ending their careers in the mid to late fifties, all except Lawrence Welk and his Champagne Orchestra—*an' uh one, an' uh two.* I still remember the policeman's generosity.

Most people have heard the remark, "A sailor has a girl in every port." The truth is a sailor has not been in every port. I did have one date and a short encounter with another girl while in San Diego, our homeport.

I was in downtown San Diego having a few *cool ones* to celebrate and remember my twenty-first birthday that the Navy took away from me on our way to Panama. By chance I met up with this sailor from Arkansas. He was most amusing to talk to. Not that I was looking to make him a buddy, just that he was country and was reminding me a little of my early farm life. He was telling his head, reminiscing about his favorite dog, farm animals, and family members. He happened to mention he had a first cousin somewhere in

San Diego. He gave me her name and enough information for me to find the number and call her. Her name was Charlene. She was delighted I had met one of her favorite kin, and readily agreed to go out with me that very afternoon. I tried to shake off the two or three beers to be presentable, but needn't have been overly concerned.

With address in hand I commandeered a taxi in manly fashion, for I was now a twenty-one year old salty sailor - off to pick up my Charlene. Luckily she lived only a short taxi ride from town, leaving me with plenty money for a good time. The cab driver must have known the address and been there before, for he rolled right up to the curb directly in front her house. She was ready and waiting, and opened the screen door just as I was about to step upon the wooden porch. I could see several family members peering and peeping out through the windows of the wooden framed house, but none peered out of the screened door.

She was a *knockout*. When I saw her I went cold sober. Not that Charlene was all that comely, for she had on the brightest orange *floral print dress,* orange socks near the same color, and *orangey* red hair, all tied up with *yellowish-orange* ribbons. She had a lively countenance of mischief. I knew I was in trouble, but my upbringing told me I had to see it through. I have often asked myself why redheaded, fair complexioned women have the unrelenting compulsion, and propensity to wear reds, orange, yellow-orange warm colors, when cool colors would be more becoming. Just as well. I did not know too much, or think about color matching in my early twenties. Charlene's brightness would be a little disconcerting should I have to introduce her to any of my shipmates.

Before I could close the car door, Charlene had flopped right in, all smiles, and with a good-time expectation. She said, "Where you from?" I told her, Texas. "You got any cows?" From there on she talked non-stop about her early farm life, her dog, and family – just like her first cousin. I thought the quickest way to get to town and Charlene back home was a two hour movie. I asked her, "What movie do you want to see?" She quickly replied, "Anchors Aweigh." I just wanted to *weigh anchor.*

At the concession stand I asked her, "What size drink do you want?" She said, "A big-un." The candy was soon gone, and I only got a handful or two of popcorn. The musical was too sweet and the sound was too loud, but Charlene did not seem to mind. I was jolted with the idea this *vixen with orange fixin's* might have been out with sailors before. My upbringing again told me I had to see this through, because she was of the fairer sex. The movie ended, I was hungry and felt I had the duty to feed Charlene. She did not want a hamburger but a cheeseburger, with everything on it, and a large fry. Now I knew why she was a bit dumpy. But as we politely said back in Texas, she was ***pleasingly plump***. She loved catsup, lots of catsup (ketchup) – to *wallar* her fries in.

Satisfied that she was full of food, sights, and sounds, I determined it was the opportune time to make an exit and take her home. I must have made a feeble excuse that I had to get back to the ship. She seemed to know the party was over.

Bolstered by sustenance and the excitement of big city sights, she *banged my ears* all the way back to curbside. "You said you had some cows; do you raise any turkeys?" Before I could answer, "No", she jumped out with alacrity and quickly stuck her head in. With her best orange lipstick smile, as warm as the color she was wearing she said, "You can call me anytime."

The expected often times becomes the unexpected. For there in early evening on a later occasion I was smitten by this petite girl with soft auburn hair, deep blue *Spanish eyes,* and a smooth olive skin complexion. She twisted and turned sprightly as if window shopping. She had on a very white full skirt imprinted with very black large Roman Numerals. The skirt was tight around her slender waist and accented her womanly figure. I knew she was my *number!* Her fresh starched white blouse was amply filled, and had puffy sleeves that fit snugly around the upper arm. Shoes were white with ankle socks like those worn in the '50's. She told me she lived with her aunt in El Cajon – a costly taxi ride, with limited bus service on Saturday and none on Sunday.

Our eyes had met with a glance at first, then a smile. I had to approach her even if it meant rejection. But no, we were soon acquainted, and found our conversation most delightful. We were drawn together with youthful laughter, and excited by the anticipated bliss only young people can know. I began dating Rita Fay, seeing her every other, or every third, night. Our short romance was interrupted by our first orders to tow two YO's (yard oilers) to Panama. Just as well, I was out of money after wining and dining Rita Fay on a Seaman's pay.

The 6,000 miles in 18 days round trip to Panama kept me away from Rita Fay long enough to dwell upon my new love life. I vaguely remembered she had mentioned something about having an old boyfriend. I was certain whatever the attraction, that was all over, and I was now the love of her life. We arrived back in port in the early afternoon, enough time for a liberty. I checked to be sure the gangplank was down, and hurried to the dock to call my Rita Fay. That night I was able to be with her as before. All was well.

After two weeks, orders came for the second time to tow two more YO's to Balboa, Panama CZ. I dreaded the mandatory five hour rock and roll along the coast of Acapulco, caused by ground swells. I had to remember to have my shoes laced to the bunk to keep them from sliding.

We were making preparations to return to San Diego, but were called out to make an emergency run to aid the Santa Rita, an ammunition ship with a fire in her #1 hold. The merchant ship's name being Rita was a coincidence. I volunteered for the excitement, but my services were not needed. There were enough experienced damage control and deck hands to handle the emergency. Twenty-five days later we were back in San Diego.

Anxious as I was to see Rita Fay, I was in the duty section the first night and not allowed to go ashore. The next day was my day of liberty and with an all night pass. I rushed to the dockside telephone and called the aunt's house with great anticipation, with not the least misgiving or trepidation. I said, "This is Jack, and I would like to speak to Rita Fay." There was a long pause, then the soft spoken heartbreaking words, ***"I'm sorry, she's married."*** I remembered at once her telling me of her civilian boyfriend. At least I had not lost my love to another sailor. Now I was mean, tough and dumped. *A girl in every port?* As it turned out I lost a girl in the only two ports I visited.

Wild Nights – Wild Nights!

Were I with thee
Wild nights should be
Our luxury!
Futile – the Winds-
To a heart in port-
Done with the Compass-
Done with the Chart!

Rowing in Eden-

Ah, the sea!
Might I but moor – tonight-
In thee!
~ Unknown

Chapter 9

The Sand, The Sea, and Waikiki

It was good to be at sea and headed back to beautiful Hawaii—my Hawaii. Now Diamond Head was just off our port bow. My heart jumped. Eventually I had to leave my favorite sitting place on the gunnels and perform detail duty of raising the *Union Jack* on the bow flag pole. The many ships and submarines tied up or anchored in the harbor cured my nostalgia, cheered my heart, and brightened my countenance. I was home!

A new ship's duty roster divided the crew into three sections. Two liberty sections or two-thirds of the ship's crew were allowed ashore because this was the peacetime Navy. One duty day on board and two days' liberty ashore was great. Sometimes we would get an overnight pass and stay at the YMCA, and not be back until Sunday night. But most of the time we lined up on deck at 1400 hours to receive permission to go ashore. AOL- *Absent On Leave* - return time was 1100 hours. With every liberty a few shipmates and I would rush to catch the bus headed for Waikiki Beach and the Waikiki Tavern, where Wally Rae played the organ and piano. The hula girls danced and played the ukulele—as only Polynesians can. I still remember the song, "Lola O'Brien, the Irish Hawaiian," done by a very pretty petite girl who really was half Irish and half Hawaiian – it made sense. Lawrence Welk and his orchestra later recorded this whimsical little number, which I sometimes listen to.

Inside Waikiki Tavern there was a long salad bar set up with fresh island fruits, tree-ripened papayas, melons, and an assortment of fresh island juices contained in very cold *sweating* crystal pitchers. All were attractively arranged and displayed on beds of crushed ice.

The soft sound of incoming waves was mingled with rustling palm branches and melodic Hawaiian music. This was the height of luxury back in the late forties and early fifties. I was a twenty-one year-old sailor, and in a hurry to get my share of adventure and excitement. An octagon bar with several stools was located just outside on the tavern grounds, adjacent to and part of the Waikiki Tavern.

It was nice to sit outside and feel the cool tropical night breeze, hear the ocean waves slap softly against the shore - then listen to Wally Rae and the ukuleles. Sometimes I would meet up with Chief Petty Officer Merrill, who had been the Chief Corpsman on our ship, and was now assigned to Tripler Army Hospital. Two Navy nurses that seemed to enjoy my company usually accompanied him. My advancement to Petty Officer and maturity allowed me to fit in, and share the company of one pretty petite nurse. The tavern is no longer there, but *ah*, the memories linger on.

One night after Parson, Parris, and I had watched the hula show, and Wally Rae had retired for the night, we left the Waikiki Tavern and ventured down Kalakaua Avenue toward the Royal Hawaiian Hotel. The hotel had been occupied and used as military headquarters after the bombing of Pearl Harbor, December 7, 1941, and continued in use until the early 1950's. We had walked past the *Pink Palace* many times, and wondered about the *goings-on* in such a lavish place. This night, it was just too enticing to pass up.

There among the swaying palms, and well-manicured lawn was a fine orchestra playing music of the isles. Officers in spiffy dress uniforms decorated with gold braid, and ladies dressed in their finest long evening dresses were in a relaxed mood. A whiff of expensive perfume mixed with the moist evening sea breeze got rid of any inhibition I might have had.

We quietly ventured in without being acknowledged, or worse, accosted, and found an unobtrusive table. The effect of the melodic Hawaiian music, rustling palm trees, and full tropical moon over Diamond Head gave me a bad case of Polynesian Paralysis—that "I don't care" feeling. I was instilled with misbegotten courage.

One well-dressed lady in particular caught my eye. Glances were exchanged, and obvious gestures were made, until I walked to the dance floor where she met me. Without a word we smiled, embraced, and began to dance. Our mutual attraction was soon and abruptly interrupted by the coarse, authoritative voice of a *four striper*, a senior officer—a Navy Captain. Fraternizing with enlisted personnel by officers and their wives was frowned upon, and in my case forbidden. I sheepishly changed my devil-may-care attitude and made a hasty exit lest I and the others be shipped to the outer edges of civilization-like the Kwajalein Atoll. I have been drawn back to Hawaii several times; could have stayed, never stayed, but remember claiming a dance once beneath the full tropical moon over Waikiki at the Royal Hawaiian Hotel – the Pink Palace.

During the next month we towed an ammunition barge to the dumping area, towed targets for the U.S.S. Norton Sound and other ships. Life was idyllic, and we had settled into the mood of the islands, until one Saturday morning. Sure enough, we left Hawaii for Kwajalein towing a YFRN (Yard Refrigeration Ship) and a barge. The U.S.S. Sunnadin ATA-197 went with us towing two barges.

The next day we reversed course to rendezvous with the U.S.S. Pussumsic AO-107, to allow a sailor with appendicitis to be high lined off the Sannadin. After the successful transfer, both ships continued with their tows to Kwajalein in the Marshall Islands.

Once we left Kwajalein our ship had to go into dry dock for eleven hot, lonely days at Guam, and then hold sea trials for another ten dreadful days. The crew, as well as I, were getting edgy, and needed something different besides hanging around a rock in the middle of nowhere. Our reprieve came at 2400 hours with us having to assist the USNS Sgt. Howard E. Woodford T-AP-191, which carried ammunition, and had a fire in its number one hold. The ship was formerly an Army Ocean Transport – MSTS, and also a United States Army Transport.

During WWII the Army transported their own troops and supplies on a fleet of Army Ships refered to now as the *Ghost Fleet,* because of lack of history. Only a few records were kept, and books are almost non-existent on the roll of Army Ships. Civilian, Coast Guard, Merchant Marine, Navy, and Army personnel manned these many ships of many designations. Most transport and supply ships had been transferred to the U. S. Navy by the late 40's and early 50's. The Army is now out of the transport business and depends on the Navy for logistics.

Another Navy cargo ship, the AKA-86, lost power and was dead in the water. We met up with the stricken vessel, made repairs, and escorted her back to Pearl Harbor. We were out again for a few days on a routine operation to relieve the U.S.S. Kaskaskia AO 27 of her tow. I believe the top administration sat around thinking up things that would disrupt our lives ashore.

Surely one of these detested necessities thought up by dizzy brass was *circling* and *wallowing* in and out of sea troughs all night, waiting for ships to come by and fire at the target sled we were towing. One early morning about 0200 hours the aircraft carrier Bairoko passed close to starboard and fired on the target. We could hear the ***wham, wham,***

wham of her guns. The next morning we looked aft and saw that we were pulling nothing but a flat piece of tangled metal. The upright metal bars holding the canvas bull's eye had been mangled or blown away. We discussed among ourselves that firing so close was of no benefit and a waste. Only one time do I remember we pulled target for a surface vessel in the day time. We cheered when a water plume rose close by the target, and was considered a hit. We laughed and jeered when their shells landed a way off target, knowing the gun **pointer** was going to get reprimanded.

A lot of excitement was caused the day our ship fired at a sleeve—an orange nylon windsock affair, towed by a single engine airplane. As soon as the sleeve was spotted a distance to starboard, the order was given to commence firing. Our twin 40s, twin 20s, and 3"50 began to fire, and kept it up until the angle of fire was becoming closer and acute, nearing the tow plane's tail. The pilot began to holler, "shut them d--things off!"

Strange how there was aggressive awareness the longer we fired, seeing tracers and shell patterns hit the target. The staccato of the small and medium anti-aircraft guns, the powerful blast of the large bow gun, the danger of a misfire, and the duty to be on target gave a high—a high that was not easy to come down from.

Another aggravating duty was anti-submarine exercises conducted at various times and hours. Duty required sudden maneuvers of stopping and starting, turning, speeding up, zigzagging, and slowing down. Every time we cut across a wave the ship rose and pitched; then when we made an evasive turn into a trough the ship would rock and roll side to side, as if in a storm. I came to dread even seeing a submarine, fearing we might be called out for an extended exercise. And subs would come in fast to port, and not give way to our ship, even if we had the right of way. Submariners were a pushy bunch, and when push came to shove, us tugs had to give way or get literally run over.

These short trips and duties interrupted our liberty in Honolulu that was always the very best. Even if you were broke, the gifts of the island were free to enjoy. Some sailors were broke because they had spent their money on tattoos, but mostly on booze and beer down on King and Hotel Streets.

The duty section was not too bad if you had the eight to twelve watch. There was always the expected excitement of a few rowdy and out of control malcontents, being escorted by the Shore Patrol. They were most unceremoniously delivered into our custody with disgusting, but sometimes humorous antics, and the customary official papers of infractions.

One night was a *doozy.* I had the watch when the SP's brought back our Chief Bos'n Mate Garfield, who was a strong, rough and tough ole cuss. He was ashore and got into a brawl with two Marines. Unconfirmed reports were that he whipped the two, and had to be restrained before he was finally arrested.

Anyway he was helped aboard and found a seat on the fire hydrant near the gangplank that conveniently extended from the bulkhead. I noticed the bridge of his large nose was skinned from the tip to the forehead. Blood had coagulated. He and his nose looked awful. He sat there, head down in a drunken stupor. I had to get three or four men to help get him to bed. We removed only his shoes, laid him on his back, and let him sleep it off. Rules were not that strict on a tugboat. I do not think he was reprimanded, surely not for fighting with the Navy's nemesis, members of the Marine Corps.

There was another incident on Guam where one of our deck crew tangled with a Marine, some said two. There may have been none, but he came back with smiles and *braggadocio.* I remember pulling Shore Patrol Duty in Japan where both a soldier and Marine were out of uniform. I excused the soldier who had just come back from fighting in

Korea, but not the Marine. I waited for him to roll down and button his sleeves, and straighten his tie, to get back in uniform. I remembered being turned back at the main gate at Pearl Harbor.

There was a lot of animosity between the Navy and the Marines because they did guard duty and held inspection on the dreaded liberty gates. Often one or more of our crew would be turned back and not allowed to pass through the main gate until they went all the way back to the ship, shined their shoes, or wore hats with an ultra clean hat band.

Other times they would not let taxis enter and take us down to the dock. The short ride or the long walk often made the difference of being logged in on time. Picky little infractions, and at times no infraction, caused our delay going ashore or late to catch the Waikiki bus.

They were also the brig security guards both on land and large ships at sea. We felt their ire, their superiority. We were adventurous sailors, free-spirited, well trained shipboard specialists who were thought to be undisciplined. We straggled. They marched—everywhere. They were *esprit d' corps* and professional. We were good-time Charley. They were Tradition and *Gung-ho.* Sailors were usually *hung-oh* with good cause, after many days at sea. The two branches of service did not understand each other, nor did they try to. They were leathernecks, *disdained for sailors,* security guards. We were *squid* or *devil dolphins.* We were *Aye, Aye*: they were *Ooh-rah.* More Marines would later become successful businessmen, but more sailors would become Presidents. Both branches were under the Department of the Navy, however, and the Marines used basic Navy terminology. Yes, we each had different jobs and knew how to perform skillfully, but our reactions to each other had been practiced, polished and honed over many years.

Tattoos were a part of the Navy in the 40's and 50's, and it was not uncommon to daily view the artistry from the beach. I noticed the sober sailors very seldom were the ones who retuned to the ship with tattoos. Drink, loud music, bright lights, and the hum of needle guns created an environment made to rid a man of his inhibitions. But you know, I don't think I ever saw a Marine get a tattoo. One of our crew, a barrel-chested sailor had a large American eagle tattooed across his chest. Another small chested sailor got a tattoo of palm trees, blue water, sea birds, and a hula girl on a tiny island. We were in and out of port so often; I wondered what would have happened had we not returned. They would have been left with a half finished tattoo. Shortly after their tattoos were finished and healed, we returned to port, and these two sailors were given a discharge. Little time was wasted in typing up their discharge papers and getting them ashore. One was athletic and elusive, the other likable, but neither fit in. I wonder at this late date if the eagle has *flown the coop* and the hula girl has lost her *charms – after sixty-two years.*

New and usually small tattoos were commonplace. Each time when naked, waiting our turn to take a shower, bodies were scrutinized for the latest art work. There was one sailor named Hall, who was very fair complexioned, red headed, and with a thin red mustache. He came back off the beach one night all smiles with two screws, *twin screws*, one on each cheek of the buttocks. Our ship only had one screw. Ships with twin screws were more maneuverable and accepted.

With many tattoo parlors lining the streets in downtown Honolulu, I was tempted to get just a small one. But I was nearing the end of my enlistment and would soon return to civilian life. My WWII brother had a medium size tattoo on his left shoulder. I could tell he had grown tired of it. A tattoo soon faded, lost its attraction, and was not appreciated in civilian life. Recently I saw a large billboard along an expressway in California that said, "Tattoo Exhibition." On the other side the sign read, "Tattoo Removal."

Life in a good port and the peacetime Navy was great for us single men. There was lots of fun, and little sea duty, just enough to keep us out until payday, and long enough to make us want to go ashore again. We had little worry, plenty of food, health care, no war, and someone to look after us. Some sailors had found a home! And I had become a Hawaiian *Kiamaaina* (old-timer), no longer a *Malihini* (newcomer). As well, I now belonged to the Realm of the Golden Dragon.

I had these two *orders* that I had purchased on the beach of Waikiki filled in and signed by *King Kanakanui, 1st*. They read:

Hawaiian Kamaaina

Greetings: Seafaring Men, Landlubbers, and All Living Creatures of Land, Sea, and Sky, Know Ye, that Billy J. McCoy

on the 3rd day of June, 1949

via U.S.S. Tawakoni ATF-114 -

A *Malihina* (newcomer) entered my Royal Domain *the Hawaiian Islands* in the Pacific and having worthily partaken Fish and Poi, drunk Okolehao *beer*, crossed the Pali, climbed the Volcanoes, ridden the Surf, combed the Beaches, and kissed the Hula Girls and done all in true Kanaka fashion,

I hereby pronounce him *Kamaaina* (old-timer).

Royal Witness: King Kanakanui, 1st

Realm of the Golden Dragon

Know ye, that B. J. McCoy on the 4-5 day of July, 1949, aboard the U.S.S. Tawakoni ATF-114 Latitude 130 degrees 42' Longitude 180 degrees 00' E appeared on the Threshold of the Far East, and having been duly inspected and found worthy, was accepted into the Ancient and Sacred Order of the Golden Dragon.

Royal Witness: Mystic Scribe, Order of the Golden Dragon – *King Kamakanui, 1st*

Most all sailors, whether they say so or not, feel a separation, an end, a parting, from the *Mistress of the Sea.* Days on end they have been in the comfort of her arms, but all the while knowing full well the dangers, and how careful one had to be lest they should feel her squeeze of death and be taken to a watery grave by her powerful pull.

She was born into a royal troubled family of Neptunus Rex – King Neptune. His name in Greek is Poseidon. Her Highness Amphitrite and King Neptune produced the Royal Baby whom every sailor reveres and fears – the *Tempest of the Sea.* She was to become the mother of Triton – *the god of water, horses and earthquakes.*

Great turmoil and strife in the Royal household caused a tremendous split among the brothers, with King Neptune's domain being the Ruler of the Sea. With him he took the Trident with which it is said he whirls when angry, causing tidal waves, tsunamis and fierce sea storms.

Davy Jones – Denizen, Menace, Ruler of the Deep, Most Royal Mushiness – Realm of the August Moon, King Neptune's temperamental assistant – is known to aid and often cause mayhem at sea as well. He took with him a temperamental razor-sharp sword. Known to every open-blue water sailor is Davy Jones, Neptune's abode, and Davy Jones' Locker. Davy Jones is believed to be the collector of the bones of dead sailors.

Adventures of the Black Fisherman

1824 Washington Irving

He came, said he, in a storm, and went in a storm;
He came nobody knows whence, and he has gone nobody knows where.
For aught I know he has gone to sea once more on his chest, and may land to bother
Some people on the other side of the world though it is a thousand pities, added he,
If he is gone to Davy Jones Locker.

King Pest

Edgar Allen Poe

"that unearthly sovereign" Tarpaulin resounds, "Whose name is Davy Jones!"

It is the Pollywog who has bothered and aroused the *Ruler of the Deep*, who has crossed the International Date Line, and entered into the realm of the Dragon. But it is the Shellback sailor who has disturbed and offended King Neptune, by entering his domain at the Equator without his permission. A raucous and rowdy shipboard ceremony with much fanfare is held to initiate and welcome those crossing the Equator for the very first time –

they become shellbacks: sons of Neptune. This is a royal shipboard occasion. Everything is *royally* planned and carried out with *royal food* and entertainment meant to appease King Neptune, the Ruler of the Deep, and celebrate the invitation into his watery domain.

But there may be hope for the souls of some sailor in the legenday and imagined afterlife found in Homer's Odyssey, Elysian Fields and the Irish myth of Fiddler's Green – where the fiddle never stops playing and the dancer never tires – more so for the worthy Old Salt who has been at sea for fifty years. (I read in the latest edition of NAFTS Towline (National Association of Tugboat Sailors) August 2012 that an Enlisted Men's Club, the Fiddler's Green had opened in Sasebo, Japan, in August 1952 – the same month and year I was discharged).

Everything was running smoothly, light duty and a carefree lifestyle until the Yeoman, Joe Knapp, took state-side leave. There were only the two of us in the office so it was necessary for me to assume his duties. They included making the Plan of the Day, issuing ID Cards and Liberty Cards, and recording Captain's Mast, of which I was to be one of the chief participants a few days later.

I discovered the importance of the ship's office and that it ran the ship. It afforded me special privileges like retaining my Liberty Card, making out my own Special Liberty Requests, and having a favorable duty station on the bow to raise and lower the forty-eight stars of the Union Jack. This forward position afforded me an ample view of each new port and little exposure to inclement weather.

Once I was greatly embarrassed and thought I might lose my favorite sea detail station by becoming lax. The two hoist lines *(lanyards) that* were used to raise and lower the flag had to be fastened to the two metal grommets by a snap. One snap was not thoroughly secured, and halfway up the mast a strong wind caused the Union Jack to come loose and flop in the air forward of the bow. I stood up on the very tip end ledge of the bow holding tightly to the mast, but could not reach the wayward insignia. All this time I was being watched from the bridge and the dock. I ran and got the long boat hook, snagged the flopping line and properly raised the flag. I expected a reprimand, but a word was never said. My job was secure, and I had had a great ride.

Later another incident happened with the Union Jack as we were attempting to dock. We had a new skipper, a Yeoman administrator, not a line officer. I noticed he was bringing the ship in too fast. Order was given to reverse engines Full, but the ship had too much way and kept coming, cracking heavy wooden timbers, and almost plowing into the stern of our sister ship. I had to take the brunt of its sailors' slurs, insults, and sarcastic remarks like, "Can't your ole man drive that thang? You almost ran into us." I hurriedly hoisted the Union Jack, secured the line, and went below.

Some of our crew drank heavily, and filled with Hawaiian Hadicol – Hawaii's local beer – got into a fight or caused mischief. The Shore Patrol became familiar with the ship named Tawakoni. I was often amazed, sometimes aggravated, and at times disgusted by their antics, fisticuffs and mayhem. Between the hours of 2200 and 0200 was when quarterdeck activity was the most active. Some of the lesser offenders would hang around, mill around the quarterdeck talking boisterously - refusing to go below to bed. Often times the duty officer would come around about midnight to check for AOLs.

Every ship, including our ship, had a drinking problem – some more serious than others. Some of our crew were teetotalers, others light drinkers. A few were habitual drinkers, and there was the pitiable young sailor who did not know how to drink or when to quit. They usually would return early thinking they were drunk, but not really, only loud and ridiculous. Most of the old salts knew how to drink and hold their liquor, and caused little trouble. Still there was apprehension and concern for crewmembers that were missing after midnight.

It was customary to log in as on-time those coming back off liberty a few minutes, or even an hour or so late, if they were not causing trouble. A deck hand named Choats was *chicken.* He habitually came back late, and I would always log him in on-time. One night I returned a few minutes late. He had logged me in late and was refusing to erase the time. I explained to him very firmly that I had done him a favor many times, and he should do the same for me, and if he didn't his liberty card and any special liberty request would be lost in the ship's office forever. He thought better, and logged me in at 2355.

The sailor I remember the most was a WWII veteran named Taylor. He was a balding, redheaded First Class Petty Officer with cirrhosis of the liver. The doctors had warned him to lay off alcohol, but he just could not. One night he and his best drinking buddy, Bardenberg, came aboard inebriated, *higher than a kite.* Taylor's legs were too wobbly to climb down the ladder to the crew's compartment. His buddy was a big man, and picked him up and began to descend the ladder. They were about half way down when they both tumbled and landed on the steel deck below, where many nuts and bolts stuck up on hatch covers. I was certain they were seriously cut or hurt, but no, neither had a scratch or bruise. Taylor was very ill the next morning and had to go to the hospital. He was gone for over a week and assigned light duty for a few days.

It was soon after that I caught Taylor *stealing* coffee from the Bread Locker. He had a sea bag, and was filling his bag with two-pound cans of coffee. When he saw me he became all nervous and started stammering. His explanation was that the coffee was to be used as a bribe to get us better movies when he was on base picking up the ship's mail. Once I knew his purpose, I gave him several more cans and told him it was okay, but to ask me next time. He came back with the best movies we had ever had—one was actually in Technicolor, a rarity for us in the fifties.

Movies were a very important part of Navy life, especially for our crew each night when we assembled on the fantail at sea. Each evening at dusk, those who had chairs would bring them aft and get ready to watch the movie. The film was considered new if it had not been shown over three times. We did not have thirty different movies when we were thirty days at sea. On these long voyages it was necessary to see the movies more than once, sometimes wound and shown in reverse! The movie may not have been exciting but the projector's sudden flapping-clicking noise of broken film with the screen going blank was.

The real excitement came when the ship rolled too far to one side and our chairs began to slide across the steel deck. When the roll was accompanied by seawater spilling on deck, there was much scrambling and grumbling, because the chairs began to slide uncontrollably, and it was necessary to put your feet down in the sloshing water to keep your balance. Then while your feet were being covered, you had to catch your balance and wayward chair. If the roll was small and water was only a little, we would just lift our feet and wait until it had drained down the sculptors. There were times the sea became too rough, and we were taking on too much water. Often word came over the speaker, "There will be no movies tonight."

Rough seas or seas becoming rough cancelled a movie many times.

It came to be a game of chance and anticipation as to whether the sea would be passive, with slow even swells or fretful, not letting us to enjoy our only nightly entertainment. At times it seemed the sea would have the proclivity to send water sloshing across the deck two or three times, a little or a lot, until our shoes, socks and pant legs were all wet. Often times we would be delighted to find a flying fish or a squid on deck in early morning. Our ship's stern *fantail* rode that close to the water, and was often awash in cloudy and turbulent weather.

I remember one night the ship was rolling pretty well. I stepped out of the hatch with my chair from the ship's office *hurriedly*, for the movie was about to begin. It was very dark that night. I reached for the metal safety line as usual. The ship rolled to port and I missed and almost went over the side – would have if the ship had not lurched in a quick roll back to starboard. I remembered what my brother had said about the sea being always hungry. I had forgotten his admonition and become over-confident.

Our first Captain Cherwood was a rough ole salt, a fine ship handler, and a swinger, with the ladies coming aboard and staying all night, and whiskey in the wardroom. I understand his previous ship had engine work with three engines down, when he was ordered to rescue a ship in rough seas with only the one engine. He refused. I believe that kept him from making Lt. Commander. Maybe that was the reason we were sent to far islands near the Equator. The whole crew respected him for his skills, but most disliked him. He robbed me of my Fourth of July in 1949. We were on our way from Honolulu to Guam. It was the 3rd of July. We crossed the International Date Line on July 3rd at 2245 hours. The date was now July 4, 2245 hours. An hour and fifteen minutes later at 2400, (0000) the date was July 5th. A day is gained going west and lost returning east. I was robbed of my favorite 4th and had to work chipping paint for the first and only time in my life.

The Captain had a black curly-haired Cocker Spaniel named Sinbad. I understand Captain Cherwood told his wife, "You can go, but the dog stays." Information was she *went.* One day we were out for target practice, to fire at a sleeve pulled by a single engine airplane. Sinbad was terrified of guns. When we began to fire all guns, the dog was so scared that he *messed* all over the upper deck. I just happened to see him run and hide under the ready box – ammunition storage box. After cease-fire the Captain and his entourage began their search, bending, looking, and calling, "Here Sindbad, here Sinbad." I never told him or anyone I knew where his dog was. I sure wanted to, but I knew if I told, and then they told, I would be in bad trouble.

Later that evening, long after the search was over, Sinbad came out of hiding and was found waiting near the ready box. We returned to Pearl and shortly after, Captain Cherwood and his dog were transferred to shore duty. There was much jubilation and little fanfare at his leaving. Our new Captain Scrivner was a kinder and gentler man you could respect, which was good, for my first encounter with him was at a Captain's Mast. I was the dubious instigator of a *foul deed.*

There was an obnoxious Fireman named Peopke, who had a dirty yellow handle bar mustache. He rolled and stiffened this *beauty* with beeswax. One day I turned a monopoly board up in his face because of his uncouth behavior.

My good buddy, D.D. Parlson, and his friend came back off liberty late one night in high spirits. He shook my bunk as usual and woke me up for a *pee call.* I said, "Parlson, why don't you get the scissors and go cut off Poepke's mustache." In a few minutes I heard a big commotion in the engineer crew compartment. Petty Officer Poepke was furious, ranting, raving, in a fit of anger and vexation. He had been so rudely awakened - minus one mustache handle bar.

The Master-at-Arms was called; lights came on in the crew's compartment waking up most of the ship's crew. The two were put on report to stand at Captain's Mast. The new skipper was congenial and fair, which was fortunate for them, and for me.

I gathered the culprits' personnel records, my number two pencils, lined yellow pad, and climbed the ladder to the

Captain's wardroom. Ship's Yeoman was still on state-side leave. All was ready at 1000 hours for the hearing. I was to witness and record the punishment. There was the Capitan, Executive Officer, Engineering Officer, Chief Master-at-Arms, the two sailors, and myself. I was verily instructed to take down with all diligence the events of the proceedings.

The time had approached for Poepke to be called in. When he entered the Captain's stateroom he had on both handlebars of his mustache. The Captain said, "Well Poepke, it looks to me like you have both sides of your mustache." Poepke's reply, "Oh no, Captain!" as he made a quick pull with his left hand and stood there at attention with only half a mustache. There were many smiles, grins and the Capitan almost bursting out with laughter. Eventually everyone regained their composure and the questioning began.

I, the innocent one and perpetrator of the whole thing, was ready to record their guilty plea. If either of the two had said, "McCoy put us up to it," I would have been cleaning the *head* for a long time. But they were my good buddies, and admitted only what they had done.

The punishment was reluctantly administered at a minimum of so many hours cleaning the head, known as the latrine in the Army. I had just completed writing everything down when the Captain said, "McCoy, I am putting you in charge to see that this punishment is carried out." I said, "Aye, Aye, Sir."

After the mast I told the two would-be barbers to show up every once in a while for a few days to appease the Master-at-Arm. Just make their presence known, but they did not have to do any work. I might have come close again to losing my Good Conduct Medal.

A month or two later I saw Poepke on the beach one night, wandering around all by himself. He was acting very strange and would not return to the ship. He came back early the next morning around 0200 or 0300. We never knew where he had been or why he stayed out so late. The next day he was issued a fire extinguisher, and assigned to a *fire watch.* Damage Control was to do some welding in a far part of the ship. He was found asleep on watch, a most serious offense. Because of his dereliction of duty, he endangered the whole ship and its crew.

The ship's new Yeoman, Whitman recorded the Court Marshall. Poepke was demoted in rank and given a discharge. His aloof, superior attitude and lack of commitment to the care and protection of the ship, and his inability to get along with crewmembers, were his greatest shortcomings. I felt a little sorry for him because he did not fit in, could not fit in, even with us giving him every chance to do so.

The crew members' antics continued to amuse me with unexpected and at times ridiculous behavior. There was Seaman Salone, a slow moving, and slow talking deck hand from down south, very congenial. One afternoon far out to sea a large brown frigate bird lit on the forward port side gunwale. Birds at sea are not afraid of man. Salone approached the bird, and carefully picked it up before I could warn him. He soon discovered he was covered with mites. We rushed him into the shower, and his clothes were quickly thrown in the washer with plenty of salt-water soap and hot water. I recognized the mites right away because it was a yearly chore to whitewash our chicken house each spring with lime. Fortunately the ship was not mite infested from this incident.

Many sea birds followed us to feed on scraps when we were thousands of miles out. It amazed me that they could dip down to catch the scraps or fish, even light and ride up and down on the waves. There were times we were rewarded to have a graceful long-winged black and white albatross follow aft or circle overhead. The albatross *goony bird* is the clumsiest bird on land and resides mostly on Midway Island. But once airborne they gracefully glide over the ocean for one year. It is great sport to see their *crash landing* when returning to nest. Yet, it was the suspicion of killing the graceful albatross that caused the doom of the ship and crew in Silas Marner – *water, water, everywhere, but not a drop to drink.* Neither do sailors whistle – only fools and sailors whistle lest there be bad luck.

I suppose the saddest sight I ever saw was our seaman crewmember, Memetz. He was assigned to permanent scullery duty, one of the lowest shipboard jobs. I viewed him sitting on his favorite wooden crate up on the boat deck peeling potatoes. There was no expression on his face, only a look of forlorn. The only time his spirits were up was when he had on his whites ready to go ashore. But I believe he was happy not to have any real responsibility and was resigned to his position. I reflected that there must be someone for every job, and I believe his job fit him well.

Tex was another deck hand, and he liked me. He was most affable and amiable. His broad grin could belay strong anger and melt the hardest heart. Never did he complain about hard work or long hours. He was truly a skilled, willing seaman. But his skill as a musician left much to be desired. He would come to me with his guitar and always play the same song – "Among My Souvenirs," by Edgar Leslie and Lawrence Wright, 1927. I would tell him, "Tex, this is the same song and the same way you played for me last time." He would give me that broad *ear-to-ear* grin and say he would practice. And sure enough he would work in some different *licks* and notes, a chord or two, until he was back to play for me again. I would brag on his effort and improvement. He would grin sheepishly, turn and go away, not to come back until he was satisfied he could again show me something better.

I was having trouble with a second-class storekeeper named Choat, who had just recently been assigned to our ship. He came aboard and bullied his way into my office, my home, and was messing up my playhouse. What was worse, he was *chicken* and liable to put me on report if I crossed him. He had this nervous habit of quickly raising his arm and scratching his head. I told Parlson that Choat was giving me a hard time, and I wondered if there was anything he could do about it.

One night on Guam I had the duty, but Choat and Parlson were ashore having beer at the EM – Enlisted Men's Club. A few beers made Choat even more obnoxious, boisterous, and irritating. He again quickly raised his arm to scratch his head when Parlson said, "You swung at me." With those words Parlson knocked him backwards off the bench. The next morning Parlson comes down the starboard side with a wide grin and an attitude of accomplishment. He said, "I got Choat for you." Our close friendship known to Choat belayed any more harassment. He took care to give me a wide berth.

This was not the last of Choat though, and not the last time he made us mad. Several of us were going to put our money together to buy a car to drive when in Honolulu. The make of the car was a Nash, and was referred to as the bug because of its rear-sloping, bug-shaped rounded back body style. Another unusual feature was that the front wheels were narrower than the back wheels. The car would not track. After WWII there were many makes and models of cars that were on the market for only a few short years. I remember the demise of the Studebaker (Golden Hawk), Hudson (Hornet), La Salle, LaFayette, DeSoto, Kaiser and Frasier, Henry J, and a few others.

Choat got word of our intentions, and bought the car for $100 above our agreed-upon offer. Naturally we felt hurt, disappointed, and betrayed. One night several of us were coming back to the ship when we spotted Choat's Nash with its back wheels hanging off the pier – over the water, almost ready to topple into the *drink*. He asked us, begged us, to help lift the rear of his car until it could get traction and move to safety, back onto the dock. We looked at the car, then at him, and with little comment continued walking to our ship.

The next morning I was anxious to see this car that wanted to be a boat. I thought this because the selling feature of the Nash automobile was the strong, flat, welded underbody – unibody. But I was not to see this strange sight again, for the Navy tow truck came early that morning, impounded the vehicle and severely chewed out the owner.

It was time for Choat to ship-over, re-enlist for six years, or get out. He decided to sign up for another six years and make a career of the Navy. His shipping over bonus was six hundred dollars, a great sum of money back then. We cautioned him to be careful with his money, not take it ashore. He was hard-headed and would not listen. That night he was ashore, drunk, and celebrating his manly decision. He was rolled, and came back to the ship beaten up and broke, with six more years to do. We all just shook our heads. He was soon transferred to another duty station, and I had my office back. A quiet, good-looking storekeeper striker named McKey came aboard for me to train.

He was a young, naive, innocent seaman apprentice just out of storekeeper's school. I took him ashore with me one night and introduced him to the lovely sounds of Wally Wray at the Waikiki Tavern, my favorite watering hole. There we met a very friendly civilian who picked up and delivered the ship's dry cleaning. He had a fifth of Jack Daniels and liberally shared his bottle with McKey until he was getting him drunk. I noticed this laundry deliveryman was moving closer, touching, and forcing himself onto McKey. I was surprised because the laundryman was very muscular and gave no indication he was other than straight.

I could see what was happening and hurriedly got McKey on the bus and back to the ship. But before we could leave, the laundry deliveryman confronted me with a threat: "If you ever bring your clothes to me again, I will throw them on the dock and stomp them." I had difficulty keeping clean white uniforms for several weeks.

Not only McKey, but also other crewmembers, were confronted in Honolulu. We were careful and diligent to inform and protect the newer sailors from these people known as *queers* back then. They were predators, preying on unsuspecting service men. Just as some good men had looked after me, it was now my turn to look after others.

There were times before the end of the month when I was low on money and had to spend my off-time on base at the Enlisted Men's Club. Seaman's pay was not enough to sustain my continuous merrymaking ashore. It was not until I was a second-class petty officer that I received a decent pay of about $142.00 per month and was allowed to go to the NCO Club for Non-Commissioned Officers. Enlistee's entry pay was no more than $90.00 per month in 1948-49, enough for necessities and a few cheap liberties. But every *swabby* who earned a sailor's pay knew he was trading fortune for adventure, and a life time of memorable sea stories.

Chapter 10

USS Tawakoni ATF-114 – Respect for the "A" Fleet

Other than knowing that the Tawakoni "TA-WA'KO-NI" was put into service at Tsingtao, China after World War II, when Chaing Kai Shek was evacuated to the island of Formosa (ROC)—the Republic of China—I knew little, but learned the history of the ship after the fact.

The U.S.S. Tawakoni and all Navy Ocean Fleet Tugs were named after Indian tribes. The Tawakoni tribe *–a river bend among red hills, or neck of land in the water* – was proximate to my hometown, since the tribe ranged along the red, sandy banks of the Red, Brazos, and Trinity Rivers between Texas and Oklahoma, during the 18th and 19th centuries.

It may sound frivolous, but I liked knowing that Tug Boats were named after Indians. Battleships were named after states; Cruisers named after large cities; Destroyers after important men; Supply and Cargo ships after constellations; Tankers after rivers; Minesweepers after birds; Aircraft Carriers after major sea battles, and Submarines – fish.

Years after I was discharged I found out there was a lake named Tawakoni located approximately 35 miles (55KM) east of Dallas, 10 miles (15KM) northeast of Willis Point, and 25 miles south of Greenville, Texas, on State Highway SH2375, and about 85 miles northwest of Cleburne. The lake, with its 200 miles of shoreline, is a 36,700 acre man-made reservoir that is an impoundment of the Sabine River, with a 5 mile spillway. The lake is recognized as the Blue Bird Capitol of America. Many visitors come not only for bird watching but for the 200 yard giant Spider Web – found stretched between seven trees and on bushes along one of its nature trails.

I tell all this because I find it fascinating that I had lived in Texas 19 years prior to my joining the Navy, and did not know the lake existed, nor did I know the ship I served on was of the same name, same Indian Tribe - never made the connection. But then I didn't get around much early in life, maybe to Fort Worth to shop, to Glen Rose for the very best Bar-B-Que, and Lake Cleburne to fish and picnic. The used cars we had back then were not fit to make the extensive trips necessary to educate us about Texas lakes and parks.

The size of the BB, battleships; CA-CL, cruisers; CV-CVE, aircraft carriers; and DD, destroyers, dwarfed our and the many smaller ships. These large ships received all the publicity, were covered on the national and local news and received all the glory. Submarines and submariners of the silent-running Navy belonged to the above group and received their recognition and glory, and justly so because of their strenuous duty, many contributions and losses during WWII. The deep-sea combat tug, *Work Horse of the fleet*, made a magnificent contribution to the Navy, Coast Guard, Army, and Merchant Marine vessels in war and peace. The National Association of Fleet Tug Sailors serves as a repository for information and artifacts concerning tugs in the military and naval service of the United States.

An introduction to the A (auxiliary fleet) is needed here to acquaint the reader and sailors who served on *ships of the line* with the various types of support ships serving the big ship *gray fleet.* The YT and YTB yard tug boat (harbor tug), YW yard water, the YO yard oiler, and AO -AOG fleet oilers, ATA tugs, ATF fleet ocean tugs, YMS motor minesweeper, AM – AMS - MS - DMS and MSC - MSI and MSO minesweepers, the ARS repair ships, AV seaplane tenders, AKS (general stores) service ship, AKA attack cargo ship, AF refrigerator stores ship, AD repair ship, AH hospital ship, and the PA - PF (MATS) troop transports, LSD dock landing ship, LST tank landing ship, LSM landing ship medium, LSMR converted LST rocket ship medium, and the LCVP (Higgins Boat) vehicle and personnel landing craft could all be classified as Auxiliary Ships—helping, aiding, assisting, and supporting craft.

These auxiliary vessels worked in relatively unknown and certainly unheralded capacities, except for hospital ships of course, until they were relegated to Davy Jones' Locker, a period of about thirty years. Or they were turned into scrap metal—often times without a trace of history, especially the WWII Army Transports.

Building of the Tawakoni was completed on May 19th, 1943 in San Francisco by the United Engineering Company. She launched in October of the same year and was commissioned in 1944. She was sold and struck from the Navy Register June 1st, 1978, under the Security Assistance Program to Taiwan, and renamed *Ta Han, Ta Mo or TAMO (A533), more officially DAHAN ATF-533. As of this date she is in service with the Taiwanese government.*

The Tawakoni's proud service record is known and recorded, but only partially recorded for her actions in the Korean War (1950-1952). Naval history credits her with downing three Japanese Kamikaze planes, known as floating chrysanthemums, in late 1945 - two at Okinawa and another at the Ie Shima invasion.

For wartime service the small ship received nine battle stars: two for service during World War II, three during the Korean War, and four stars for duty in Vietnam. The ship saw duty in the Marshall and Mariana Islands, the Philippine Sea, Sea of Japan (East Sea), Yellow Sea (West Sea), South China Sea—Tsingtao, China, Guam, Saipan, Eniwetok, Iwo Jima, Okinawa; Inchon, Sok-cho, Yang Yang, South Korea, and Wonsan and Hungnam, North Korea; Alaska, and at Danang, South Vietnam at what was called Yankee Station.

No, Tawakoni was not a beautiful ship, a large ship, a man o' war—but a *tugger*, a deep-sea 205'3" long plodding, floating workhorse, auxiliary rescue ship. Tugboat crews had to be physically strong, agile and rugged. They weren't considered ships of the line like the sleek cruisers, dreadnaught battleships, menacing destroyers, exclusive aircraft carriers, and deep-six submarines. But an ocean tug probably had more firepower per ton than any ship in the Navy at that time. The ship's personnel at full wartime complement were listed as eight officers and sixty-eight enlisted men.

The ship's propulsion was 4 ALCOA diesel main engines providing 3000 horsepower and a single four-bladed screw (propeller). The fuel capacity of 95,000 gallons gave an estimated cruising distance, at 12 knots without a tow, of 9,000 miles. A fleet tug could tow an aircraft carrier weighing 60,000 tons 2,000 miles without refueling. The towing winch was wound with 2,100' of heavy oversized 2' twisted wire towing cable, and had a towline pull of approximately 49,000-60,000 pounds.. A set of beach gear with anchors and underwater divers' gear were standard for repairs and rescue of crippled ships. Her salvage pumps could remove water from flooded compartments at the rate of 6,000 gallons per minute.

The reputation of the tugboat sailor was both myth and fact. The myth was they never left port or went to sea because the ships were seldom seen on the horizon, or in close company of the larger ships. It was reasoned a ship so small and low in the water was not sea worthy, not able to take the roll and pitch, tossing and pounding of a *fickle sea.* The facts were that the fleet ocean tug was designed for the high seas and to operate in all kinds of weather - not to roll over or capsize with the strain of an extremely heavy tow. Tugs possessed superb endurance and an enormous fuel capacity for the ship's stability with its long range and large ballast capacity. It could be said, "She had a *pair of good sea legs.*" The ship was quite safe with thick steel plates and bulkheads. But the rounded bottom, necessary for towing and to carry large quantities of fuel, caused the ship to experience safe but very large rolls. The ranchmen from Texas and Oklahoma might say, "You'd have to wear your spurs to ride one of them things." Sailors on larger ships would ask, "What's it like to ride on a small ship like yours? Do you ever get seasick?" We shrugged these questions off with little comment and a feeling of nautical superiority. After all, we were *tugboat sailors,* and their ships were at our mercy should they be damaged, lose power, or be in danger of breaking up.

There was some animosity and a little jealously between the crews of gigantic war ships carrying personnel in the thousands and armed with enormous guns, and the deep sea rescue *tugmen* of the A Fleet. This feeling was carried over to the beach at times.

We weren't impressed. Were they really sailors if they had never been close enough to the water to experience salt spray in their faces, never endured winds and waves in order to rescue a ship that was stranded dead in the water in the middle of strong gale force winds, or never weathered waves breaking over the bow and bridge that inundated the ship? Were they really sailors who had to do their individual jobs so well that each life depended on the other, and the life of the ship depended on each man individually and collectively? I will paraphrase a saying I read once, *We made her the ship she was. She made us the men we were.*

There was praise but it came only recently. *The Towline*, the publication of the National Association of Fleet Tug Sailors (NAFTS), April 2007, noted:

They're squat little ships, lacking the glamour, speed and sleekness of the Battleship, Destroyer or Cruiser, but they're industrious, sturdy and essential. Their work is never done. They salvage, tow, haul, patrol, rescue and when the occasion demands, FIGHT.

Such is the nature of the front line Tugs, operation in considerable numbers for Service Force, Pacific Fleet, doing their work quickly, bravely, tenaciously, and efficiently, and more often than not, under extreme duress.

The Tug, in its homely plodding way, IS APPRAISED ONE OF THE SERVICE FORCE'S MOST ESSENTIAL SHIPS.

Thanksgiving Day, November 22, 1951, sixteen days out of Guam towing an ARD floating dry-dock, Jack Pollard, EN3, USN wrote a poignant poem for the crew titled,

A SHIP of the FLEET

Many a ship has been christened for sea;
But none so great as the Might "T".
She has no armor, neither bow nor stern,
Only the will to live and to learn.
Her armament too, at no great excess,
Hardens the burden, to remain at crest.
She'll do her job, no matter the task;
With flying colors, from her invincible mast.
She'll fight for her country, til lost to the sea;
But no higher record, have any yet shown.
Mile after mile has resisted her keel;
The pounding of seas is not a new feel;
Nor is her job, of rescue and tow.
Operations procedures, salvage and so;

Her speed is slow, but destination assured;
Nothing enroute will get her allured.
Shipboard routine is familiar to all;
There is no difference just 'cause' we are small.
The plan of the day is even at sight;
Turn to all day, stand watches at night.
The engines pound and motors whine,
But she'll get us home on scheduled time.
There may be a tow to take by the way;
To lengthen our trip to thirty more days.
But we won't mind, we're a happy crew;
We'll do our job, as most sailors do.
We're a tugboat crew, of that we're proud;
Of what we do, with what we are allowed.
As for combat duty, we're far from the best;
That's not our job, but leave us the rest.
We evacuate harbors, or sweep for mines;
Or plant marked buoys, to designate signs.
Our tasks are many, our failures are few.
We will succeed, with our present crew.
She's known to most as a plain ole tug;
But to us she's home with a friendly hug.
She comes and goes, as most ships do;
Far away: in that misty blue.
But wherever she goes, no matter the place;
She stands for our country with utmost faith.
Her ensigns fly high, its colors are clear;
Courtesy's extended for all ships near.
And yet a warning to whoever starts war;
The Navy gets mean whenever they are sore.
She's just another of our great fleet;
But one you'll find that's hard to beat.

I never thought I would be retyping this stenciled mimeographed poem from the ship's Thanksgiving Day menu sixty-one years later.

Chapter 11

Mine Clearing Operations

When you can't go where you want to, you haven't got command of the sea.

-Admiral Forrest Sherman,
Chief of Naval Operations

From October 2nd to October 29th, 1950, we had been underway from Hawaii to Sasebo, Japan. It had taken us twelve days to Kwajalein, seven days to Guam, and eight more days to Japan—a total of twenty-seven days at sea. This lengthy, arduous trip was different. The crew was tense and edgy with a sense of coming danger. The calm placid waters of the Pacific throughout the voyage and the antics of dolphins leaping, spinning, and riding our bow wake were little noticed, of little concern to the more seasoned of our crew.

I felt I had been cheated out of WWII because I was too young to enlist. Now, I was excited, elated even, with a diminished remembrance of World War II and its many losses. The ship with me aboard was sailing into harm's way. Fear of the unknown and uncertainty explained the crew's somber attitude as Japan's southernmost island of Kyushu came into view. It wasn't until much later that the reason for our being there was scripted into words—***to face danger, injury, death even, in order to stop the tide of Communism in Asia, and to free a people who had been under Japanese occupation, rule, and abuse from 1910-1945.*** But now, I asked myself, "Are these the people thousands of Americans fought so hard against." Some WWII sailors who saw combat duty in the Pacific refused to go ashore to fraternize with the *enemy.* I was quite uneasy when they did go ashore because of their hatred and bitterness towards all *Gooks, Nips, and Japs.* I never saw any compassion from these hardened veterans. I myself had to do some soul searching.

The monotonous and continuous droning of the diesel engines, located only one deck below the crew's compartment was bringing us closer to an ill-defined war in an ill-fated country – the Hermit Kingdom, the Land of the Morning Calm – unheard of, and into a war without a name.

When we reached our new liberty port we knew there would be new sights to see – exciting, and certainly different. As we drew near to our destination of Sasebo, Japan, we were greeted with unfamiliar, pungent, strange, even peculiar smells and odors. And it was a land that resonated with uncustomary and indescribable sounds. Strange, at a day or two out, and in the clean crisp sea air, how you are able to detect the foreign smells wafting from a foreign country. People of different dress, customs, color, and features, whose language we were never to master observed us with expressionless, quick, dark eyes. Behind their masks I wondered if there was animosity and anger for losing the war, their destitute condition, and our dropping the atomic bomb on Nagasaki and Hiroshima that ended the war.

My feelings were mixed with compassion for the impoverished Japanese population, especially the little children who were without adequate food and had insufficient winter clothing. I came to see they were the victims, not the perpetrators, the innocent, who were suffering because of their Sun God, Emperor Hirohito, and Japan's military leader and later Minister of War, Head of Imperial Cabinet, and Prime Minister – General Hideki Tojo.

Later in my married life, I learned my mother-in-law had a sneaky black and white Terrier – a real mean dog. She named him ***Tojo.*** The worst name she could think of. He would never warn with his bark and had the propensity to sneak up and bite the heels of strangers as they stepped off the porch. She also had thrown away her large collection of Made-in-Japan porcelain shoes. She and thousands like her did not want anything that was stamped – Made in Japan. To older Americans of the *Greatest Generation* this aversion, though lessened, to Japanese made products still exists.

It was very hard to remember the sacrifices of our country, to acknowledge the ravages of World War II, our many ships, planes and lives lost in the Pacific, and then suddenly be cast on the shores of this former enemy. It was many years later before this experience and my maturity let me see the enemy was not the Japanese people, but greed and the desire for power, the expansionist policies of the Japanese leaders.

I noticed other things: the long-tailed Yokohama Minohiki or perhaps Onagador - Japanese long-tailed fowl, crowed differently than ours. The few Japanese HI KE cats I saw scampering had no tails. And night soil was gathered in wooden containers called ***honey buckets*** to be used as fruit and vegetable fertilizer. This was the main reason we could not eat the vegetables, especially the lettuce and leafy vegetables, because there was the likelihood of ingesting soil microbes and bacteria, causing severe dysentery.

The many drab shades of gray, faded brown, and smoked black covered everything – the buildings, the streets, and the clothing – of a deprived people. This lack of color caused me to have an eerie feeling, a feeling that these people could be from another planet. The monochromatic colors all blended together, and there was too much sameness, even the people looked the same. What a depressing land we had come to! Granted, Sasebo was a fishing village, a seaport town located on Kyushu, Japan's poorest and most southern island, only a short overnight's run to Pusan, South Korea. But what a contrast to Hawaii—the topography, the sky, the climate, the music, the architecture, the pungent smell.

The few old cars were driven on the wrong side of the road and continuously honked their horn to let the pedestrians and bikers know the car was coming— not a warning to get out of the way. A very old car was later to completely ruin my favorite white hat. We were in Tokyo looking for a taxi. The taxi we found had a body style like maybe an old 1932 Ford or early French Citroen. Before we could open the rear door and get in, the driver motioned to the rear of the car to what looked like a luggage compartment. On the right side I perceived him to operate a *pump* with several up and down strokes. Soon he was satisfied and we jumped in with me riding on someone's lap. I didn't pay any attention that my white hat was rubbing the car's headliner and becoming all black. The car must have been an antique coal burner because of the oily soot.

Later my duties as a Storekeeper necessitated me getting a Japanese driver's license in order to drive a jeep. Driving in Japan later led to indecision, confusion, and insecurity when I returned home. After two-and-a-half years in the Far East, I became disoriented, confused and almost panicked, not knowing which side of the once familiar Mansfield Road to drive on. Not until I saw a car coming was I sure to drive on the right, not on the left. Even today I have noticed the paradox between East and West. The most noticeable and opposite difference is the United States emergency and information numbers of 911 and 411 respectively. It's just the opposite in Japan, Taiwan, South Korea —119 and 114 with some variations to fire and police being separated.

We could not eat Japanese food or drink the water, not until much later, when the ***Off Limits*** sign came down and one restaurant was approved for military personnel. I distinctly remember my first meal of ham and eggs. I did not know the Asian custom of layering the food together. My ham was covered in an opaque layer of egg whites with two small yellow-orange egg yolks sitting brightly sunny side up. The toast was a very light crunchy rice cake, without taste and of little substance. No way could it be used as *bread sop* for the runny eggs. And the ham, when exposed, with the egg whites removed, was different in texture and in taste from the Texas/Oklahoma corn fed Poland China hog meat I was raised on.

The exchange rate at that time was 360 Yen to the US dollar or 3,600 Yen to the American $10.00. We were paid in what I believe was a bluish, later greenish colored script because the US dollar was not allowed for exchange ashore. Five dollars worth of Yen would get me a very good cheap liberty, including a ride back to the pier. The bicycle *petty cab* ride from town to the whaleboat-landing site was only 60 Yen, about eighteen cents.

It was necessary to catch the last whaleboat at 2200 hours back to our ship moored to a buoy, or anchored out in the harbor. Several of our crew tried, and some succeeded, in smuggling foul tasting Suntory Whiskey back aboard. Shore Patrol duty guards stood on either side of the landing and patted down the drunkest and the sailors most likely to break the rules. But they could not catch them all. A half-pint fit nicely in the inside ankle sock.

I saw a British sailor trying to make it back to his ship with two tall opened bottles of Japanese Asahi beer, one in each coat pocket. I never knew if he was successful, or if his purchase was confiscated. All booze taken by the SP was thrown and broken against the rocks that lined either side of the boat landing. That was bad and thoughtless, but it seemed the right thing to do almost sixty years ago. After all, we were in *Occupied Japan.*

I only know we did not get along with the limy sailors too well. They were called *limies* because in early years their Department of the Navy mandated all British sailing ships stock up and carry a good supply of limes to prevent scurvy. I went aboard a British light cruiser once when dockside in Yokohama—just out of curiosity. I noticed many huge rust spots and bubbles, indicating paint failure. The crew's compartment was in disarray, strewn with dingy clothes, piled high on lowered bunks. Our bunks were always triced up with all clothing stored, or in the laundry bag. I was mystified as to the method the British ship's crew used to separate their clothes too. A sweet musty smell permeated the sleeping area due to untidiness, and poor ventilation. I was treated well with courtesy by my British sailor escort, but had soon smelled enough. I thanked my host after only a short stay and bid him farewell. My curiosity was satisfied, except one more thing. I often wondered why British warships had portholes running along both port and starboard side near the waterline, and why did the frigates' stern slope near the water line. French warships had a similar configuration. All American warships had solid steel sides of approximate height that I deemed stronger, safer, and more watertight.

Our crew's compartment at times had some odor when we were in moist hot air down by the Equator, or when hatches had to be dogged down in rough, rainy, sultry weather. Ship's regulations called for our crewmembers to bathe and change underclothes daily, wash dirty clothes weekly, and change the mattress cover regularly. There was a saying that went with all that tidiness—*Sailors make the best husbands.*

I remember only one British ship anchored out and an admiral's barge tied up alongside a most convenient dock at Sasebo. Mail and messages were brought to the Admiral by a single engine seaplane each morning, usually around 0900. I tried to be topside to see this novelty, and if choppy harbor water would impede his take off and landing. It occurred to me the plane would dart in and out of Sasebo harbor like the fast beating transparent winged *Damsel* or *Dragon Fly* of summer that flitted on the river, creeks and ponds back home. We called them *snake doctors*. The little seaplane would stay only a short thirty minutes or so, and with a high-pitched revved up engine break water with its skis and be gone. Often times I would see the Admiral's gig cutting through the water at a high speed heading toward a big British warship, maybe his flagship.

The USS Tawakoni ATF-114 was the first of many ships to ride anchor or be tied up to a buoy in this, Japan's best and most beautiful harbor, in spite of its location in one of the poorest districts of Kyushu Island. There were a few auxiliary ships, but really no big ships present - only the destroyer USS Ernest G. Small DD 838. She had been damaged after striking an underwater mine at Tanchon, North Korea. The stem and bow were blown off with nine sailors killed and eighteen wounded, October 7, 1950. The damage was so severe that the bow and 5"/38 guns broke off four days later on her way back to Sasebo, Japan. I understand the damage and uneven weight distribution caused the ship to ride high behind with the screw nearly out of the water. The USS Small with an LST escort slowly limped back to port under her own power. We were surprised and shocked at the sight of the severely damaged Small - with her makeshift steel plated *false bow*. It was the first time the crew realized what mines could do and that destruction and death lay just a few feet below the surface.

A mine is a self-contained explosive device placed in the water to destroy ships and submarines. The deadly explosives are of various sizes and can weigh from 1,000 to 3,000 pounds and are triggered in various ways by an approaching ship.

Russia in August 1950, sent down an estimated 5,000-6,000 mines, of which approximately 3,000 had been planted. Russian technicians had trained North Koreans to lay selected patterns, and supervised the laying on both coasts and at the mouth of Korean navigable rivers. The USS Manchester (CA-83) with her big guns destroyed a boxcar loaded with an estimated 2,000-3,000 of these mines.

Russian mines were of three types: first were floating and submerged buoyant contact/pressure mines attached to a tether (cable) anchored to the sea bottom, with the hidden mine lurking below the surface ready to explode when approached or hit by a passing ship. Acoustic mines were planted on the sea floor and triggered by the sound of a ship's engines. And magnetic mines were set off by the ship's electric field. We became acquainted with all three kinds because the Tawakoni was also used as a minesweeper, as were various small craft including the LCM, LCVP and Motor Launch. We were soon to see snow-covered mountains and the icy coastlines of North Korea, where mines would be our greatest threat. Oh, how I dreaded the thought and consequences of sinking in frigid Korean waters.

The USS Hoquiam PF-5 was our harbor contact, to prepare us for a safe but short stay in Hungnam, straight up the coast from Pusan (Busan) in South Korea. The next day at 0700, we were underway south from Hungnam to Wonsan, North Korea to relieve the USS Askari ARL-30. This was to be the start of a six-month tour of duty. However, the tour was extended to another six months; then to another two months.

Before August, 1950 United States ships and ships of the coalition—Britain, Australia, Canada, France and other countries—were relatively free to carry out the directives of the United Nations command to blockade all ports, destroy shore batteries, interdict small mine planting craft, bombard and destroy supply lines, disrupt enemy troop movements, and prevent the re-supply of enemy troops by sea. The Navy's dominance of the sea came to a halt in October 1950, with the sinking of the minesweepers USS Magpie AMS-25, the USS Pirate AM-275, the USS Pledge AMS-277, USS Partridge AMS- 31, and the ocean tug USS Sarsi ATF-111. The Magpie lost 21 members of her 33 man crew to the mine blast. Minesweepers suffered at least 14 hits from shore batteries. The largest single Navy loss occurred on the USS St. Paul on April 21, 1952, while it was giving fire support off Wonsan. The cruiser experienced a powder fire that claimed the lives of thirty sailors. Six larger ships struck mines with extensive damage and loss of life, but did not sink - USS Bush DD-745, USS Mansfield DD-728, USS Walke DD-723, USS Ernest G. Small DDR-838, and USS Barton DD-722. Some UN ships were damaged with loss of life but did not sink because of their size and water tight compartments. I thought of this line: ***"Over a sailor's grave, no roses bloom."***

The South Korean ROK (Republic of Korea) Navy lost seven ships to mines and shore fire. They gained our respect with minesweeping skills, and as a valued, professional, hard-hitting force attacking enemy-held islands and interdicting special units, and with guerrilla landings. ROKN Paektusan (PC -701) engaged and sunk a North Korean 1,000 ton armed transport headed for Pusan, South Korea with 600 KPA (Korean Peoples Army) soldiers aboard – even before the war began.

The sudden damage of these ships and loss of life to underwater mines brought a halt to sea traffic near and around both Korean coasts - and to General MacArthur's landing force, Task Force TF-98 made up of 50,000 troops of X Corps and Marines contained in a large flotilla of 250 ships. He had landed successfully at Inchon, South Korea and planned the same kind of assault at Wonsan, North Korea - MacArthur's Operation was named Chromite. The number of troops had to be downsized, delayed, and off-loaded south of Wonsan due to the mine scare. Admiral Allan Smith fumed, "The US Navy has lost control of the sea."

The delayed landing at Wonsan may have saved the lives of many American military personnel, because Wonsan was soon to be evacuated – just prior to the evacuation at Hungnam, North Korea. And too, ROK troops had marched north overland during the mine delay and now occupied the port of Wonsan.

Minesweeping measures were the inglorious side of the Navy's auxiliary fleet of sweeps and buoy-laying ocean tugs. Once the channel was supposedly swept clean, our ship and other tugs would mark the entrance with designated buoys. After a *check-sweep* for mines and the channels secured, ships of all types, especially destroyers, were allowed through. The destroyers gave fire cover for not only minesweepers but for tugs and other auxiliary vessels.

Mine countermeasures had names like counter-mining, de-mining, remediation and neutralization. Whatever the names, it was a relentless effort to detect and destroy mines and to interdict and destroy the enemy who tried to lay more. The *minemen* and *tuggers* had to cautiously ply uncharted mine-infested waters, cutting loose, exploding, sinking, destroying – *harvesting* – every mine found and planting marker buoys in cleared channels.

While the large ships avoided the mine-plagued waters, minesweepers, tugs, LST's and other auxiliaries worked the coastline day and night looking for and destroying the large, ugly explosive menace. Minesweepers were equipped with a forward-winged floating torpedo-shaped device, attached to saw-tooth cutters, called a *paravane,* to cut mine mooring lines at a prescribed depth.

The *oropesa*, named after the early Spanish minesweeper HMS Oropesa, was another minesweeping control device that kept cutters and cables at certain depths and widths. Many other methods, both old and modern, were used to detect and eliminate the mine menace.

A US raiding party destroyed three steel-decked North Korean junks that imitated the formidable turtle ships, as they were known, and collectively named Kobukson, by the Koreans. Kobukson were invented and commanded by master naval tactician, Korean Admiral, Lee Soon Shin. Admiral Lee Soon-Shin defeated a huge Japanese armada at the battle of Hansan in the IM JIN WAR, 1592-1598. For his feats in more than twice destroying the Japanese Navy, he was given the honored title, Choon-Moo or Chung-mu, meaning *Loyalty-Chivalry*.

The turtle ship was the first iron clad armed battleship, sea tank, or tank of the sea, to wreak havoc on a far superior enemy. The design was slightly rounded like a turtle with steel plates fitted with sharp metal spikes protruding upward and outward. The spikes prevented boarding, which was the usual way of fighting back then. Another clever feature was retractable oars and a *fire breathing dragon* bow head.

At the beginning of the Korean War, the North Korean Navy consisted of only forty-five small ships. Altogether approximately 1,000 various types of enemy boats were used for infiltration and mine laying. They were all either destroyed or captured.

Land demolition teams, South Korea Commandoes, Special Forces, U. S. Marines, British Royal Marines, Navy Seals and Under Water Demolition Teams (UDT) destroyed bridges, supply depots and tunnels on both coasts and coastal islands and aided in mine eradication. The UDT teams also worked with the Navy to locate and cut loose many underwater mines that were later destroyed.

The French frigate La Guere spotted fifty-four mines and is reported to have used their larger 40mm anti-aircraft guns to sink four of the mines. Each detonation and explosion sent a massive geyser of water with a huge plume of black and white smoke high into the air. The explosive energy reinforced the realization that our ship was in continuous danger of being damaged or more possibly, sunk.

One night we had anchored close ashore with *Lights Out/Darken Ship* and instruction given to all personnel to announce when they were coming out on deck. I had been assigned guard duty with a new seaman, who was unaware of the danger. Our ship was darkened to be undetected against shore batteries, or those who would try to board by way of the low gunnels that formed a ledge near the water line.

It was a little past 0200 and I was manning the starboard side and the seaman was guarding the port side. As I walked aft, I saw the young sailor to my right and at the same time saw a dark figure with his leg slung over the fantail (stern). I quickly dropped down low in the shadows and clicked my M-1 rifle off safety. I had the figure in my gun sights, my finger on the trigger. Just then I saw him glance over to where I was kneeling in the shadows with the muzzle of my rifle pointed directly at him. He said a few indistinguishable English words to the seaman, looked my way again, then went quickly below. I never knew if I could kill a man close up, but had he moved erratically toward the seaman, or spoken in Korean or Chinese, I believe I would have defended the ship and the sleeping crew. His purpose for being on deck without permission was to check the ship's swing at anchor and see if the anchor chain had fouled the screw.

The man in error was the Chief Bosun - Chief Master-at-Arms. He and I had always been at odds - conflict of personalities I suppose. I believe our dislike for each other was mutual. But I know after his error in judgment, he never spoke or tried to give me orders again. The incident left me with sweaty palms and the shakes. The incident could have been a tragedy. The young sailor never knew. I never told him.

Another hair-raising night was when our *ole man* got off course, missed the cleared channel, and took us out across a mine field. I hurried topside to the boat deck and stayed until we were back in the safe channel. For the first time I was terrified and on the verge of panic. Tugs have only one watertight compartment up by the foc's' le, just before you get to the bridge. The area is usually referred to as the forward hold or paint locker. A mine striking the side of our ship would undoubtedly be lethal, flood the engine room and the crew's compartment and cause us to sink within minutes.

The ROKN (Republic of Korea Navy) assisted with a few YMS's (yard minesweepers). The British and Thailand had furnished one YMS each, for which we were grateful. Japan and the US government contracted for eight Japanese minesweepers early in the war. Eventually, there were about twenty contracted for, plus a few Japanese old patrol boats and two guinea pig boats sent ahead to detect mines.

The Japanese had gained valuable experience clearing their harbors of mines after WWII. Near the end of the war US forces mined the harbors to prevent any Japanese warships or supply ships from entering or leaving port. It might be a little ironic that the first ship to enter Tokyo Harbor with the Japanese surrender was the minesweeper USS Renege AM-110 and the last ship lost in WWII was the minesweeper USS Minivet AM-37. The ship was lost at Tsushima Strait, Kyushu Island, Japan on December 29, 1945.

Mines posed the most serious and persistent threat to both ship and personnel. Even if none of our ships were hit, the impact of the mine campaign disrupted landings and logistics along both coasts, not to mention the constant strain on sailors, whatever their ship. North Korea was a minor power using inexpensive means to thwart our military efforts that caused major chaos and sometimes disaster.

The mines were often laid in shallow water by motor sampans, junks, shallow metal and even wooden craft. Many moored mines were left exposed at Inchon on the West Sea (Yellow Sea) because the tide fluctuates from 26'- 32' at high tide. These high tides can occur every two or three days each month in the daylight hours, especially with the fall full moon. At low tide the mud banks at Inchon extend 6,000 yards (5,400 meters). Korea has the second highest tide in the world, the highest tide being at Wolfville, Nova Scotia, Canada in the Bay of Fundy. Low tide that exposed mud flats allowed the destruction of many mines on the Inchon coast. The mine threat on this coast, though crucial, was not as severe and demanding as on the Sea of Japan (East Sea) at Wonsan and Hungnam. The Tawakoni had work and was continuously engaged with duties on the East Sea-Sea of Japan, mostly along the coast of North Korea.

The United States had contracted with the Japanese early in the war to sweep mines both north and south of the 38th parallel. The sudden sinking of the two Japanese minesweepers caused much consternation and the cessation of all sweeping operations.

The Japanese skippers refused to return north because of rough and icy waters, the loss of two ships, and the influence of family members who didn't want them to go. It was said that three of the ships' captains were pressured and then forced to retire. One captain said that to "attempt duties beyond our ability is extremely dangerous." Admiral Yamanoue Kamez, Commander of First Minesweeping Division, noted that it was "difficult to search for advanced mines using such old and weak techniques and mine sweeping equipment" and clearing mines "in the most bitter cold of the winter seas in nearby North Korea" was a task so difficult "that we could not complete our duty was more clear than light itself." To us it was a matter of not refusing to do what we had to do—what we were ordered to do, as part of this *police action*, now labeled a *Korean conflict,* heading surely for all-out War with a capital W – the Korean War 1950-1953.

After considerable delay an agreement was reached that Japanese minesweepers would drag the coastline south in deep waters of 200 fathoms – deep, at least for minesweepers, although not for large ships – to destroy any mines that had washed ashore south of the 38th parallel. Their duty was less difficult because most of the mines were found in the north East Sea (Sea of Japan). Later, the Japanese' efforts accounted for the destruction or sinking of over fifty underwater and beached mines. Mines were found south of Wonsan all the way up north to Hungnam and on the Korean west coast, north from Inchon to Pyongyang, and in the mouths of navigable rivers.

The Japanese government was cautious about not getting into the war, but courageous enough to open its ports and air fields and to use her ships to transport American troops at Inchon, and much needed supplies to Pusan, Korea. We were always relieved to see a Japanese ships and minesweepers flying the modified international red or orange/red *Echo flag*. Japanese ships working for the US had identifying names and numbers removed to not disclose they were helping UN forces. Japanese minesweeping efforts between 1950-1952 accounted for the removal of 229 mines from the East Sea (Sea of Japan). Their efforts helped clear the southern waters, giving us safe passage between Japan and the lower half of the Korean Peninsula below the 38th Parallel.

For many weeks our ship had been assigned to MinRon3 (Mine Sweeping Squadron 3) and various Task groups – 90.2, 90.8, 95.2, 95.6, 96.2. Sometimes the group consisted of a large fleet of ships; other times a few ships, or in our case, a single ship. Anytime we were patrolling, towing, leading or escorting ships we were assigned a Task Group number. This work was in addition to our other duties of surveillance, interdiction of sampans and junks, traffic control, retrieval, transport and assist.

"--- in our convoy were other ships and ocean tugs with their floating stage elements etc. We sailed through the channel at low speed slowing ever more and occasionally stopping when it appear a mine threaten us."

"The channel was heavily mined and we had a hair rising navigation in this channel to protect our troop ships."-Leon C. Rochotte, Ex Petty Officer, French Frigate FMS Grandiere (F-731).

"One of two small ships was kept in the offing guided the ship down the swept channel and lead the loaded ship down the mine-free lane on her return." –Admiral James K. Doyle.

By the middle of October, 1950, after a stalwart effort, minesweepers, tugs, ARS rescue and salvage ships and other auxiliary craft operating close ashore and without any, or with only limited, fire cover from destroyers, had successfully opened up harbors and coast lines for the larger ships. By November 17, 1950 all ports were opened, both north and south – 270 miles of cleared channels.

The small ships of the Auxiliary Fleet, with small crews and few amenities, and using antiquated equipment, accomplished a great task that kept the fleet moving and supplies coming. Destroyers and destroyer escorts that went everywhere along the coastal waters especially from Wonsan, Hungnam to Inchon, standing by and giving protection were most important to the operation. I particularly remember the USS Endicott DMS-35 and the USS Thompson DMS-38. Both ships were each hit three times by shell fire. The Thompson sustained many dead and wounded. Ships of the line such as American battleships, heavy cruisers, aircraft carriers, and UN heavy and light cruisers, operated in deep water away from the coast. The larger ships were rotated in and out of the war zone because there were not enough targets for their planes or large caliber guns. They were mostly effective in interrupting supply and troop movement, thereby containing the enemy during the evacuation of both the city of Hamhung and Hungnam. These large ships expended an enormous amount of ammunition, and effected complete destruction and devastation on designated targets, especially trains, bridges, tunnels and rolling stock.

Eighty thousand enemy troops were unable to move south along the east coast due to the numerous air strikes and naval firepower. Navy carriers had ultimate freedom to come close ashore to launch sortie after sortie, bombard installations, stall and disrupt troop movements, and give quick air support to our troops on the ground, especially when urgently needed. This was more evident during the evacuation of Hungnam in late November and December 1950. Superiority of the air and sea controlled and contained enemy troops and brought the North Koreans and Chinese to an early bargaining table at Panmunjom.

After completing the phase that provided access to all ports both north and south, there were still monumental tasks ahead. Ships were still being hit with mines, fired on, and damaged. The work continued until a thirty-mile firing line was provided at Wonsan, and a firing line marked with buoys was on either side of Hungnam, North Korea. Previously, five patterns of Russian mines of undetermined number had been spotted in shallow water within the thirty-mile curve near Hungnam.

Sweeping and laying buoys along the coast of Hungnam and Wonsan after minesweepers had detected, and hopefully destroyed, all mines in the designated shipping channel, was constant and ongoing. Because there was not enough equipment or the kinds of craft to work the minefields, it was twice necessary to leave the East Sea (Sea of Japan) and plant marker buoys on the west side of Korea at Inchon and northern coast. Larger ships continued to stay in deep water and were unable to give fire cover at first because a marked firing line channel free of mines had not been provided. The deep draft ships were to stay out of the 100 fathom waters and to operate in the 200-fathom waters outside of the danger zone until a close-in, safe channel could be provided—it would eventually happen with a buoy marked channel approximately 280 miles long, from Pusan to Hungnam. A fathom is a 6' measured depth – the distance between a man's outstretched arms.

Without any fire cover and with enemy shellfire from shore batteries, it was necessary to sweep at night. Daylight and night-time sweeping necessitated using an oil-vapor-smoke system that hid our ship and the *sweeps* from shore batteries. We too had smoke pots on board when working close to shore where enemy batteries might fire on us. At those times I wished the Tawakoni was completely invisible! For many days we were towing the mine detector *George Peter.* We named the George Peter after the semaphore call letters G-George and P-Peter. Other ships named the small iron boat the *Lock nes Monster* – we did not know it had been given that name. We handed off George Peter to ANS-16. Another time we handed off to YTB-415. Japan furnished two old often remote controlled *guinea pig* ships in addition to giving us *George Peter*.

We felt like sitting ducks on a pond. Often our duty was to stand guard all night, going in circles to keep larger ships out of unswept waters, and be there to show them the channel entrance at early dawn. Before allowing any ship to enter very early in the morning, night time sweeping had to be done in case mines had been planted under cover of darkness. Once the *check sweeping* was done, large ships would be let in the swept channel with our ship in the lead. Mines continued to be planted all through the war. There were plans in 1952 to plant 3,500 underwater shallow Russian R type chemical horned contact mines. Hungnam, North Korea had been evacuated, but mines continued to be laid making it necessary to go back way north and sweep the channels previously marked during the evacuation.

There was always the immediate danger that the ship could be damaged or sunk by shore batteries, or sunk by undetected or floating mines. Totally dark nights when the water was *pitch black* were the worst and unnerving. While anchored I felt relatively safe. How I dreaded to get underway down *ulcer gulch* in the thick of night. The light of a rare full moon was a welcome sight to aid in spotting floating mines. I remember an anonymous quote*: Any ship can be a minesweeper once.* We were more uneasy too, because the enemy shore batteries were getting better fire control, range and accuracy.

We had been underway for fourteen Sundays – three months on the run up and down, in and out, around the coasts of Korea. I believe the engines never cooled down. Nonstop duty was changing us from seasoned sailors who had moved freely through the wide expanse of the Pacific, where we practiced nautical skills and maneuvers, into sea-soldiers, who were trapped on a *liquid battlefield* with the enemy, human, and manmade, on every side. Strain took its toll on body and nerves. Every trip south out of hostile waters was greeted with *euphoria.* Each time we fired the engines to return to the waters of North Korea, fear and tension returned – paralyzing, suffocating. Yet, there was no grumbling, no expression of feelings, maybe a little mumbling. We returned with steely determination and a firm conviction about what we had to do. It was routine – unnerving as it was. The thought that we might lose our lives was commonplace and unsaid.

A special recognition should be given to the officers and crews of these auxiliary ships of few amenities - the YMS – AM – AMS – ATA – ATF – ARS – LST – that operated in shallow coastal waters and braved the dangers of daylight and nighttime sweeping, and danning – laying marker buoys. Arduous, uncomfortable winter weather, high winds, and freezing salt spray were endured by these men to open up the Korean coast to allied shipping. Icy sea water froze on decks, hatches, anchor chains, gun mounts - the weight destabilizing the ship. The whole crew had to *turn-to* with axe, pick and scraper to remove the enormous ice build-up that destabilized the ship.

Many are the memories of shared hardship, required-skilled seamanship, unique camaraderie and respect - a history to be proud of. Auxiliary crews, which made up only two percent (2%) of the fleet in Korea, suffered 20% of the casualties. Auxiliary ships, especially the minesweepers and fleet tugs, suffered 25% of ships damaged. The first two years of the war mines caused 70% of all naval casualties. Most naval causalities occurred early in the war to auxiliaries and the protecting destroyers attached to the Mobile Logistic Support Force. The United States had five ships sunk and eighty-seven damaged in the Korean War.

I like and concur with the Minemen Motto: "Where the fleet goes, we have *already been."* There is an unspoken consensus among the rare, special breed of sailors of the small ship navy: *"Little ships do all the work; big ships get the glory."* At least in the Korean War.

Ships sunk by mines with casualties:
USS Sarsi ATF-111, 2 killed, **Sank** in 21 minutes
USS Pirate AM-275, 1 dead – 12 missing, **sank** in 4 minutes
USS Pledge AM-277, 6 missing – 40 injured
USS Magpie AMS-25, 21 killed – 12 survivors, **Sank**
USS Partridge AMS-31, 8 killed, 6 seriously wounded, **Sank**
ROKN YMS-306 – **Sunk**, unknown casualties
ROKN YMS-516 – **Sunk** (formerly YMS-148). Exploded by Magnetic Mine – 1/2 crew lost
ROKN PC-704 Sub-chaser – **Sunk**, unknown casualties

ROKN PC-740 Sub-chaser **Sunk**, unknown casualties
ROKN 760 Lost, possibly to mine, unknown casualties
JMS-14 Minesweeper – unknown casualties
JML-301 Minesweeper – 1 killed

Ships damaged by mines, but not sunk:
USS Mansfield DD-728, 5 missing – 28 wounded
USS Walke DD-723, 26 killed, 40 – wounded
USS Earnest G. Small DDR-838, 9 killed – 18 wounded
USS Barton DD-722, 11 casualties
USS Brush DD-745, 11 killed, 3 missing, 10 wounded
ROKN YMS-509 – unknown casualties

American ships damaged by shore batteries with casualties:
USS Gull AMS-16, 2 casualties
USS Kite AMS-22, 5 casualties
USS Swift AM-122, 1 casualty
USS Redstart AM -378, 1 killed, 2 casualties
USS Dexterous AM-341 1 killed, 1 wounded
USS Dexterous AM-341, 3 casualties
USS Grapple ARS-7, 2 Killed, 11 critically wounded by friendly fire from Minesweeper
USS Brush DD-745, 9 casualties
USS Thompson DDS-38, 3 killed, 10 casualties
USS Thompson DDS-38, 1 casualty
USS Small DD-838, 9 killed, 18 wounded
USS Osprey AMS-28, 1 casualty
USS Osprey AMS-28, 4 casualties including Executive Officer
USS Osprey AMS-28, No casualties
USS James E. Keys DD-787, 4 Casualties
USS Walke DD-723, 26 Killed, 35 Wounded
USS Ozbourn DD-846, 2 casualties
USS Burke DD-783, No casualties
USS Hoquiam PF-5, 1 casualty

USS New Jersey BB-62, 4 casualties
USS Brinkley Bass DD-887, 8 casualties
USS Brinkley Bass DD-887, 5 casualties
USS Frank E. Evans DD-754, 4 casualties
USS Barton DD-722, 1 killed, 1 casualties
USS Barton DD-722, 5 missing, 6 casualties
USS Agerholm DD-826, 1 casualty
USS Alfred A. Cunningham DD-752, 8 casualties
USS Perkins DDR-87, 1 killed, 17 casualties
USS Everett PF-8, 8 casualties
USS Helena CA-75, 2 casualties
USS Helena CA-75, 4 casualties
USS Renshaw DDE-499, 1 casualty
USS Samuel N. Moore DD-747, 1 killed, 2 casualties
USS Glouchester PF-22, 1 killed, 11 casualties
USS Wisconsin BB-64, 3 casualties
USS Cabildo LSD-16, 2 casualties
USS James C. Owens DD-776, 10 casualties
USS Douglas H. Fox DD-779, 2 casualties
USS Buck DD-761, 2 casualties
USS Orleck DD-886, 5 casualties
USS John R. Pierce DD-753, 10 casualties
USS Lewis DE-535, 7 killed, 1 casualty
USS Shelton DD-790, 12 casualties
USS Samuel N. Moore DD-747, 3 casualties
USS Uhllmann DD-687, 13 casualties
USS Hanna DE-449, 1 casualty
USS Taussig DD-746, 1 casualty
USS Hasley Powell DD-686, 2 casualties
USS James E. Keys DD-787, 4 to 9 casualties
USS Bremerton CA-130, 2 casualties
USS Irwin DD-794, 5 casualties 18 June ‘53
USS Irwin DD-794, 5 casualties 8 July ‘53
USS Rowan DD-782, 3 to 9 casualties
USS Gurke DD-783, 3 casualties
USS Wiltsie DD-716, 5 casualties

USS Los Angeles CA-135, 13 casualties
USS Maddox DD-731, 3 casualties
USS Southerland DDR-743, 8 casualties
USS Henry W. Tucker DDE-875, 1 casualty
James C. Owens DD-776, 2 killed, 7 casualties
*USS Lyman K. Swenson DD-729, 1 killed
USS Clarion River LSMR-409, 5 casualties
USS Clarion River LSMR-409, 5 casualties
USS Albuquerque PF-7, 1 casualty
USS O'Brien DD-21, 1 casualty
USS Grapple ARS –7 Fired on by USS Chief AM – 315, 2 killed, 9 wounded by friendly fire.
LCPL (Landing Craft Personnel (Large) of LST-561 - foundered with twelve lost to sea – 2 USN Officers of COMLSTDIV, 2 US Army Officers, 1 ROKN Officer, 5 USN Sailors, and 2 Royal Marines.
*The ship USS Lyman K. Swenson DD-729 was not damaged, but the airburst of an exploding enemy shell killed Lieutenant David H. Swenson at Wolmi-do Island. He was buried at sea at Inchon, Korea from aboard the cruiser USS Toledo (CA-133).

American ships damaged by shore batteries without casualties:
USS Heron AMS-18
USS Redstart AM-378
USS Redstart AM-378
USS Redstart AM-378
USS Mulberry AN-27
USS Mainstay AM-261
USS Grapple ARS-7
USS Firecrest AMS-10
USS Firecrest AMS-10
USS Firecrest AMS-10
USS Pelican Am-27
USS Endicott DMS-35

USS Waxbill AMS-39
USS Swallow AMS-26
USS Murrelet AM-37
USS Chief AM-315
USS Endicott DMS-35
USS Endicott DMS-35
USS Colahan DD-650
USS Competent AM-316
USS Heron AMS-18
USS Osprey AMS-28
USS Thompson DMS-38
USS Firecrest AMS-10, damaged four times
USS Cook County LST-611
USS Mc Dermut DD-677
USS Maddox DD-731
USS Charles S. Sperry DD-697
USS Henry W. Tucker DDR-875
USS Leonard F. Mason DD-852
USS Herbert J. Thomas DDR-833
USS William Seiverling DE-441
USS Hyman DD-732
USS Porterfield DD-682
USS Rowan DD-782
USS Henderson DD-785
USS Laffey DD-724
USS Charles S. Perry DD-697
USS Henry W. Tucker DDR-875
USS Thompson DD760
USS Frank E. Evans DD-754
USS Mansfield DD-728
USS Owen DD-536
USS Samuel N. Moore DD-747
USS Collett DD-730
USS Manchester CL-83
USS De Haven DD-727
USS Shelton DD-790

USS Wisconsin – BB-64
USS James C. Owens DD-774
USS St. Paul CA-73
USS Eversole DD-789, strafed
USS Croix River LSMR 525
USS LST-661
USS Duncan DDR-874
USS Los Angeles CA-135
USS Rupertus DD-851

Ships with crewmembers killed or wounded by various causes:
USS St. Paul CA-73 – Explosion in gun mount, 30 killed - support effort at Kojo, Is
USS Oriskany CVA-34, 2 Killed, 13 wounded by a Navy Corsair F4U crash – 250 lb. bomb explosion
USS Antietam CV-36, 4 Killed, 8 casualties by a F9F air crash
USS Essex CV-9, 3 killed, 4 missing, 27 injured – F2H aircraft crash landed
USS Mount Baker AE – 4, rammed ROKN APNOK PF – 61 amidships, 25 dead
USS Rochester CA-124 –Bombed by two Russian YAK aircraft – no casualties
Thai Frigate HMTS Prasai TG-695-Corvette, Beached – Had to be sunk by friendly fire
LCPL of LST-561 floundered off Yangpyong-do, 2 USN Officers, 2 Army Officers, 1 ROKN Officer, seven US Military Personnel (Sailors), and 2 Marines lost their lives

ROKN and United Nations Ships damaged by shore fire with and without casualties.
ROKN JML-301, 1 killed
ROKN PC-705, no casualties
ROKN 504, damaged – unknown casualties
ROKN FS-905, no casualties

ROKN AMS-506, 5 casualties
ROKN AMS-510, casualties
ROKN Frigate PF-62, 3 casualties
ROKN YMS-148, unknown casualties
USS PC-810 -3 casualties
HNS Mounts Bay (PF), 1 killed
HMS Belfast (CL) no casualties
HMS Belfast (CL), 4 casualties
HMS Sparrow (PF), no casualties
HMCS Iroquois DE-217, 2 killed, 8 casualties
HNMS Johan Maurits Von Nassau (DD), 1 killed, 1 ROKN wounded by friendly fire
HMAS Murchison, 2 casualties
HMAS Murchison, 3 casualties
HMCS Cayuga (DD), no casualties
HMS Morecambe Bay (PF), no casualties
HMS Alacrity (PF), no casualties
HMS Bataan (DD), no casualties
HMS Bataan (DD), no casualties
HMS Constance (DD), 2 casualties
HMS Constance (DD), no casualties
HMS Crane (PF), no casualties
HMS Tobruk (DD), no casualties
HMS Cockade (DD), 1 killed
HMS Concord (DD) 2 killed, 4 casualties
HMCS Huron (DE), no casualties
HMS Comus 1 killed, 1 wounded by Russian IL10 Sturmovik aircraft
Later Lieutenant Commander, I. M. Mc Lachlan died of wounds and was buried with full honors from aboard HMS Triumph.
HMS Jamaica 6 killed (5 soldiers, 1 sailor), 5 wounded. Six buried at sea from aboard the HMS Jamaica, 7 killed, 8 wounded total
HMS Jamaica strafed by two Russian IL-10 YKS, 1 killed 2 casualties. Boy Seaman Ron Godsall buried at sea.

HMS Kenya – Petty Officer Tate – Killed at Chosin
HNS Triumph – 1 killed, 1 wounded by North Korean Aircraft
USS Perch SS-313 (submarine) 1 killed, Royal Marine Commando P. R. Jones – Shore Mission. Buried at sea from aboard the submarine Perch.

The Japanese freighter, Senzansan Maru SS 152 struck a floating mine near Hungnam, North Korea. Miraculously, she stayed afloat. Most of her 50,000 bags of flour not damaged had to be jettisoned or off-loaded. Her bow was 8' down at freeboard. We slowly eased along-side and took off several bags, all we had space for. USS Tawakoni ATF-114 stood by the stricken vessel until the next morning, until the repair ship USS Askari ARL-30 arrived. After ten days, with the flour off-loaded or moved aft and fifty-gallon oil drums ingenuously affixed for flotation, the stricken ship was raised and proceeded to Japan for repairs. Casualties are unknown.

David Bushnell, an American inventor from Connecticut, invented the first submarine and first sea mine (explosive torpedo) and used it to attack the British ship, HMS Eagle, in New York Harbor. His submarine was referred to as the Marine Turtle, American Turtle or The Maine Torpedo. Her oak hull was covered with a semblance of a turtle's shell, with an auger for a head. Bushnell's ideas and testing of his invention made for a humorous story with a sad ending.

The Turtle was launched in 1776 and attacked the British galley, Eagle, in 1777. His idea was to drill a hole in the enemy ship's hull and plant a bomb. He discovered the British ship was clad with a copper bottom that caused the drill bit to break. His plan was foiled, but not entirely. One of the bombs exploded underwater causing the fleet commander to remove all his ships from the harbor. One British ship Captain said only this brand of warfare was considered a devilish device and only *unchivalrous* nations would use it.

Bushnell had a plan for a more deadly torpedo. Contact triggers would be attached to powder kegs and floated down the Delaware to the mouth of the river and into the British blockade. That very night the temperature dropped below 0 degrees Fahrenheit and slowed the flow of the river. No damage was done from the *floating mines,* except for one British boatswain who was blown to bits trying to retrieve a keg from the ice.

This episode of the Revolutionary War is known as the *Battle of the Powder Kegs*. Bushnell was jeered, laughed at, kidded, ridiculed, and lost all support for his inventions. He changed his name, moved to a remote area in Georgia, became the head of a private school, and later practiced medicine.

A portion of a poem taken from Your Navy Handbook has been written about him:

Kegs of 1776 Rev. War NY POEM

Twas early day as poets say,
Just as the sun was rising,
A soldier stood on a log of wood
And saw a sight surprising.
As in amaze he stood to gaze,
The truth can't be denied sir,
He spied a score of kegs or more,
Gone floating down the tide, sir.
Now up and down throughout the town
Most frantic scenes were acted,
And some ran here and some ran there
Like me almost distracted.
"There prepare for bloody war
These kegs must all be routed,
Or surely we despised shall be,
And British courage doubted!"

The cannon roar from shore to shore,
The small arms loud do rattle,
Since time began, I'm sure no man,
E'er saw so strange a battle.

Except for David Bushnell, this saying might not be: ***"Damn the torpedoes! Full speed ahead!"***
Admiral David Farragut, United States Navy.

The urgency to remove the Russian menace can be seen in the mobilization of various ships, boats, planes, demolition teams and tactics to gain mastery of the seas. The assemblage consisted of motor launches, whaleboats, small landing craft, the larger LCVP (landing craft personnel), yard tugs, ocean tugs rigged with sweep gear, shallow 4' draft LST –"Gator Navy" that acted as mother ship to the minesweepers with a helipad installed to quickly rescue for downed Navy fliers. Twenty-four airmen were saved at Wonsan. ARS-auxiliary repair and salvage ships, various other auxiliary ships, a HRP-1 helicopter successfully rigged to tow sweep gear, HU-1 and HU-2 helicopters to spot, destroy or mark mines with dye packs, Navy amphibious mine spotter planes, Navy propeller driven WWII F4U Corsairs and Air Force jet aircraft that strafed and dropped 1,000 lb. bombs, Royal Navy Sunderland aircraft machine gunned mines, the destroyers Mansfield, DeHaven, Lyman K. Swenson and Henderson eliminated mines at Inchon with their guns, and the large DMS (destroyer minesweeper) was deployed to give protective fire cover to minesweepers and small minesweeping craft. I suppose the most unorthodox method to rid the harbors and coastline of mines was the dropping of depth charges. This expensive method was used very little and soon abandoned as means of mine eradication.

Another real or supposed threat during minesweeping operations was the report of mine laying Russian submarines. The US Navy dispatched several subs to counteract any Russian activity along the coasts of Korea, and the Strait of

Formosa. Twice the French Frigate LaGuere dropped depth charges on an unidentified object. And the New Zealand ship HMNZS (Her Majesty's New Zealand Ship) Hawae (FF) fired *squid* similar to the *hedgehog* after tracking an unidentified underwater object for over twenty minutes. Results were inconclusive in both attacks.

One of our destroyers was severely damaged along the water line, and there was much discussion and speculation, but no real conclusion. that the damage was not caused by a Russian torpedo. The final determination was that a floating mine *(floater)* caused all the damage. The mine menace we could handle, but the likelihood of being sunk by a submarine only added to our apprehension. Obscured history now reveals our Navy destroyers – USS Francis Knox DDR 742, USS Mc Kean (Rancher) DD 784, destroyer minesweeper USS Endicott DMS 35 and the USS Tassig DD746, dropped depth charges on a sonar *'solid ping'* moving object, December, 1950. Overhead aircraft spotted a silhouette and a torpedo wake passing close astern of the USS McKean. The McKean's depth charge expenditure was eighty-four in twenty-four hours. There were actually two unidentified underwater contacts. The latter contact disappeared but left an oil slick and some floating debris. Divers from the recovery ship, USS Greent ASR-10 were called out from Sasebo. A pair of field glasses without barnacles, or any evidence of being long underwater, were found. Other secret documents were determined to have been recovered, as well as a top secret Russian device that mimicked a submarine's sound. Officially, the underwater find was that of a Japanese sunken freighter, the Iona Maru. A crew member aboard the *Ranche*r DD-784 is purported to have said when hearing the official story, "We sunk a hulk ship that was doing five knots."

Chapter 12

Evacuation

I think often of that voyage. I think of how such a small vessel was able to hold so many persons and surmount endless perils without harm to a soul. The clear, unmistakable message comes to me that on that Christmas, in the bleak and bitter waters off the shores of Korea, God's own hand was at the helm of my ship.

Captain Leonard P. La Rue
(*The New York Times*, October 20, 2001)

We were soon to play our part in amphibious operations in reverse – the Asian Dunkirk. The evacuation of Hungnam, North Korea, was the largest redeployment of men, ships, materials, and supplies – plus the thousands of North Korean refuges – since WWII.

We had total control of the seas around the Korean Peninsula. How could it be that we would have to undo everything we had worked so hard and sacrificed so much to put in place? The answer would come too soon, after only a few days' liberty in Japan.

Our ship was released from Task Force 90, Amphibious Force, Far East, and we returned to Sasebo, Japan for pay, provisions, and R&R. We were surprised and annoyed to see so many large ships, American ships, and ships with foreign flags in the harbor. Thousands of sailors were going ashore and the price of everything had skyrocketed, but still very affordable with the exchange rate of 360 Yen to the Dollar.

A new beer hall with a large dance floor had opened up while we were gone. It was located on a slight, but beautiful rise some distance from, and overlooking, one of the finest harbors in Japan. The name of the establishment escapes me, but I remember it because it was my friend Bill Bate's favorite *performance hall.*

He was an active reserve call-up from Fort Worth, Texas, an excellent dancer, and had come aboard in Hawaii shortly before we left for Japan. Every third night was an occasion. Only one-third of the ship's company was allowed liberty to go ashore, the rest had to remain aboard should the ship have to get underway. Those in the duty section sorely missed seeing Bill's dancing skills.

Bill had danced with several partners and was impressive each time. When he matched up with a rather tall, slender, good-looking, fun-loving dancer who could really move, could keep up, and matched his style, the floor would clear and give way.

Exuberant cheers fortified with tall bottles of Asahi beer, foul tasting Suntory Whiskey or warm Sake, whose bubbles tickled the nose, went up from all quarters. For a few hours our stress and tension abated, and the fourteen consecutive Sundays at sea forgotten.

The irony of this story is that when I was discharged and working at Safeway Grocery while attending Texas Christian University (TCU), I was transferred to another company store on the East side of Fort Worth. When I walked in, I immediately recognized the store manager – Bill Bate. We had a *shipmate's reunion* right there – disregarding the staring customers. I knew he and I would have fun again and that my job would be easy and secure: We did, and it was!

When I reflect back, there were fun times and good times all up and down the coast of Japan from Sasebo to Yokohama, Yokosuka, Kamakura and Tokyo. The sea stories I have told and will later tell are as true as I can tell them, and for the most part without any or only very little embellishment.

We had a motor mach engineer with a terrible disposition. He was sullen, pouty, and had disdain for our very able coxswain. I dreaded to ride the whale boat ashore when the two were working together. Things kept getting worse until one day the mechanic disregarded the bells of the coxswain. Bells are used on small boats to tell the mechanic to speed up, slow down or stop – because the loud bell can be heard over the roar of the engine.

We were headed to the dock on our way to liberty at Sasebo, Japan. The whaleboat engineer in his displeasure opened the engine up full throttle. Furiously, the coxswain began *ding-ding-dinging* his bell to slow down. We were nearing the dock way too fast. The command was ignored until the very last minute. The engine was finally reversed to back down full, but it was too late. There was too much way and not enough time for the screw to bite into the water. I saw the danger, stood up on the bow and jumped just as the boat crashed into the dock. There was a thud and a creaking, cracking sound of breaking, and splitting wood. The mechanic was court-martialed and relieved of his duty. He was later booted-out of the Navy.

Many times the last whaleboat run to pick up the remaining crew ashore came back with sailors in various degrees of inebriation after excess libation. This one dark night the liberty boat was making good headway, purring right along on its way back to the ship. Two buddies, one with a newly purchased Japanese stringed musical instrument, got into an argument. The first thing we knew the instrument is thrown over the side. Quickly, unexpectedly, almost immediately, the young sailor rolled over the gunnel and into the water to retrieve his instrument. We knew he could not stay afloat long in the cold water in his dress blues, shoes, and heavy P-coat.

Fortunately our experienced coxswain saw everything, swung the boat quickly around, came along side, and stopped. We pulled the dripping cold and wet sailor back into the boat. How foolish. Quick work by the seasoned sailors and my engineer friend D. D. Parlson is all that saved this young kid from hypothermia and drowning. I suppose his instrument is still on the ocean floor – playing Davy Jones a *soggy serenade*.

Though our ship and crew were small, it seemed we had an undue number of times to do Shore Patrol Duty. One time I was assigned to work with a fine Marine from Tennessee, whose speech pattern was similar to mine. He is the only Marine I ever really liked. We were having a quiet night until we got a call of some sailor sticking his fist through the door of a Japanese establishment. We found the unruly culprit with a bloody hand, and a decimated fragile paper wooden door with holes in its covering. Just as we were to take him into custody he put his bloody hand on the Marine's *braided folia (folium), epaulette (epaulet)-aiguillette-fourragere accouterment and uniform.* It made me sick and ashamed that this individual had on the Navy uniform.

We managed to get him into the back of the pick-up *paddy wagon,* but had to continuously guard against him jumping out the back. This constant restraint continued until we pulled up at dockside of his small ship. The gangplank was lower than the dock because the tide was out. When we got him on the gangplank we gave him a slight but solid shove. Surprisingly, he bounced off the bulkhead sustaining no injury, nothing hurt except his feelings. Before we left we noticed his demeanor was much improved. He had a vague realization that he was in bad trouble. I felt sorry for this good Marine. His crisp pressed uniform was disheveled and soiled with dried blood.

Two hundred thousand Red Chinese – Chinese Liberation Army, later named People's Volunteer Army (PVA) - had invaded North Korea on November 26, 1950, while we were in Sasebo. Our fine liberty was cut short, and we were ordered back to Hungnam to help sweep an eight mile firing channel, lay marker buoys, red and black spherical buoys, and assist with the evacuation.

Salvage and rescue operations got underway on the morning of December 11, 1950 with the merchant cargo ship Enid Victory aground. The ship left at night, and cut too close to Ritsu Gan Pinnacle at Hungnam. The bottom was severely punctured on the hidden rock. Early that morning we hooked onto her and pulled until our towline was at the maximum - strained and stretched, flopping out of the water. There was great danger the tow line would snap, whip back and cut into or severely injure anyone on deck. I cannot recall exactly, but I think our tow cable broke one time.

The Askari ARL-30 came to help as well as two YTB's maybe, and LST. The Enid Victory was pulled free after much effort and sailed with an escort vessel back to Japan for repairs. She had sustained major damage because of the tremendous pull and damage necessary to get her free.

We were working close ashore in shallow water just after freeing the Enid Victory, and the sonar was useless at these shallow depths. We had to resort to the old fashioned way of measuring – the sounding line or lead line, marked off in fathoms. The measurement was marked off in fathoms this way: Mark 2 – two leather strips; Mark 3 and Mark 13 – three leather strips; Mark 5 and 15 – white cloth; Mark 7 and 17 – red cloth; Mark 10 – leather strip with hole; Mark 20 – two knots; Mark 25 – one knot. (Samuel Longhorne Clemens, 1839-1910, derived his pen name, **Mark Twain** while a steamboat Captain measuring the shallow waters on the Mississippi.)

We were attempting to rescue an LCVP, and as we crouched closer to the beach, the second class deck hand was heard to call out ***by the mark, twain*** as he continuously threw out and retrieved the lead line. Suddenly the ship scraped bottom - we stumbled abruptly forward. The engines were quickly reversed; the ship's powerful screw caused the ship to literally shudder. Mud and sand boiled up from the bottom, discoloring the water. Soon we backed off the rocks and were free, afloat again without any hull damage. We returned to Sasebo to act as an escort for four AMS's when our orders were changed to return to Hungnam. The four AMS's were given over to the ATF Cree, with the big E – for ***Excellence*****!**

From Hungnam we towed an Army crane barge and carried a LCVP down to Pusan, then made a trip back to Sasebo for another load of buoys and the installation of an LCM rack. With the LCM secured to the rack and a load of buoys in place, we left Sasebo towing an LCVP. The LCVP sunk in rough seas. The load on our fantail was found to make the ship top heavy, too dangerous. The LCM and two excess buoys were off-loaded by the Bolster (ARS-23). We continued to plant several buoys in the eight mile firing channel, which was both North and South of Hungnam. The firing channel was greatly needed and heavily used during the evacuation of Hungnam Harbor.

The news came on April 1, 1951 that President Truman had extended our enlistment by one year. Simultaneous news came that we were to serve another six months in the forward area. The news was met with disappointment, but with little comment, a numbness, and resolve.

For months we had no news, the days were the same, and the months did not matter, only the temperature and sea condition. Thanksgiving and Christmas did matter, just those two. We were laboriously and continuously doing jobs we thought were important and had to be done. And danger was a necessary, even common, part of our job, to bring peace to the two Koreas.

Twice we had to drag for two anchors – bow and stern – belonging to the heavy cruiser, USS St Paul (CA-73), and one for the British Frigate Alacrity PF-60. The Alacrity's anchor was never found. Both ships had been fired on by shore batteries and had slipped their anchors. They had returned fire with their 5" and 6" guns, and large fires were seen along the waters edge.

For two days the British Frigate Massey and two American ***tin cans*** (destroyers) gave us fire cover, and the minesweeper, Kite, swept for mines-looked out for *floaters* – as our divers searched the sea floor. From the 14th to the 21st at Hyon-an, our divers made their search. The St. Paul was lying off 6,000 yards; we were working 600 to 800 yards from breakwater. After three or four days the USS Incredible AM-249 and the USS Gull AM-74 each tied up to our port and starboard sides.

Our divers were in old cumbersome diving suits with a large metal helmet, leaded shoes, and a leaded waist belt. The diving suit was hooked by air to an onboard air compressor. All this time we were sitting close to shore. I was anxious for our ship, especially the divers, should we be fired upon by shore batteries. Would we slip our anchor and leave the divers down? Would the divers be killed by the concussion of an exploding shell? If our ship was hit, would the air supply be cut? Or the compressor damaged? Would there be enough time to retire the divers without them getting the fatal *bends*? Fortunately none of this happened, but the divers did earn hazardous duty pay of $50.00 a month, if I remember correctly.

After our three divers, and I believe our diver in training, made several attempts, the St. Paul's starboard anchor was found. The St. Paul offered one of her deep sea divers *after* the anchor was found, but before it was harnessed to our boom. The big ship eased her bow very close to our stern at a great height and risk. The use of our boom with much skill and effort was needed to attach the extremely heavy anchor chain. I believe the Alacrity's anchor was never found. Our ship's complement of about 60 men was given a three gallon carton of vanilla ice cream as a token of appreciation – 20 men to the gallon, about 6oz to the man. We were *taken* by their appreciation and generosity!

The St. Paul with her many amenities – library, barber shop, indoor movies and lounge area – was due back in the States. She could not return embarrassed with one huge costly anchor missing. We later learned the Navy had enough anchors to last for 99 years. The St. Paul and Alacrity moved away. We stayed at anchor all night with a ROK minesweeper.

The windlass on HMS Comus would not retract, and we had to hoist her anchor and chain. We should have shouted, *Anchors Away.* We left underway back to Hungnam to help the hospital ship Consolation. She had swung at anchor and needed a shove. We placed our bow on her port side and swung her to the right position and into the wind. An Army tanker Y-108 was adrift with her main engines full of water. We made the run to retrieve her loosened cable, pump her out, and tow her back to Yokosuka. A menial job came up with us having to pick up pieces of wreckage and place a red and black spherical warning buoy. We returned to port and were at anchor when the USS Mulberry AN-27 attempted to tie up to our port side. Extensive damage was done to her gig, davits, and a gasoline rack. Our ship received slight damage. Again we were underway from Wonsan to Hungnam with an Army crane barge where we handed the barge to Army Tug LT-535. Then back to Wonsan to tow Army barge 1070 and a LCM to Hungnam – handed off to YTB-420. Later USS Tawakoni ATF-114 headed a task element of LST-799 and the SCAJAP LST's Q-017, Q-018, Q-012, and Q-019 to Hungnam during the evacuation. We returned to Sasebo, Japan on 1-31-50 –**three Christmases and two birthdays -** I had been at sea. Once tied up, we had to *dress ship* in honor of Princess Beatrix of the Netherlands, ***as if there was no war.***

An unusual event happened when we had to tow a Japanese barge loaded with WWII Japanese rifles to the dumping area. This was an afternoon run, and by the time the obsolete guns were cast overboard it was getting dark. The wind and sea had picked up, causing the barge to take on water and eventually swamping it. I was in the wheel house when the ship began to swing uncontrollably at the stern. It was impossible to keep the ship on course. The large search light was ordered on. There we saw the barge dive underwater, rise above water, swinging back and forth and plow through the water erratically, like a dolphin at play.

The captain shouted, "Don't cut that line." Just then a Bos'n's knife parted the line and the barge entered Davy Jones' locker. I was glad we lost the barge because this was to have been my liberty night to see Bill Bate dance. This trip was not an emergency, did not contribute to the war effort, and I thought it totally unnecessary. I heard it said, ***There is the right way, the wrong way and the Navy Way.*** I shook my head and thought to myself, **"This is *the Navy way.*"**

Orders were for us to head for Wonsan to relieve the USS Grasp ARS-23. But first we had to go alongside the USS Prairie (AD-15) to install two racks for a mine sweeping motor launch with crew and buoys. We got underway for Wonsan with the USS Endicot (DMS-35), USS Incredible (AM-249), USS Curlew (AMS-8), and USS Swallow (AMS-36).

The trip was uneventful, fairly smooth waters and no GQ alarms. Russian MiGs often annoyed us with having to go to General Quarters at anytime. Many times we saw MiG-15's rushing for the Yalu River with friendly aircraft in hot pursuit.

The last time we were dockside at Wonsan we had acquired a dog, a ship's mascot we named Rex. I had grown rather fond of him. He was a mid-size Korean dog, smart, with brown hair sprinkled with black color undertones. The black was more pronounced on his nose, feet and ear tips. He was fat and healthy. Our ship docked again at Wonsan and the gunnel (gunwhale) being low let the dog jump ashore. He never came back. I am sure he made a fine meal of health food for some old Korean man or family. It was thought that dog meat would give stamina to old people, especially old men. This custom or rather the necessity for this custom has almost faded from Korean culture, and is now discouraged. The new, modern South Korea has plenty of healthy food, more than adequate nutrition for its people.

It occurred to me while over there that dog meat was not so bad. The French eat slimy snails (escargot) and tripe (pig's small intestine). When we killed hogs back home we gave all the internals including the brain, *lights,* lungs and organs to a neighbor and her son who lived a ways from us. I believe she cleaned and boiled the pig's small intestine to make chitterlings *(chittlings).* I only know chitterlings smelled to *high Heaven* when boiled or spoiled, when I worked at Bill Gray's grocery store on the East side in Cleburne.

Spam! I must say a word about Spam. Koreans eat more Spam than any country in the world, and they continue to like it because of its versatility. WWII was what introduced the populace to the *benefits* of this product of mysterious ingredients. No one knows or can tell you what it is made of. I contend its contents will continue to remain a mystery for all time.

There was never any news of how the war was going, only scuttlebutt. But we all had earlier noticed and experienced an atmosphere of winning and believed soon the war would be over, not knowing the Red Chinese Army with 12 battalions had crossed over the Yalu River into North Korea.

Wonsan soon had to be evacuated and we were to see a partial destruction of the port. I remember when we left the dock there were the few old weathered warehouses and an antique hand drawn iron wheeled wagon. Earlier there were two small girls in ragged clothes on the dock selling Korean pears. I wanted to buy the pears but we were warned not to eat raw fruits and vegetables. Even today I regret that did not lean over the gunnel and just hand the two little girls a five or ten dollar bill. They would have been rich. My plan was to return to Wonsan someday to find the two girls and make amends. But I was young at the time. This was just the way it was in war time. I still have the two girls' picture. My hope is that they were evacuated down south and safe below the 38th parallel.

As we were ready to move away from the dock at Wonsan, large explosions could be heard, and then several rockets began swishing, making erratic moves just above the ground. I supposed the Marine Air Wing had left them behind when they had evacuated their planes to Yonpo airfield near Hungnam. We quickly fired-off the engines, threw off lines, and backed away. We proceeded to Hungnam with a crane barge and an LCM in tow. We became snowbound with 40mph winds for 36 hours in a swept channel. Four LCM's were adrift because of the storm. They were later found and rescued. More shipping channels had to be opened up to accommodate the evacuation ships. Our schedule called for more buoy planting.

The evacuation of Wonsan was complete; Hungnam and Inchon had begun. The Marine Air Wing that had located from Wonsan to Compo just south of Hamhung on December the 15th had to be relocated again below the 38th parallel. Navy carrier aircraft had to increase flights to give close support and effect a successful withdrawal from Hungnam. Hungnam is 112 miles north of the 38th parallel.

The battleship BB63 USS Missouri, and the heavy cruisers St. Paul-73 and Rochester CA-124, along with several destroyers and at least three rocket ships lay off shore and gave tremendous fire cover. Day and night around the clock, the First Marine Division and U.S. Army 7th Division were redeployed in landing craft. The LSD's downloaded ballasts and awaited the continuous circle of evacuation boats waiting to unload. Round and round, day and night, various watercraft, amphibious craft, and the LVT we called *alligator,* because of its bright raised headlights, brought load after load of soldiers and Marines to the ships.

On December 3rd, 1950 11 LST's were beached with their doors open and loading ramps down. Seven more ships were double-decked, banked and loaded from the other side. Trucks, tanks, tracked vehicles, troops, and equipment, including all locomotives, even those needing repair, were taken south. APA's, cargo ships, WWII Victory ships were furiously loading men and material to take south to Pusan. Twelve hundred Japanese dock workers were hired to help with the outloading.

The influx initially overloaded the port of Pusan's capacity, and refugees had to be deposited on Koje Island, the main island for holding refugees. After clean sweeping Muko-hang for mines, the evacuated ROK Army and 700 trucks were off-loaded. This was an amphibious operation in reverse.

By the 11th of December, the 1st Marine Division had arrived at Hungnam harbor after a *seventy-eight or eighty-two mile walk* from the Chosin Reservoir, *the Frozen Chosin.* They were met by one APA, one AKA, 3 AP's, 13 LST's, 3 LSD's, seven time-chartered merchant ships and Merchant Marine vessels. Embarkation began on December 15, 1950. An estimated 200 ships were needed to redeploy troops and material of the American X Corps, 1st ROK Corps and fleeing civilians. Eventually 6 APA, 6 AKA, 12 TAP, 76 Time Charger, 81 LST and other auxiliary ships, including Amphibian Truck water craft, were added.

The battleship Missouri BB-63, USS St. Paul and three other heavy cruisers, eight destroyers and three LSMR's with 5' rockets, secured the port and laid a protective ring of fire around the city of Hamhung in support of American and ROK troops. Four aircraft carriers operated off the coast to provide air cover during the evacuation – the USS Philippine Sea (CV-47), Valley Forge (CV-45), Princeton (CV-37) and Leyte (CV-32). The light carrier Bataan (CVL-29) and the escort carriers Sicily (CVE-118) and Baedong Strait (CVE-116) supported the larger carriers. Even Admiral James H. Doyle's flag ship, the USS Mount Mc Kinley – Auxiliary General Command(AGC-7) – fired from a marked channel. Four battleships saw action in the Korean War, the USS Wisconsin (BB-64), New Jersey (BB-62), Iowa (BB-61) and the Missouri (BB-63). The Missouri was the only battleship to participate in the Hungnam evacuation, and the USS Begor APD-127 – high speed transport – was the last ship to leave Hungnam.

The battleship's 16" guns could fire a 2,700 pound projectile twenty miles, the weight of a small car. The heavy cruisers carried large 8" guns, and destroyers carried 5" guns. Tugboats and most auxiliary craft had one 3"50 mount plus twin 40mm and twin 20mm mounts. More ammunition was used at Hungnam – 34,000 projectiles of various sizes, and 12,500 5" rockets were expended. More shells were fired than at the Inchon landing, although the Hungnam evacuation was longer. Navy and Marine aircraft – propeller, jet, helicopter and bomber – flew 270,000 combat missions (sorties), only 7,000 fewer sorties than WWII in all theaters - 177,000 tons of bombs were dropped - greater by 74,000 tons. The number of rockets fired was greater by 60,000; 17,500 vehicles including 10,000 tanks and trucks. Stores and supplies; greater than the Berlin Airlift.

Other than the Battleships previous listed, the Navy's extensive fleet in Korean waters consisted of the following ships and type of ships – aircraft carriers, cruisers, destroyers, destroyer escorts, the flag ship USS Eldorado AGC-11, Estes AGC-12, Mt. McKinley AGC-7, and Tacomic AGC-17, AKS, AKA, APA, APD, AK, AW, TAP, ATA and ATF. Ocean tugs, oilers, frigates, hospital ships, LSD, LSM, LSMP, LST, AM and AMS minesweepers, DMS - destroyer minesweepers, and AR-ARS repair ships, ATA and ATF Ocean Tug, and submarines. Still the Red Chinese kept coming. I determined we did not have enough ordnance and firepower to defeat a nation of 1.2 billion people. A ceasefire at the 38th Parallel was the best the US and United Nations Forces could do.

The LSMR's rockets would *whump, swish, and flash,* row after row, in a zigzagging motion across the night sky and splatter up, down, and over the side of mountains and hills. The rocket ship was very effective in routing enemy troops from reverse sides of mountain slopes that the large ships and airplanes were unable to do. Star shells were fired by ships or dropped by Navy spotter planes to illuminate enemy targets. Constant, random, harassing and interdiction naval gunfire provided a *no man's land* and prevented the Chinese Communist Forces from regrouping for an attack – as well as allowing for a frantic, but orderly, withdrawal from Hungnam.

Spotters ashore would identify targets for ships to fire on at night. Fighter planes would dive between the mountains both day and night firing rockets, bombing, and strafing. Sometimes I would see them pull up after a steep dive, sometimes not. I wondered if they had been shot down or crashed into the side of a mountain. I know the soldiers and Marines pinned down and those who struggled to make their way to Hungnam Harbor greatly appreciated the menacing Navy and Marine planes giving close support, especially the close support WWII propeller driven F4U Corsair Fighter.

Close ashore one day about noon, we heard this loud noise of sputtering and backfiring coming from over the mountain behind our ship. The damaged Navy F4U Corsair barely cleared the trees, flew low over our ship and went in the *drink*, only a few yards starboard. A nearby rescue ship fired off its engines, blowing black smoke to get underway. Just then a helicopter aboard an LST lifted off and quickly plucked the pilot out of the water before the plane went under. One LST and more later had heli pads installed to quickly rescue downed fliers. The first H-13 helicopters, *angel choppers,* were used at Bokoko-ko to communicate with, spot, and rescue damaged and downed F4U Corsair airmen at Wonsan. The US Air Force was not as effective for quick close support. Its planes had to fly from South Korean airfields or from Japan and were unable to be readily called on because of distance and limited fuel.

Heavy cruisers and larger ships far off shore continued to give heavy fire coverage for our troops working their way from the *Frozen Chosin* to the forced evacuation port of Hungnam. LSMR's were launching rack after rack of streaming rockets from the beach to maintain a one mile *zone of fire* around the port city of Hamhung. The fusillade of fire made for one hellish fireworks display. Unexpectedly, the battleship Missouri had pulled up closer off ashore, near where we were anchored. I was suddenly awakened at about 2000 hours with a *wham* and *bang* on the starboard side. The concussion caused the sleeping compartment to vibrate. Sound resonated throughout the ship. When the Missouri would fire her 16" broadside our whole ship would light up like daylight, light enough to read a newspaper. The blast rippled the waters. I was aware that many, maybe hundreds of the enemy were being killed by these salvos. When large ships fired their big guns and the shells left the barrels (muzzles) they first glowed a bright hot yellow, cooling to reddish orange, then changing to red. There were times I would watch the large shells arc, floating *slowly* across the sky. Sometimes the shells would disappear over a mountain, or quickly start a fire on some convoy, or enemy grouping along the shore. We were that close, and all this firing over our heads made us uneasy and tense. A shell could fall short.

The coldest winter in 200 years was experienced on the 16th of December, 1950, with forty-knot winds that worked up the sea westerly. Under these severe conditions three ROK South Korean Divisions, ROK Marines, I Corps as well the KATUSA – Korean Augmentation Troops to the United States, and the SVA – Student Volunteer Army, were evacuated on the 17th. The U.S. Army 7th Infantry Division evacuated Hungnam on December 20th. The last to go was the 1st Marine Division. I and II Corps, 3rd Capital Infantry Division and all American forces of X Corp of the Eighth Army were .evacuated, including the 5th and 7th Marine Infantry Division, 1st Marine Division, and the Army 3rd Infantry Division. The list of fighting units evacuated may not be in the exact order, or dates, or because of the confusion and me not knowing exactly their military structures. I have tried to include and not overlook any designations or men who fought an unparalleled fierce battle in severe weather with frostbite and much difficulty. Especially those who fought their way out at the reservoir known as the *Outbreak of the Chosin Few.*

They began embarkation the eleventh and continued until December 22, 1950. The 1st Marines – ***The Old Breed –*** the Eighth and I (whose barracks at eighth and I streets, Washington, D.C.), are our nations oldest Marine regiment. In three years, at the Battle of Inchon, and the Battle of Chosin Reservoir – Choson Chin Jaeng – Changin (Chosin), they lost 4,000 killed and 25,864 wounded. I say to all Marines, ***Semper-Fi!***

Civilian evacuation was continuous after December 19th in –l0C (14 degree Fahrenheit) weather. As the evacuation neared an end the refuges began to push toward the docks and suddenly broke into a hectic rush to board any ship with space to take them. I am reminded of a quote, ***Men of the sea have seen the works of the Lord.***

I believe it was truly a miracle that Russian MiGs did not attack, bomb, or strafe the concentration of men, women and children, ships and refugees. Russia was not willing to sustain a large loss of aircraft, get her pilots captured, maybe spread the conflict. The large number of carrier aircraft ready on our four carriers undoubtedly deterred and thwarted any Russian plans of attack.

Our tug was kept in the offing until needed to guide a loaded ship out of the channel, and as a harbor entrance control vessel to keep ships out, or lead an empty incoming replacement ship down the mine-free channel. Tugs were also used to position incoming vessels at a berth or assist the port loading area.

When not working the harbor, we and other tugs were running to aid stricken ships – a Japanese LST with lost power, ships with fouled screws, the Thai Naval Frigate (Corvette), Prase – formerly the Betony – that broached on the beach and had to be destroyed, the loss of the ROK Navy ship, Munsan, formerly LST 120, that broached near Pohang and sank, the Zenzan Maru, a Japanese charter ship that missed the entrance of a swept channel and hit a mine in the morning darkness.

The most serious was the ROKN LST, loaded with 7,400 North Korean refugees that fouled its shaft as it tried to retract from the beach. The USS Conserver freed the line, but again both shafts were fouled with eight turns of 1/8" wire port, and manila line starboard shaft. The engine and gyro compass were broken and had to be repaired as well.

The USS Askari LST-1131 donated 26,000 gallons of fresh water. 1,500 loaves of bread and a large quantity of rice were supplied by other ships. Eight tons of food were given the refugees by the Navy and US Army. The ship was freed and escorted safely to a southern port. A special recognition was given to the USS Conserver, its crew, and underwater divers, for their great effort in saving the ship and all refugees.

The enormous amount of materials and the number of military personnel and refugees rescued in this two week period at Hungnam is truly astounding. Three hundred and fifty thousand (350,000) measurement tons of cargo, 17,500 vehicles, 9,000 tons of ammunition, 29,500 drums of petroleum products, and 105,000 troops were pulled out from the port of Hungnam, North Korea on 193 ships. This was like the Inchon invasion in reverse – *The Korean War's Dunkirk, Dun Kirk of Korea.*

The number of refugees reported evacuated varies from 91,000, to 98,100, or to an even number of 100,000. LST's that normally carried 1,000 were loaded with 5,000 Korean civilians trying to flee. The sad part of the rescue operation was that there were not enough ships to take out the remaining panic-stricken civilians who were suffering from the frigid Siberian wind. It is estimated there were as many refugees left stranded on the dock as were rescued. There was just not enough time, not enough ships, nor dock space.

Hamhung, North Korea was a political, cultural and educational center and is known as the birthplace of Yi Tae Jo, who founded the Yi Dynasty. Hungnam was a strong center of Christian influence and the most Westernized city, aside from the capitol of North Korea, Pyongyang. Hamhung was blessed with many churches, clinics, and a western-style Presbyterian Church. The fall of Hungnam/Hamhung to Communist forces meant imprisonment, torture or massacre of the Western-educated intellectuals, local civic leaders, UN people, all Christians, and suspected South Korean sympathizers. A plea was made by one of the city leaders, "You know what will happen to us after the Americans leave. Please save us." Marine Colonel Edward Forney, who efficiently supervised the evacuation at Hungnam, must have heard their plea, for many of those most in danger of their lives were the first to be evacuated.

A little after 2 PM on December 23rd most of the supplies and equipment were gone, and by mid-day on the

24th the last troops had boarded LCVP's and LSTs. The amount of supplies left on the dock to be destroyed by 12 UDT demolition teams were 400 tons of dangerous half-frozen dynamite, 500 1,000 pound aerial bombs, a few hundred empty oil drums, and some equipment. Shortly after 2 pm (1400hrs) on December 25, 1950, UDT teams and UN demolition teams blew up cranes, piers, equipment and retaining walls. Anything left that could be used by the enemy was destroyed by naval gunfire. The USS Begor APD-127 lay off shore to embark the last landing craft and to witness demolition of Hungnam's port facilities.

Curious enemy troops appeared along the mountain ridges overlooking the harbor, *some for the last time.* The cruisers and destroyers laid heavy fire along the ridge line as the last ships pulled away.

The evacuation of Wonsan with 64,200 refugees had been completed earlier – December 4-5, 1950. The cities of Pusan, Pohang and the islands of Je-ju do (Che-ju do) and Koje were most used to off-load refugees from both Wonsan and Hungnam. The island of Wolmi-do was used for approximately 37,000 refugees evacuated from Inchon on January 4, 1951. The number of American troops evacuated from Inchon numbered 69,000.

The greatest amphibious operation in reverse rescue was accomplished by a single ship with 47 crew members on a 455' Moore – McCormick Line ship. The SS Meredith Victory, licensed to carry only twelve passengers, was commanded by Captain Leonard P. LaRue. Capitan LaRue remarked, "God's own hand was on the helm of my ship."

The Unit Citation from the US Department of Commerce reads, *At the height of the epoch-making event of Hungnam, Korea, by the United Nations Forces in December 1950, the Meredith Victory was requested to assist in the removal of Koreans trapped and threatened with death by the encircling enemy armies. Most of the military personnel had been pulled out, and the city was aflame from enemy gunfire.*

Despite imminent danger of artillery and air attack, and while her escape route became more precarious by the hour, the Meredith Victory, her tanks full of jet fuel, held her position in the shell-torn harbor until 14,000 men, women and children had crowded into the ship. One of the last ships to leave Hungnam, the Meredith Victory, set her course through enemy mine fields, and although having little food and water, and neither doctor nor interpreter, accomplished in the three-day voyage to safety at Pusan with her human cargo including several babies born enroute, without loss of a single life.

The Presidential Unit Citation awarded by the South Korean government in 1958 reads in part, *The arrival of the Meredith Victory in Pusan after a three-day voyage through dangerous waters was a memorable occasion for all who participated in this humanitarian mission and is remembered by the people of Korea as an inspiring example of Christian faith in action.* The ship also received the Gallant Ship Award from the US Department of Commerce-Maritime Administration.

Upon arrival at Pusan, the Meredith Victory was turned away because the influx of so many refugees had overloaded dock facilities. The ship with its human cargo was directed to Koje Do (Goeje Do) Island about 50 miles to the southwest. The dock was too small, and the ship, crew, and refugees had to ride anchor – this was the third day. Two LSTs came out the next day, tied up to the freighter and safely took off all the refugees. The five babies born at sea were delivered by the Meredith Victory's First Mate, Savasti. The ship left port with 14,000 and arrived with 14,005! Truly this was a ***Christmas Cargo***.

I believe the observation made by J. Robert Lunney, a WWII Navy Veteran and an officer on the Meredith Victory needs to be weighed: "We were impressed by the conduct of the refugees, despite their desperate plight. We were touched by it."

Our ship was ordered to proceed to Pusan with our tow. We arrived at 0900 hours Christmas Day, 1950 - *my third Christmas at sea.* The ship's company had just sat down to what we thought would be a peaceful Christmas Dinner and Christmas Day, when orders came to fire off the engines, and man our duty stations to get underway. The hospital ship USS Consolation had arrived from Hungnam and had run aground on the mud in the port's shallow water. I was disheartened. The selection of food had been limited because I had to draw stores off supply ships returning from the States, but I had managed to obtain for the crew some traditional morale foods. The Christmas evening meal turned out to be cold cuts. A time was now to contemplate on our part in an *amphibious landing in reverse.*

A word needs to be said about the 600 Navy nurses who served in MASH (Mobile Army Surgical Hospital) units, in Korea hospitals in Japan, or aboard one of the Navy hospital ships stationed off the Korean coast; the USS Repose AH 16 (*Angel of the Orient*), USS Haven AH 12, and USS Consolation AH 15 – renamed HOPE. The hospital ship Benevolence T-AH 13 was conducting sea trials before preparing to do duty in Korea when she was rammed by the SS Mary Huckaback and sunk.

The Danish hospital ship Jutlandia served the evacuated wounded off the West Sea (Yellow Sea) coast at Inchon. The hospital ships treated the more serious wounded who were ferried to the Jutlandia and Consolation by helicopter as was done in the movie MASH. The Marines referred to Nurses as the ***Quiet Hearts***.

General Roy Davis, USMC (Ret.) is quoted saying, "Were it not for the Navy Hospital in Yokosuka, Japan there would be fewer of us to show them our appreciation on this the 50th anniversary of the Korean War." The dedication and sacrifice of Nurses, the quiet heroes of the Korean War, was mostly overlooked until corrected by the Reader's Digest article, ***"Veterans of a Forgotten Victory."***

Lest we forget, four Navy nurses, one Army nurse, and one Air Force nurse were killed in action in Korea. Another four nurses (two Navy and two Air Force) were killed by non-hostile causes. Eleven Navy Nurses died in the Marshall Islands on their way to Korea. Three Air Force nurses were killed in a plane crash on the island of Okinawa. Five hundred nurses served in combat. A mark of appreciation came to Navy Nurses on June 24, 2000, with the designation: ***Navy Nurses of the Korean War Day.***

NURSES:

God protect the women who
In service, faith in Thee renew
O guide devoted hand of skill
And bless their work within thy will.
Inspire their lives that they may be
Example fair on land and sea.

Lines 1-4, Merle E. Strickland (1972) and adapted by James D. Shannon (1973),
Lines 5-6, Beatrice M. Truitt (1948).

"I hate war as only a soldier who has lived it can, only as one who has seen its brutality – its futility, its stupidity."
- Dwight D. Eisenhower

We left Pusan (Busan) and arrived at Sasebo, Japan, at 0830 with much relief and great expectation to receive our long awaited mail, packages and pay. Money had not been a problem because we had no place to spend it. But now we could load up with Japanese Yen. We were to be in port for five days, enough time for one section to go ashore *once* and the other two sections *twice*. There would also be ample time for me to requisition much needed stores. Five days later we were on the go again, headed north of the 38th parallel.

The United Nations Memorial Cemetery, now designated as the UN Memorial Park, is the only of its kind in the world. The location is Daeyon-Ong, Pusan, consisting of 35.62 acres or 14.39 hectares, and is held in perpetuity. The cemetery is maintained by mandated funds from eleven nations and a Korean Support Commission. Sixteen nations and six medical support groups are represented. There are two Marine Monuments: **Monument of Marine Corps** – which honors the ROK/Marine and all Soldiers who fought in the Korean War, and **The ROK/US Marine Corps Monument** – erected in remembrance of their sacrifice in recapturing Seoul with the Han River crossing. Other military cemeteries are at **Kaesong, Inchon, Tae-jon (Dae-jon), Tae-gue (Dae-gu), Mir-Yang and Masan, South Korea.**

Partial list of those buried at **Daeyon-Ong Memorial Cemetery:**

UN – 54,000
US – 81
Australia – 378
Canada – 44
France – 117
Netherlands – 34
New Zealand – 1
Norway – 50
Turkey – 884 (1109)
The United Kingdom – 34

The three-year Korean War was one of the bloodiest, most horrendous wars in history. Men from many nations, especially ground forces who fought in the rugged mountains, endured extreme cold, frostbite, hardship, and long tours of duty for the freedom of a downtrodden Korean people – the freedom of a foreign nation, freedom of

American men, women, and children, and the ideals of the United Nations that all people should be free.

Lest the Forgotten War be forgotten, a war that was only a conflict in the minds of the American people – a possible substitute of WWII – our nation needs to remember the sacrifice of our service, and that ***Freedom is not free.***

World War I (1914-1918) – 4,272,000 served; 117,000 killed; and 204,000 wounded – 4 years

World War II (1939-1945) – 16,112,566 served; 291,557 killed; and 670,846 wounded – 5 years

Korean War (1950-1953) – 1,789,000 served; 54,246 killed; 103,284 wounded – 3 years

Vietnam War (1959-1975) – 1,170,000 served; 58,209 killed; 153,303 wounded – 16 years

My admonition to our future generations and peoples of all nations is that we come to know and try to understand one another in brotherly love – that the world might have peace and freedom, and most certainly ***religious freedom***. Yet we must be diligent to remember the main cause of past wars with untold deaths, terrible suffering and total destruction is one man's obsessive *greed,* and desire for total *power,* or *religious fanaticism* that has no scruples – believing the ends justifies the means, including the use of nuclear weapons. One world government and one world religion does not mean one world *Individual Freedom* or *Individual Religious Freedom.* We all know that one leader, or a one world leader, even with best intentions, will eventually become a dictator – thinking he knows what is best for the people, even at the killing and imprisonment of his own people. Religious freedom is not the right of one religion or ideology to enforce its belief on another of unlike belief. Religious freedom stops when religious beliefs are held within the individual and respect for another's beliefs. "You believe like I believe or I will kill you" is not religious freedom. Either we stand for something, or we will stand for anything – including the loss of our religious and personal freedoms. American Statesman and Patriot Patrick Henry said it best, **"Give me liberty or give me death."**

The Korean War Veterans Recognition Act (H. R. 2632) was signed by President Obama after a vote of 421-0. "Fly Flag," The Bill sponsored by Rep. Charles Rangel, D-NY, added **National Korean War Veterans Armistice Day** to the list of days on which the flag can be flown over government buildings, homes, and businesses. The Act especially encourages all Americans to fly our flag ***Old Glory*** on July 27 each year, in remembrance of the Korean Veteran – the Veterans of the Forgotten War.

Chapter 13

USS Castor AKS-1

Logistics and Support Activities

May 5, 1951 at 1000 hours we were finally relieved by Ocean Fleet Tug USS Hitchita ATF – 103, and proceeded to Sasebo, Japan, a short 165 miles from Pusan, where I was told of my two month extension in the Far East.

I wished we would stay at Sasebo for the two months and rest, but that was not to be. At 2000 the first night back an emergency put us underway to assist a LST that had engine trouble. One fourth of our crew - about 15 men on liberty – were left ashore. After we rescued the LST we had orders to proceed to Yokohama, Japan.

The liberty party returned to find our ship gone. Only an old receiving barge Y-108 was accessible for their temporary assignment. Most had spent all their money, had on only their dress uniforms, no cosmetics, no clean socks or clean underwear. The few sailors in transient shared what they could.

An appeal was made to the Red Cross for a change of clothes, tooth brush and razor. The Red Cross flatly refused to give them anything except a tooth brush and tooth paste. If they wanted clothes they would have to make arrangements with the ship's disbursing officer to repay the Red Cross. Our ship was small and did not have a disbursing officer, and our ship was not in port where a disbursing officer could be assigned to debit their pay. They were on their own in a foreign country without the help of the International Red Cross. The Red Cross charged the GI's for donuts in WWII; the Salvation Army gave them away – Free!

Several days passed, from February 28 to March 10, before crewmembers found transportation from Sasebo to Yokohama. They looked awful. Some had gotten into trouble and had a Captain's Mast. The consensus was if they had had assistance from the Red Cross for necessities and a little spending money, they would have returned to the ship sooner, not been in so much trouble, and in much better shape. Most WWII and Korean Veterans have a low opinion of the Red Cross.

A tumultuous greeting awaited our tug boat at Yokohama. There was a dress blue Navy Band playing rousing music and Japanese Dancing Girls decked out in the traditional and colorful Kimonos. The greeting was much appreciated, and we took a lot of pictures. I thought to myself, "I sure wish I could play the horn!" The sailors left in Sasebo missed out on this fine welcome of appreciation. I was sorry for them.

May the 16th we began two months of towing targets for the repair ship Hector, and a cold storage ship, a *reefer,* and doing anti-sub exercises with two Navy PB4Y's, as well a firing practice at an orange nylon sleeve towed by a single engine airplane. We returned to port after the first exercise at 1030 hours on May 18, my birthday. These exercises were tedious, tiring, exhausting, and depressing. We would leave port early in the morning and stay out all night crisscrossing, zigzagging, rolling and wallowing, cutting across waves, going in circles, and rendezvousing with subs. The crew was disappointed and disgruntled after returning from Korea, because we were on the Japanese island of Honshu, seven hundred miles from the fighting, but with only 17 liberties in 50 days – nine port liberties and eight starboard.

Music to our ears came on June 24, 1951 at 1:00 pm – 1300 hours - with the announcement we were to get underway for Pearl Harbor, Hawaii. Ten days later, July 4th, 1951, we were welcomed by a full Navy Band blasting out Souza marches, and six Hula Dancers swaying gracefully - telling beautiful stories of the islands. We were home at last. The scuttlebutt and expectation of a peaceful trip to Alaska to see the glaciers and ice floes was well received. But first we had to return to the Marshall and Mariana Islands.

The first trip was to Eniwetok Atoll towing an AFDL-5 dry dock with a barge inside. We deposited our tow and left the same day for Midway, Island. There we hooked our tow line to a barge and returned to Pearl. We left again for Midway to wait for the Tawasa ATF-92. On September 25 at 1430 hours we rendezvoused and relieved her of her tow – ARD-28 dry dock, with the US Corps of Engineers and a barge berthed inside. Orders were for us to meet the tug USS Cocopa ATF-101, 750 miles north of Guam, and pass her our tow. We got underway from Guam for Pearl on November 8th, towing another ARD-22. I had completed three years of service: two years and five months on the USS Tawakoni ATF-114, and now would start on President Truman's one year extension.

Three days out of Pearl I received the news that I was to be transferred to another ship – USS Castor AKS-1. This time I knew an AKS was designated a General Cargo Ship or General Stores Issue Ship. The USS Pollux AKS-2 was our ship's twin. Castor is the most northern of the two twin bright stars in the Constellation Gemini.

The USS Castor AKS-1 (C-2 cargo ship) was launched May 20, 1939, as the SS Challenger and commissioned March 12, 1941. The ship was acquired by the Navy October 23, 1945, with a displacement of 7,350 (lt) and 13,910 t (fl), Length 459'2", Beam 63', Draft 26;5", Speed 15.5-16 knots, Complement 315, Armament – 1 5"/38 dual purpose gun mount, 4 3"50 gun mounts, 8 20mm guns. Propulsion: Geared Turbine Engine, Single shaft – 6,000shp.

The Castor was tied up forward of the tanker Neosho AO-23, when the Japanese launched their surprise attack on Pearl Harbor on December 7, 1941. She was also tied up to a lighter barge loaded with 450 aerial depth charges. During the attack the red powder warning flag was removed and the barge towed across the harbor by the ship's boat crew.

The ship may have been credited with blowing away the rear fuselage of a Japanese zero, but was unsure because of all the smoke and flak. The Castor was awarded five bronze stars for extensive action in WWII and Korea War service. She was decommissioned at Sasebo, Japan and sold September 9, 1969 to Mitsui and Co. of Japan.

Supply ships are the clumsy looking *mother hens* of the fleet providing food, general stores, fuel, parts, and ammunition. I was not seeking anything glorious, but there was really nothing glorious about a slow, thin hulled, top heavy hole in the water supply ship unceremoniously named by the crew – the Ichiban Maru (number one ship) because of so much Asian Pacific duty. Again I was disappointed. I believe the Castor's and all supply ships motto is: ***You call, we haul.***

My new assignment on the Castor prevented me from manning a silhouetted low riding, heavy armament battle ship - the long and trim menacing cruiser, or the tough distinctive sharp lined destroyer. But somehow all Man O War's were now commonplace, not that important to me anymore. The important thing was that the Castor was in Yokosuka, Japan. I was to fly back to Japan and Korean plod waters. I was full of dread and dejected, and it was unfair. I had given much, and served my time in Korea. I had stayed too long!

The same day, three days later, my beloved Tawakoni sailed with my many friends and memories to its new home port at San Diego. I flew out of Hickham Field-Air Force Base, Hawaii, on a Marine (Convair) R5D, four prop cargo plane. We flew to Johnston, Island, on to Kwajalein, Guam, past Mount Fuji, and on to Haneda airbase in Tokyo. Mount Fuji or Fujiyama was clear of clouds the morning we flew by. A rare and beautiful sight this was - Japan's most noted landmark with its pristine snow-covered volcanic peak. The bright sun sparkled and glistened off the pure white snow as we flew low and slow at ten o'clock that morning. It had been necessary for our heavy loaded transport plane to land and refuel on Guam. I was hoping they would check out the generator real good, because it had to be replaced before we left Hickham Field.

We would have a lay over of about four hours, so I made off down the vegetation-lined small dirt road to the EM (enlisted men's) Club. I looked behind me and here came several young sailors following close behind. I hung around until about 2100 hours and began to wander back to the flight line. There was some commotion among the new sailors, and I had to go back and get them lined out, and on their way back to catch the plane. They had had a few beers too many. When it was time to board, the flight officer saw their inebriated condition and gave me a real hard time. I had not been assigned to be in charge, but I was the leading Petty Officer. The plane took off and soon they were laying on each other asleep on the long canvas seats. Their bodies' metabolism responded more adversely to alcohol at our high altitude. I was grateful only one had to use the *barf bag*.

Soon after landing at Haneda airport I was taken into the Air Force chow hall. I was pleasantly surprised. There in the dining room were large round tables covered with white linen table cloths and napkins, shiny silverware, sparkling water goblets, and Japanese waitresses. I thought to myself, "I should have joined the Air Force."

Just as I was anticipating a fine fare, here placed before me was a whole fish, complete with eyes, fins, and I just imagined what was inside. My stomach was weak from flying so long and with little sleep. Also, we did not eat fish with heads and eyes looking up at you down in Texas. What was I to do? I took my knife, cut the head off and hid the staring eye under the rim of my plate. The fish was surprisingly good and I ate most of both sides.

Later that afternoon I was summarily taken by military pickup to Yokosuka where I went aboard the USS Castor AKS-1 at 1800 hours for permanent duty. The next morning it was soon apparent that I was the ranking storekeeper in charge of the supply office and disbursing office. The ship had just been reconditioned and was short on personnel.

Coming off a small ship and experiencing the vastness and formality of a working supply ship made me feel like a fish out of the water. I had to learn and learn fast. My immediate superior was the ship's supply officer who was a full *scrambled egg* Commander. There was plenty of opportunity to quickly learn supply procedure. We were issuing and receiving stores twenty-four hours a day - around the clock. Two weeks later an Ensign (officer) came aboard and took charge of the disbursing office. I was very much relieved.

We made one trip to Sasebo, Japan, and then to the Koreas' two-mile limit danger zone to replenish ships of Task Force 77 operating off the Korean coast. Two more trips were to be made to the *"two mile"* area via Yokohama before returning to Yokosuka. We stayed in port at Yokosuka issuing stores until March 18, 1952.

Japanese stevedores were hired to assist with the enormous amount of loading and unloading in port. I was amused to see the lead man vigorously flap and wave his red flags giving directions to lift, lower, move right or left, or stop. The whining sound of wench motors, hoisting cables and banging booms was heard day and night all over the ship. I never got used to the mixed and irritating sounds.

There was always coffee left over after breakfast, and by ten o'clock it was getting strong and bitter, but still good. I asked the Japanese foreman if he would like some coffee. He gave me a puzzled look because his workers had never had coffee before. Their amusing word for coffee was ***kopi***. I showed the *head honcho* where the coffee was and filled his half gallon tin can. This was a mistake, for there was no mid-morning coffee left for the crew. I explained the *proper etiquette* to honcho-foreman. The problem was solved immediately.

One day I went down in the hold and heard a great commotion. Honcho had a worker up against the bulkhead, beating him something awful. I went over and observed the punishment, not knowing what it was for. Honcho's voice was raised on high; the countenance of the worker was very low. The beating and loud voice continued until finally the worker opened his quilted coat and exposed a bright red Japanese ladies kimono that was wrapped around his waist. It belonged to one of our crew and had been taken it from the crew's compartment. The man was fired from government work, and had to do hard labor at reduced pay. I felt sorry for him and for his wife, or girlfriend, for not getting such a nice surprise.

One Lead Man had served on cruise ships before the war and had a good command of the English language. I visited with him down in the hold on several occasions where we got well acquainted. He invited me and a shipmate to his home for dinner one night. I was greatly appreciative because I had had mostly Navy chow and not been in a home for many months. We were graciously greeted and ask to take a seat at the table. To my surprise there was a square hole in the floor. The raised table was built over the hole. When I sat down, my legs hung over warm coals. My feet and body were warm, my back cold.

We were served Japanese traditional sukiyaki with a raw egg on the side. I saw the sukiyaki was dipped in the raw egg for flavor and then eaten with chop sticks. I could not bring myself to do that. The bowl of beef and vegetables was very hot, hot enough to cook my beaten egg. Sukiyaki continues to be my favorite Japanese food, but without the egg.

My world would be turned topsy-turvy with a reserve Lieutenant Junior Grade coming aboard to take command of the supply office. The Lieutenant, *Mr. Lieutenant Banks, Sir.* He was a nervous *spit and polish* unsure reserve *call-up* supply officer who did not know his job. I could soon tell he was running scared and possibly dangerous.

My intention was that we would run the supply office together. I answered his questions and freely volunteered information. That is, until he began to use what he had learned against me. Cooperation was one-sided and without any semblance of gratitude. I quickly saw I had to protect myself and was sorry I had taught him as much as I had. A fiasco was to follow.

My first real encounter came one day after the supply crew asked me to intervene on their behalf for a day or two of liberty. We had been working for days, issuing stores from one side and taking on stores on the other. I was a hardened tugboat sailor by now and asked to speak to him man-to-man. I should have known better. Word of my request was passed on to the Supply Commander. I was called out into the passageway and chewed out royally. I took it that the Lieutenant felt threatened by me, though I had given him no reason to.

Mr. Banks had the propensity to run up and down the ladders to inspect ship's holds fore and aft. Only he climbed with his hands on the rungs - instead of sailor fashion, using the side rails. Once he came back in the office complaining that some seaman had stepped on his fingers. No one responded, only grinned.

Another time there was spray painting being done in a cage in #2 hold. Just as he raced down the ladder the painter swung his spray gun full blast. The bill of his hat changed from shiny black to battleship gray. He thought he was spray painted on purpose. Word of his *accidents* and misfortunes soon spread throughout the supply office.

What could have been a fatal incident happened one mid-morning while off-loading stores at Yokohama. Booms were swinging, rising and falling, smoothly and rhythmically, lifting and lowering their nets of cargo. For an unknown reason one of the heavy iron shackles fell suddenly from one of the booms. Lt. Banks had just moved one step to the right when the shackle landed hard on the very spot where he had been standing. He undoubtedly would have been killed should the shackle have fallen on his head. He became paranoid and complained that there was a conspiracy; someone was trying to kill him.

The engineering officer and I were having a heated tit-for-tat about parts, budget, and inventory. The divided doors to the supply office were swollen and shut. I pushed on the upper door. It did not budge. I pushed again; again, it did not open. I pushed very hard the third time. The door struck Mr. Banks on the side of the head, knocking his hat off. He wobbled in a daze. He said, "I told you to wait a minute." I replied, "I did not hear you, Sir." He had been bent over trying to unlatch the lower door without me knowing. I was sorry I had hurt him, yet a little pleased.

Our last misunderstanding was one night after we made port at Pearl Harbor. I had the mid-watch from 2400 hours to 0400 hours and had sacked out early. Mr. Banks came down to the crew's compartment and woke me up. I told him I had the mid-watch, but he said, "I do not care; I want you to drive me to my apartment." His wife was living in Hawaii at the time. Reluctantly I got up, got dressed, and met him at the end of the gangplank. The ship had been assigned a new Chevrolet pick-up with brakes that suddenly *grabbed.* I asked which way, and we were off at speeds exceeding the 20 mph speed zone. He remarked, "This is a twenty mile per hour speed limit." I said, "I know."

We pulled up to his apartment, and I could see all the lights were on. I waited and waited, thinking I might get back in time for another nap before going on mid-watch. He finally came out. By this time I was *hot under the collar* and asked myself why I ever got a driver's license.

We made the trip back to the ship in short time. As I slowed and rolled to a stop, he opened the door to jump out. I tapped the brake just then; it grabbed and threw Mr. Banks forward. His hat and head caught between the door and car frame. He straightened his hat and said nothing. I said nothing. I believe we had a personality conflict.

The Castor had left Japan for the States via Pearl on March 18, 1952. On March 22nd we hit a severe storm that caused our reduction gear to go out. We were without our screw, without power, dead in the water, and at the sea's mercy, for 22 hours. This happened right at evening meal time. The mess hall was full of food, drink and sailors - some without their *sea legs*. The ship was in a trough rolling from side to side.

Young sailors began to slip, slide, and drop their trays. The deck became slick with food and drink. Tables and benches began to fall, collapse, and slide with great force. I saw the danger and ran with the next roll to the port bulkhead where I jumped up on a small ledge. Just as I jumped, a sliding bench was skidding across the deck, about to crush my leg. One sailor kicked it with his foot in the nick of time. I sustained only a severe bruise by the glancing blow. The mess hall by now was in complete disarray with folded, collapsed tables and benches, trays, food, drink, silverware and broken glass all mixed together and crashing against the bulkhead with each roll. For two days the cooks could only prepare not much more than black coffee and toast.

Shoes, maybe a hundred pair not laced to the bunks, were sliding to and fro across the deck and down into the stairwell. I had learned while on the tug to tie my shoes to the bunk rail at night and in rough weather. How they later determined whose shoes were whose I do not know.

I ran topside to my abandon ship station, found my life jacket, and observed my assigned motor launch. No way could I get aboard. When the ship rolled to starboard, the motor launch was almost touching the water. When the ship rolled back to port, it was pressed in its davits pointing skyward. It would be impossible; the lines would have to be cut. Hopefully the boat would drop into the water right-side-up without swamping or turning over, and I could manage to get aboard. This would all have to be done quickly because of the very cold water and hypothermia.

I would have to jump into the cold black waters and pray I would not be crushed between the boat and the side of the ship. I could quickly see the situation was not good. I went back below to the crew's quarters where the ship's Clinometer – inclinometer – swung dangerously close to the maximum 52 degree roll. By this time the clothes lockers were breaking their welds, falling and sliding erratically across the steel deck. We all had to find line to tie and secure the heavy lockers. The ship made a sudden roll on its side and stayed there for what seemed like an eternity, shuddering greatly – deciding whether to go over or not. I anxiously waited to see if the ship would right itself. She broke free of the grip of the strong wave just in time and swung back and forth greatly until settled down to a less onerous rolls.

A large roll of wire cable in #3 hold aft had broken through its wire cage. Every roll, lurch, and pitch sent the wire twirling erratically. It would crash into the thin steel bulkhead with a loud bang. Enough force I thought to cause a crack in the hull to flood the compartment. My resolve to help tie the wayward roll of wire cable vanished once I saw the great danger. This was a job for the more experienced Deck Force.

About this time, there was a clanking, banging, and sometimes a loud thud heard on deck. A cargo boom had broken loose. The Captain stepped out onto the darkened hatch...a shackle caught him on the forehead. He was out cold and blood was flowing from the wound. The chief corpsman ran to give aid. A large lurch sent the corpsman sliding backward down the steel deck and into a bulkhead. He was either unconscious or severely dazed. More help arrived and the Captain was taken to sick bay for treatment. He was lucky to be alive; he could have had a broken skull - been killed.

The supply office and the engineering office were a complete disaster. Desks had broken their weld; file cabinets had fallen over; typewriters and calculators slid back and forth. Papers were torn, marred and ripped covering the deck two or three inches deep, and too slick to walk on. Two days later began the clean up. The severe storm had lasted for 22 hours and we without power. I believe I can verify the old saying that there are no Atheist sailors in a storm.

A Seaman's Version of the Twenty-third Psalm

The Lord is my Pilot, I shall not drift.
He lighteth me across the dark waters.
He steereth me in steep channels.
He keepeth my log book.
He guideth me by the star of Holiness
For His Name's sake.
Yea, though I sail 'mid the thunders and tempests of life,
I will dread no danger, for Thou art with me.
Thy love and Thy care, they shelter me.
Thou preparest a harbor before me in the homeland of eternity.

Thou anointeth the waves with oil – my ship rideth calmly.
Surely sunlight and starlight shall favor me on the journey I take,
And I will rest in the port of my God forever.

The damage we incurred was all uncalled for. The Ocean Tug, USS Yuma, was sent out to take us in tow that first evening. She hooked on and began to pull, and did pull until her tow line was at times out of the water. The tug's skipper was fearful that the tow line would break. He cut us loose. He could have at least held us straight to buck the waves until the storm subsided.

I was mad and disgusted, thinking back to when we pulled the Enid Victory off the rocks at Hungnam, and the time we caught the outer edge of a typhoon three days out of Guam towing a huge dry dock. The line kept coming out of the water; there was banging when the tow gauge hit bottom, but we did not cut our tow lose, even when we took an estimated 62 degree roll. The USS Tawakoni ATF-114 would have brought the Castor back to port. I am certain of that.

Three days later the USS Greenlet ASR-10 took us in tow in fairly calm waters and deposited us dockside in Yokosuka. Repairs were made and we left again for the States via Pearl Harbor, April 4, 1952. We arrived at Pearl on April 15th and sailed for the states on the 18th, arriving in Oakland, California April 25th. I had only one last liberty to visit Wall Rae and Waikiki Tavern. By the time I returned in 1967, it was gone.

I took a twenty-day leave, why I do not know. I should have stayed aboard and took pay for my days' leave. It might have been because I could only accumulate thirty days' leave maximum. I returned to the ship May 17 and soon transferred to the Naval Hospital in San Diego, California on July 28 with a stomach problem. Four days later I was released and transferred to the Naval Receiving

Station, San Diego. It was good to be in downtown San Diego and have a few days free.

I arrived back at the Naval Supply Center, Oakland. I looked up, saw the tide was in, and the gangplank would be a very steep climb. On deck was a crewmember using a lesser boom. I motioned for him to lower the boom, attached my sea bag and had it hoisted on deck. I climbed the gangplank, saluted the flag aft and found an able-bodied seaman who volunteered to take my bag below.

The ship moved away from the dock and anchored at Vallejo, California. There was little work required riding at anchor, except to pull Shore Patrol duty several times. Vallejo was covered with sailors on liberty each night, but there was little disturbance. Easy duty, but boring duty, continued until August 18, when I received orders to be transferred to Treasure Island for discharge.

Many things had changed. I had changed since I first came through the infamous T.I. - Treasure Island. I was a lowly SKSA back then, abused and browbeaten by a Second Class Petty Officer while assigned to mess duty (KP). I looked for him, on the chance he might be still be there, or in the process of being discharged. I really did want to cross paths with him again.

Boredom, bunk time, and chow line were the plan of the day while awaiting discharge. A little stir was created when some seaman or third class came into the barracks looking for a work detail. We either scattered or looked askance because we were first or second class petty officers and out ranked the intruders. I did not envy their assignment. We were short timers with a *short timer's attitude.*

Chance meetings of former shipmates were commonplace. In my case there was Sanders, a fair complectioned, wavy redhead who we had high-lined off the Tawakoni to a larger ship one night because he had appendicitis. He told me the story of his successful operation and assignment to a tanker. The tanker had caught fire at dockside in South America. He had to jump into the fiery, oily water and swim to safety. His burns were treated and he recovered without serious scarring. But he had lost everything, all his clothes and personal effects.

By chance I talked to someone who knew D. L. Orr, the yeoman and my shipmate on the Tawakoni in Japan and Korea. He was cutting orders – discharge papers. We had a fine reunion in the personnel office where he found me a temporary typing job. I could have typed my own discharge papers, but I declined.

He had bought a small Chrysler Corporation Desoto while in Hawaii, and had it shipped over. Chrysler stopped making the Desoto in 1954. We arranged to be discharged the same day and for him to drive me to Texas on his way home to Arkansas.

Orr's wife had come to California to meet him and we three rode back together. I remember the first night we stayed at a motel; there was no room for me. I asked the lady, "Don't you have anything?" She said, "Well, I have the 'Blue Goose' out back." It was the smallest (blue) trailer house I had ever seen, clean and comfortable, and afforded me a very good night's sleep. The drive home was pleasant and peaceful. I felt free for the first time in a long time.

Orr pulled his Desoto up to the Central Texas Bus Terminal in Ft. Worth, Texas and let me out. We said our goodbyes wishing each other well. I was saddened to see him go. I knew he would be the last to understand and my last contact with what had been a lifetime of adventure. I would not take a million dollars for some of my experiences, but would not do it again for a million either.

I waited around for what amounted to two hours, maybe to 4 pm, for the bus to take me on the last leg of my journey - to my hometown of Cleburne, Texas. The ride was a short forty minutes, but I was not in any hurry. The City Cab taxi stand was near the bus station. I gathered up my small blue hand bag, and with my stuffed sea bag on my shoulder walked around the corner and asked a driver to take me home. I arrived at 615 Mansfield Road unannounced and hesitated to go in right then. Everything was brown and dead from the Texas August heat. So quiet! I walked to the back door near where we drew water for the cattle. I opened the screen door on the back porch and entered the house through the kitchen. The first words I was to hear were, "Well, I see you are back."

One last word needs to be said on behalf of the Auxiliary Fleet and logistics support ships. Trans-oceanic shipping to replenish all ships and ground forces required dedication and skilled seamanship. Seventy-five percent (75%) or more of the equipment, fuel, food and supplies, bullets and ordnance for the war was carried by ships with the designation AK, AKA, AKS, AO, AOG, AE, AG, AF, or MSTS – Military Sea Transport Service. MSTS also transported soldiers and Marines and many tons of dry stores as well as huge quantities of munitions.

These Navy cargo and supply ships, MSTS and Merchant Marine ships had to bring their cargoes 5,000 miles over the ***ocean highway*** from San Francisco/Oakland to the Far East. The maximum number of round trips each supply ship could make was one per month, or 10,000 miles at 15 knots. Vital logistic roles were played by these men and ships to tirelessly transport tanks, trucks, fuel, ammunition, spare parts, food, clothing and supplies. Ours was not the glorious navy, but the service fleet with a tireless work ethic with crews that operated in the most adverse conditions imaginable. There is no better example than the small fleet tug with a big heart. These various and specialized ships and their crews who weathered storms at sea and the vagaries of nature to sustain war operations and maintain United States global presence need to be awarded special recognition.

The invasion of Inchon saw the largest sea lift since Okinawa in 1945. The Inchon Armada consisted of 261 vessels – 194 American, 32 Japanese leased (mostly LST's),

15 South Korea, 12 British, 3 Canadian, 2 Australians, 2 New Zealand and 1 French ship. A soldier's rations and needs were figured to be 60 pounds per day.

High priority items flown in to the forward areas accounted for only about three percent of the total. Air Force C-119's and C-164's were bringing 100 tons a day to Japan by December 1950 – exceeding at times that war needs in the Pacific 1941-1945. Soon after secession of hostilities in Korea, auxiliaries were relegated to a mothball obscurity, sold to a foreign country, or scrapped.

I came to realize the reason Navy auxiliary ships did not get deserved recognition. It is because they were usually small, a long time at sea, with no boundaries and no frontiers, had a different type of staff, and ships were specialized and not visible on the map. Their exploits to control the sea and sea coasts, the continuous movement of troops and supplies, is unseen and the image of the auxiliary Navy has little public appeal. The far flung United States Navy has never received the recognition of branches of service whose actions can be pin-pointed on a map.

There is a poem from The Silent Defenders article entitled "Eternally" that sums up my Navy enlistment.

ETERNALLY

I made a choice some years ago
To sail the sea no more.
I don't regret the life and love
I've made here on the shore.

But I'm haunted by a temptress,
My first true love, the sea.
My dark and stormy mistress,
I hear her call to me.

I'm torn between my life ashore

And the call to sail away.
My love, my life is needed here,
I'm duty bound to stay.

Yet, often I will walk the beach
Throughout the darkest hours.
To hear my lover's mournful call
To feel her awesome power.

Oh, cradle of all Earthly life,
Great mother of the sea,
Cast off the lines that hold my heart
And let my soul sail free.

In the end I will return to you,
My final love, the deep.
I'll pull your waters over me
Eternally to sleep.

~ Sailor ~

Chapter 14

From Kochosun to Korea

Korea is no longer known as the Hermit Kingdom. In forty years it has risen to be the United States' seventh largest trading partner, the third largest in Asia, the thirteenth largest economy in the world, with an annual foreign trade growth rate of eleven percent. Besides being one of the leading nations in growth and gross national product, the country is first in shipbuilding, first in high-speed internet, third in tire manufacturing, fifth in manufacturing the Hyundai, Kia, and GM Daewoo. Local makes of cars and trucks are the Ssangyoung-subsidarary of Shanghai Automotive Industry Corporation, SM (Samsung Motors)-subsidiary of Renault Samsung Motors. Samsung is the world's #2 semi-conductor maker. Samsung-LG TV is the maker of cell phones and cameras as well as other high quality electronic products. South Korea is the most *hardwired* country in the world. The country refers to their growth and prosperity as ***The Miracle of the `80's***, or ***the Miracle of the Han (River).*** Koguryo, now Korea, is one of the four *dragons* (TATSU) of East Asia, the other three being Taiwan, Hong Kong, and Singapore.

The Republic of Korea accuses Japan of illegally changing the map during the Japanese Colonial Rule (1910-1945) renaming the East Sea the Sea of Japan, and the West Sea to Yellow Sea. Korea was annexed by the Japanese and could not have a government representative at the Monaco Conference in 1929 of the International Hydrograhphic Organization (IHO). For the first time the IHO had bowed to Japanese wishes and deleted the name East Sea to replace it with Sea of Japan. Korean maps use only the East Sea and West Sea designation. Some map makers (cartographers) include both of the names: East Sea/Sea of Japan, and West Sea/Yellow Sea. In fact, the sea has had many names over the centuries, but each refers to East Sea with these ancient names - Mer de Coree, *Mer di Coree,* Sea of Korea, Oriental Sea *Mare Orientale,* Sea of Joseon (Choseon), Manchurian Sea, China Sea or China Ocean, East (Oriental Sea). Two-thirds of very old maps, maps of 37-53BC refer to the Sea of Corea. North Korea uses the designation East Sea of Korea. Koreans identify with and place great importance in their national identity, culture, language and history, on the proper name of these seas. Japan was jealous and wanted the name changed from Corea to Korea whereby the superior **J (Sea of Japan)** would precede **K** in alphabetical order.

Map importance can be seen in the Matteo Ricci Map. The 400 year old massive map (5 feet high and 12 feet wide) was created by Matteo Ricci in 1602 at the request of the Chinese Emperor. The map shows China in the center, with Europe and other countries in surrounding positions. Demand for the map was so great that the map acquired the name, **Impossible Black Tulip of Cartography**, because of its rarity and importance to scholars, explorers and trade. Only six copies remain today with centrist China in the center of the world. The IHO needs to address the unfairness and reinstate the name East-West Seas, and erase the legacy of Japan's colonial rule. Fifty-one times from 1550 to 1800 the sea was Sea of Korea. The East Sea terminates with the

Korea Strait, and the East China Sea to the far south. Korea's large, sub-tropical Je-ju do (Che-ju do) Island extends farther south and is surrounded by the Pacific Ocean. Je-ju do is known for its very sweet and easy to peel tangerines and excellent sushi, and as Korean's favorite vacation and honeymoon resort. Jeju (Che-ju) Island and South Korea itself is one of tourism's best kept vacation secrets.

South Korea is about the size of Portugal, slightly larger than Hungary, about the size of Kentucky, and a little larger than Indiana, with a land area of 38,022 square miles, and a population of 48 million people. North Korea is a little smaller than Mississippi with a population of 24 million. The peninsula is very mountainous with only about 20% arable and productive land, more so on the southern plains further south and to the west. South Korean countrymen feel they are a *shrimp* caught between two whales – China and Japan.

The national flower Mugunghwa reflects the perseverance and determination of the indomitable and dynamic Korean through their long struggle for freedom. The Korean people have been referred to as the **Irish of Asia.** I suppose the comparison is because of the Irish people's long suffering, their tenacity, and similar characteristics – great love of freedom, love of literature, sad bagpipe music, and extensive use of drums, all similar to Korean music. Other characteristics are warm hospitality, importance of family, ironic-sad-funny humor, stubbornness, and quick temper. Today the Korean person (saram) is Han Guk Saram with the local name Tae Han Min' Guk. The name for South Korea ***Nam-Han*** is the Republic of Korea (ROK). North Korea's people's name ***Puk-Han*** is today's Democratic Peoples Republic of Korea (DPRK).

The common name for the Mugunghwa flower in Texas and Oklahoma is the Rose of Sharon or Althea, *hypericum calyclnum***.** It blooms continuously in Korea from

June or July to October. There is a Korean designation for the Mugunghwa, *Eternal Flower*, with Mugung being a symbolic root word meaning immortality. The tough, tenacious Mugunghwa (hwa-flower) is affected little by blight or insects and can withstand and survive in very harsh conditions. The flower truly represents the long history of Korea's remarkable people. They suffered greatly, endured cruelty, strived for freedom only to have it taken away - time after time. At the end of the Korean War the country was completely devastated, not only by the Korean War, but by the many wars with China and Japan dating back to the middle fifteen hundreds and up to liberation in 1945.

I have found the Hangul speaking Korean, with their customs, culture, and its Hungul language, meaning *Great Script, One Script*, or today Urigeul/urikul *Our Script*, to be hospitable, generous, warm, kind, caring, fun-loving as well as very hard workers. The country's noted leader, King Sejong and his selected learned group began work in 1443 on a *common man's language* with completion in 1449. Hungul is the only *true language* with the most logical writing systems in the world. Chinese characters were adequate for the intellectuals, but not for the common people to clearly express their ideas. The Korean people are Hanguk: ***han*** south, *guk* country, and *in* people, thus Hangukin.

Early Korea was called Dong-yi and the people were known as Han-Gook – *guk*... They were referred by the name Bak-Yi-Min-Jok – *white clad peoples.* The Korean nationality is made up of descendants of peoples from the Altaic Region near Lake Baikal, Mongol, South Pacific, and tribes from East Asia Lowlands. The Korean language comes from the URAL/Altaic language groups and roots of Hungarian, Turkic, Mongolian, Tun Gusic and Magyar Finno-Ugric tongues. Japanese language comes mainly from an assemblage of Chinese and a combination of indistinguishable tongues.

Religion plays a large role in Korean society, especially Presbyterian, and to a lesser degree Methodism. Many evangelical non-denominational churches, such as the Yoido Full Gospel Church, whose members number over 800,000, the Pentecostal Church, the Assembly of God, the Catholic Church, and Baptist Church have influenced a nation whose people are forty-six percent Christian. The country has complete religious freedom, and is the second largest country compared to the United States to send out overseas missionaries.

Koreans place a high priority on and readily sacrifice for the husbands', wives', or children's higher education - even if it means living abroad and separated for months, even years if necessary. Both students and parents excel academically. Strict study habits have lead Koreans to surpass other Asian students with honors, high honors, and scholastic awards, often resulting in the selection of Summa Cum Laude, especially at Oklahoma City University and University of Central Oklahoma.

The forerunner of the current Korean flag is thought to be the battle flag of Dong-yi – the Eastern Barbarian *Red Devil* King, about 2700 BC. He controlled much of China, Manchuria, Siberia and lands beyond.

The Korean flag, the Taegeukgi – Tae Geuk-gi was believed to be taken from I Chung or Korean Yeok *Book of Change* and symbolizes oriental thinking, principles, and philosophy. Adopted January 25, 1950, it has a round red and blue divided Korean um-yang, (Chinese yin-yang) symbol in the center, on a pure white background with four black Trigrams – one in each corner. The circle is characterized as the sphere of infinity and continuous motion, and is surrounded by four ancient Trigrams, one in each corner with four symbols called *kwae* – olden times eight *kwai.*

The carliest surviving flag is the four trigram flag of 1882. With the signing of the Korean-American Treaty of

Commerce June 6, 1883, the country saw the need for a new four trigram Taegukgi. The Taegukki, *flag* means ***Great Extremes.*** After a few minor changes an official flag was adopted in 1897 by *King Gojong,* who proclaimed Korea an Empire. The Korean Empire lasted until 1910 when Korea came under Japanese rule with the duress Annexation Treaty of 1910. This period is known in Japan as *The Korea under Japanese Rule*. Japan's rule lasted until 1945. An official flag was adopted October 15, 1945, and with minor changes, another and last flag was officially adopted January 1, 1950.

The Trigram has evolved over the centuries with name changes and meanings that are difficult to describe. Each Trigram is of a three bar configuration: Kwae-Geo, *Kun-Kon* - the upper left Heaven-Summer with three bars denotes Heaven as KUM or Geon; Gon, *Kon* – lower right with three broken bars denotes Earth-Winter; Gam, *Kam* – upper right with two broken bars and one solid center line denotes Water-Autumn; *Li, Yi-Ri* – lower left Trigram with two solid bars and one center broken bar denotes Fire-Spring. The other four former trigrams were represented as: *Ken* – mountains; stopping or stillness; *Chen*-thunder, initiative; action; *Tui* – lake, joy, attraction; and *Sun* – wind-penetrating.

The upper half, red section of *Yang,* man-masculine, bright-hot, represents *plus*. The lower half-blue section *Um yin,* woman-feminine represents *dark and cold – the negative cosmic force*. Taken together, the Taegeukgi - Korean Flag symbolizes **resistance** and **independence, universal balance and harmony, and unity.** Other great aspects of the land of white clad people are their innate desire for *purity, sincerity, respect and peace.*

Korean history and continuity of its ancestors that date back to 5,000 BC, *legend age*, only a thousand years less than China's record of six-thousand years, is hard to explain in a memoir and a book not of history. I ask the reader to bear with me as I try to unfold the more important historical events leading up to the Korean War. My intent is for the reader to come away with a greater appreciation of a warm, loving people with a rich history who over the centuries had their great potential thwarted time and time again up until the end of WWII and Japanese occupation.

The Old Choson founded by King Tan'gun was made up of strong migratory hunters of northern mountainous tribes near Lake Baikal. The three early Sam, *Han* (sam is the number three in Korean) regions were inhabited by the **Jin-han** – in Manchuria, the **Ma-han** in Korea and the **Bun-han** in Beijing, China. The Hun is also found in the far countries of Turkey, Hungary - *Han* or *Hun* - and parts of Europe. The early Koguryo, *Old Go Joseon,* was a large feudal state from 277 BC to 688 AD, and believed to be founded in 2333 BC.

Korean history begins in 2333 BC with a beautiful story of when the legendary figure, Tan' gun, *also Tan-Gun, Dan-Gun, Tan'jin,* was born of the Sun of Heaven and of a Bear-Totem Tribe. His true beginning has been disputed, but is believed to be that of the real **Tan'gun,** who called his land early Choson – *Land of the Morning Calm, Land of the Dawn,* or *Land of the Morning Freshness.*

The story of Old Choson – Go Joseon, *meaning morning freshness* or *morning dew*, begins in ancient times when **Hwan-ung,** *the lord of heaven,* king of the eastern heavens, descended to earth at Taebeak Mountain, Land of God or City of Go. He established the new nation of Go Joseon that lasted for one-thousand years, a place where his subjects were treated fairly, were happy, and prospered. Near Mount Taebaek-san, where the nation was founded, lived a large Siberian tiger, and a she-bear. The two saw how munificent Hwan-ung's rule was, and how the people loved their King. They were jealous and wanted to be men to enjoy life under Hwan-ung's benevolent rule. They approached Hwan-ung and asked if there was a way they could become men. The answer was, "Yes there is, but it is very difficult.

You must have great patience." Their answer was, "We are willing to try."

They were given simple instructions to eat nothing but 20 cloves of garlic and a bundle of mugwort, and stay secluded out of the sunlight for 100 days. After 80 days the tiger failed his test and left the cave to find food. *He has been a fierce enemy of man ever since.*

The bear endured the hunger and close confinement through patience and much prayer. Some time during the night on the hundredth day a miraculous transformation took place. Out of the dark cave stepped a beautiful bear-woman. She looked toward Heaven, prayed and went straight to Hwan-ung for his blessing and to seek a way to repay her debt. Hwan-ung was struck by the bear-woman's beauty. Many times she prayed under a certain tree to have a child. Eventually Hwan-ung asked her to marry him. At that time he gave her a new name, **Ung-yo or Ung-yeo** meaning *the girl incarnate from a bear.*

Not long after they were married, Ung-yo gave birth to a son in the shade of a birch tree. He was given the name, **Tan'gun** - *Dan-gun, Wanggeom or Tan-jin,* Lord of the Birch, meaning *high priest or founder.*

Hwan-in or Hwanin, the Ruler of Heaven, was the God of All and the ruler of Heaven. Hwan-ung is the Son of Hwanin. Tan'gun is the grandson of Hwan-in and the god-man. The three constitute the divine *Sam-shin-trinity.* Sam is the number three in Korean, and sin is the spirit – three spirits. The Bible speaks of **God the Father, the Son, and the Holy Spirit** being one, thus the **Triune** is found in Hwan-in, Hwan-ung and Tan'gun.

Hwan-ung, *Heavenly King* departed the earth in 2333 BC, and not long after his son Tan'gun – Tan'gun Wan Go, *King of Sandalwood,* began to rule. *Whether legend or not, twenty or thirty years before Christ*, the name Tan' gun was mentioned in ancient Chinese records. Nevertheless, Tan' gun became the Tiger of Shinshi, *City of God*, the Defender,

Protector, and Guardian, the *Golden Thread* of the Taehan Min'guk or Hanguk people. Tan' gun has protected the people through 3000 years through determination, perseverance, strength and cunning. The long ancient history, teachings, and legacy handed down to each new generation are what ties and binds the Korean people even today.

To know and understand the Korean people even more, we must go back to the legend of the shameful, impatient tiger in the 99th and last year of Tan' gun's reign. The old tiger approached Tan' gun and asked, "Must all tigers live in shame forever because of impatience?" Tan' gun, the father of Korea, replied that it need not be and granted him the opportunity to become man, but at a great price.

The tiger was warned before he agreed that he would enjoy the mountains and valleys, the beauty, sights and sounds of The Land of the Morning Calm, but there would be more. He would experience despair, frustration, pain, subjugation and hopelessness for many long undetermined years. He would be an outcast and live in the solitude of a hermit.

The last things told to the tiger were that he would have power to be man for short periods of time; a curse would be upon him if he became impatient; he would not grow older; and he would have the power to live until Choson became sovereign and the people became free. In the story, *Korea in the Eye of the Tiger,* history unfolds and we witness the joys and upheavals of the Korean people until today when The Republic of Korea is strong, and the land is free and *calm…the tiger prevails*!

The good nature of the Korean people led the nation to be known as the *Eastern Land of Courtesy.* Their kind, charitable, trusting disposition may have partially led to subjugation by other nations and colonial rule by Japan. We know from history Korea never developed imperialistic tendencies outside their given boundaries or invaded an overseas country.

A thread of fatalism, an action through non-action derived from Confucianism, is apparent even today. As well we see the traits of Confucian thought in the gentle, humble Korean, with filial duty, generosity, hospitality, empathy, valor, hard work, justice, loyalty and trustworthiness.

The nation's *spiritual* founding, varied topography, magnificent mountains, many rivers, temperate climate, and striking beauty have fostered excessive zeal and adulation for their country, *that almost amounts to an aversion toward other lands.* The pride of Korea's turbulent past, brave feats of resistance, and miraculous survival to become one of the four dragons, continues to be passed on to succeeding generations.

The 4th century BC saw the states of Puyo in the north rise from communities and clans only to be absorbed by the powerful nation of Koguryo. Koguryo lasted from 37 BC to 667-668 AD, a period of 700 years. Though the Chinese came and conquered the fertile Korean coastal plains on the West and dominated the people there, Koguryo grew strong and challenged the Chinese by conquering the Okcho tribes all the way to Vladivostok, Russia, and the Ye tribes south to Pusan, Korea. Mighty Old Koguryo waned during the last decades and lost lands because of a decadent ruling class who disregarded the hardship and misery of the poor and the encroachment by the Chinese into Manchuria.

The land was now divided into the Three Kingdoms, Koguryo (north), Paekche (middle), and Shilla (south). The three kingdoms occupied land from the southern tip of the peninsula and to the far north Chinese/Korean kingdom known as Parhae, with Kirin being the capital in Manchuria.

There was a resurgence of the Chinese T'ang Empire. T'ang armies crossed the Yalu River and became involved in an all out war with Koguryo. Shilla (Silla) to the south had remained neutral, but when she saw the T'ang winning she joined in the fight against Koguryo and Paekche. Chinese/Korean kingdoms established the new nation of Parhae from the old north Koguryo domain. But China was not satisfied with the defeat of Koguryo and later of Paekche. She wanted to rule the conquered lands and the Korean Peninsula as a separate independent military dependency. Shilla wanted an independent unified state of all Korea and turned south to Pyon Han, to face Japanese encroachment.

A six year hard-fought rebellion and struggle began for independence between Shilla's former allies, with Shilla's forces driving the Chinese troops back into China, and unifying all of Korea under one ruler for the very first time. The Shilla Dynasty or Kingdom of Shilla (Silla) was founded in 668 AD and lasted until 935 AD. Shilla is noted for consolidating all of Korea for the very first time, the strong significant influence of Korea on world history,and cultural achievement. *Cheomseongdae*, the star-gazing tower at Gyeongju, is one of the oldest scientific observatories on Earth, dating back to the 7th century.

Paekche (Baekje) (18 BC - 660 AD) had made an early alliance with Yamato of Japan to supply horses, craftsmen, metal workers, potters etc. Japan absorbed a wave of Korean culture during this period through the port at Osaka, including marriages between Korean Princes and Japanese court royalty. Confucian teachings entered Japan for the first time in 513 AD, and a large Buddha statue was sent to Yamato from Paekche in 552 AD. Reading and writing entered Japan for the first time in 587 AD. Paekche later called upon Yamato for help in its fight against China and Shilla, but to no avail, and was ultimately defeated.

Isoroku Yamato of Japan set up the State of Yamato (300 – 550 AD) that grew to be the Japanese Yamato Kingdom. He built a fighting force of thousands and laid the foundation of Japanese imperialism and colonization. His army garrison had occupied Kaya – petty state of Kaya, and Imna - the Japanese Mimana on the southern tip of the

Korean peninsula, where a Japanese colony was formed. But he was defeated and withdrew his troops to Japan, and set up defenses expecting an attack from Shilla. Japan, *the land of the rising sun*, remained closed to the outside world, but Yamato had set the stage for continuous arming and Japanese expansion.

Relations with China's T'ang Dynasty and neighbors had been good and allowed Korea to progress in art, science and government. But the rise and resurgence of the Chinese Empire, *the Middle Kingdom,* brought conflict with both Paekche and Koguryo. China's Emperors had always felt they had a *mandate from Heaven* to rule all nations. Chinese Emperors believed China was the Celestial Empire, T'ien Chao, Heavenly Dynasty, *celestial kingdom, celestial thrones*, as early as 604 AD, and that their rule was *concentric,* covering all of East Asia, Manchuria, Tibet, and Southeast Asia.

The Chinese Emperor's view was that of a sovereign, and he viewed dealings with a foreign country on the level of a vassal, or tributary, not nation-to-nation or as equals, but under suzerainty, though Asian suzerainty differed from that of Europe. Only through his *kindness* did the Chinese Emperor allow trade. Any profit, whether equal or greater, would be acknowledged as a gift of benevolence and generosity of the Emperor.

The dragon has played and continues to play an important role in Asian leaders' thinking and attitudes, toward themselves and toward other nations. The idea of the dragon first began with Kao Tsu (T'ang Dynasty 206 BC), who proclaimed themselves to be *Lung Tik Chuan Ren* – Descendants of the Dragon. The Chinese Emperor, the *descendant of the dragon* and China's Imperial power, is symbolized by its five-clawed dragon with these attributes: *Protector, Controller, Guardian, Wealth and Fortune.* Powerful but Just, and Benevolent, with the fifth claw – *Celestial Rule*, a Mandate from Heaven.

Korea's dragon has four claws, representing *family, intelligence, and strength of purpose.* Korean women believed that if they dreamed of a dragon their baby would grow up to be a great person. A male child born under the celestial sign of the dragon would be strong, wealthy and wise. This is the Year of the Dragon, and Korea is overburdened with expectant mothers waiting to have their '*dragon'* babies.

Japan's dragon has three claws, representing nobility. The Japanese**,** *Descendants of the Grown Dragon,* thought their dragon was born with three claws, and would grow extra claws the farther he traveled west – toward Korea, China, and Southeast Asia. Conversely he would lose claws the further he withdrew to the East away from China. Mythical flying animals have figured greatly in Japanese perception of their country's origin, power, and protection. From the Japanese leader Yamato (250-710 AD) it is believed came the mythical name for Japan.

During WWII the *dragon flying* aircraft carriers and two cruisers of Japan's Imperial Navy's *dragon fleet* were the: **RUYSO** –such as a Dragon Builds, *Sacred Dragon*, **SORYO** – *Blue-Gray Dragon*, **HIRYU** – *Dragon flying in Heaven*, *Flying Dragon,* **UNRYU** – *Cloud of a Heaven, Flying Dragon, Dragon in the Clouds,* **RYUHO** - *Dragon and Phoenix,* **JUNYO** – *Peregrine – Falcon*, **SHOKAHU** – *Crane Flying in Heaven*, **TENRYU** – *Heaven's Dragon* and, **TATSUTA** – *Dragon Field.* The USS Battleship New Jersey BB-62 was referred to as the *Black Dragon* or *Big J.* The Vikings had their dragon-headed Dragon Ships that brought dread and fear. And now there is an area 100 kilometers south of Tokyo named the Devil's Sea or Dragon's Triangle, similar to the Bermuda Triangle where ships and planes are disoriented and lost.

The dragon was always a type of serpent, whether scaled or feathered, and the belief was that they lived in palaces under the sea with a treasure of gold and silver.

More specifically, the Chinese Dragon was a symbol of gold, fortune and fertility, that was amphibious and lived in the ocean, rivers, streams, and even in rain drops. Chinese expectant mothers believed if they dreamed of a dragon they would have a son who would be strong, lucky, and powerful.

The Asian Dragon was also believed to unleash rain in time of droughts and figured extensively in the hopes and superstitions of the local people. The original serpentine creature took on a more exotic shape and features over time including wings of a bat, and large stag deer type horns. The loud, colorful and scary Dragon Dance with fireworks that is performed even today in Asia and Asian Communities is a throw-back to earlier times when the Dragon was thought to ward off evil spirits and bring good luck. The Bible refers to the Dragon this way: *"the viper and flying fiery serpent, they shall carry their riches"* (Isaiah 30:6 KJV); *"The Lord said to Moses, make thee a fiery serpent* (Nehushtan or Nehustan *– thing of brass), and set it upon a pole"* (Numbers 22:8 KJV); *"And the Lord laid hold of the Dragon, who is the Devil and Satan."* (Rev. 20:2 KJV).

European dragons were thought to be fire-spewing reptiles or lizards with forked tongues split like a snake's. They were accused of imprisoning maidens, destroying villages and hovering over mountains of gold.

The battle dragon of England, Scotland, Wales and Ireland was a serpent that awakened on February 1st and caused thunderstorms. A world of myths has been attributed to the dragon and caught the imagination of children and adults alike. The lyrics to ***Puff the Magic Dragon*** that Peter, Paul and Mary recorded and made famous come to mind – *"Puff the Magic Dragon lived by the sea and frolicked in the autumn mist in a land called Honah Lee."*

This theme of the central government's mandate from heaven – that it was *divine authority*, *national unity*, and *filial obedience* of the Chinese people to *do the right thing to preserve and promote the nation* – allowed emperors to control and maintain order and security without question to their legitimacy, fairness, or effectiveness.

The color yellow and the wearing of the Yellow Dragon Robe defined the Emperor's divine authority to rule, and was reserved for the celestial son of heaven and his household. These *royal* thread colors were strictly reserved for the emperor: Emperor – *yellow*, Empress, descendent from the Phoenix - *golden yellow*, Crown Prince and other wives - *apricot*.

Even today this mandate idea of being descendants of the Dragon prevails as seen in the naming and launch (October 2005) of the Chinese space craft Shenzhou, which means *heavenly vessel*. The ramifications of Chinese centralist idea can be seen in the past, and can be expected in the future, with China wanting to be treated today as in past trade relations like *tien-tse*, *the Son of Heaven* - auspiciousness and nobility, bravery, and an all-conquering force of the Tyrant when deemed necessary.

Another kingdom, the Kingdom of Koryo - Goryeo, founded by King T'aejo, Wang Kon in (918-1392 AD) was ascending and warring with the last of the Shilla family. Koryo prevailed and ruled in peace for 200 years over a consolidated people. This unity allowed the military to build up strong forces for the many defensive wars with raiders from the north and to subjugate all peoples south on the peninsula.

The government was enhanced with the institution of civil service, officials of merit, lifetime ownership of farm land, social reforms, and expansion of the number of schools and universities. The bright spot of the Koryo Dynasty was the discovery of how to make the famous Korean **celadon green pottery** (1022 AD), inlaid ceramics, earthen ware, art, and the metal printing press.

Korean culture was enhanced by higher education and moral thinking under the teachings of Buddhism, and especially Confucianism. The importation of Buddhism from

India and the embracing of Confucius' teachings were the country's phychological underpinning of national unity and solidarity. The Confucian moral system, cultural growth, new inventions, and discoveries brought the Korean civilization higher than any other in the world at the time. The compulsory teaching of Confucius, with his 300 rules of major rituals and 3,000 rules of minor observances, began in 551-479 BC. The teachings of public ethics, family values, private congruity, and order at any price began in 1912. The name Confucius was Latinized in the 16th century by the Jesuits. His real name was Kong Fuzi, Master Kong or Great Kongzi. The surname Kong was known as the, first family under Heaven. He was born in Ou Fu, *Ou Lu – pronounced Chu Foo*, China.

With the coming of Mao Tse Tung and Communism in 1949, Confucianism fell out of favor in China. His teachings condemned and the burning of *Spiritual Money* was banned. Under the acts of the Gang of Four (1966-1968), Confucius' teachings were criticized and said to be an unhealthy ideal. The Cultural Revolution began with the cry, *Down with Confucius' curiosity shop!* The Red Guard tied a truck to the statue of Confucius, pulled it down, and dragged his statue through the streets. All seventy-two sages were also pulled down and burned. Many tablets and records were destroyed. When I was in Nanjing in 2008, I observed this. Teachings of Confucius are on the way back. Both the Temple and Mansion have been declared a museum. The Temple has been repaired and restored, but isnot the majestic place it once was.

Numerous clashes by warring clans, warring states, warring factions, tribes and armies occurred up and down the Korean peninsula, into Manchuria, and deep into China, lasting until the 1800's. The most important two involved the nomadic Khitan tribe, who ranged from eastern Mongolia, ***Land of the Great Blue Sky***, and Manchuria to northern China. The Khitans conquered Parhae (old north

Kugoryo) in 926 AD and changed the name to Liao, which became the Liao Dynasty.

The other, the Jurchen (Jin) tribe, in 1115 AD captured what was former Parhae - (Liao) Dynasty, and continued the invasion of the Song Dynasties of China - North Song (960-1125) and South Song (1127 – 1279).

Jin forces pushed across the Yangtze River and captured the *Northern Song* including the capitol, Beijing. The Jurchen (Jin) Empire fell to the Mongols in 1215, but not before trade, ideas, and Chinese influence had reached Manchuria, Mongolia and the northern territories. South Song fled before the Jurchen/Jin Dynasty and remained unconquered until the coming of Kublai Khan.

In 1238 the peninsula was once more to experience an invasion and turmoil. This time invasion by a fierce people from the remote interior of Mongolia and Manchuria, under the leadership of Kublai Khan - the grandson of Timujin-Genghis Khan, Jenghis-Khan - ***Greatest Ruler, Emperor of All Men, or Universal Ruler***. He came in killing, looting, destroying temples and shrines. The Chinese had much resentment, even contempt, for these uncouth invaders.

Koryo fought against the barbaric hordes of the north until the Mongol weakened from internal struggles and made peace. The Asian nation of Koryo was the only one to resist the Mongols and maintain the nation's sovereignty as a vassal.

Genghis Khan had entered China in 1229, 1241 and 1279, founded the Yuan Dynasty, took the title Yuan Emperor of China, succeeded in subduing all of China, and made the seat of Mongol power Peiking - Beijing – **Cambaluc**. The *City of the Khan* was named by Marco Polo – Dadu by Mongols, and Yanshi by Korea. His Mongol Empire stretched from Eastern Europe, to the Middle East, to Russia, China, large parts of Southeast Asia, and into Korea.

The Mongols or Monguls had come into China bringing their own language, dress, values, food, cuisine, way of cooking, and beliefs of life. They were always the foreigner. The Chinese viewed the Mongol as inferior and themselves as superior. The Chinese also despised the Mongol for his crude ways, and that he would not respect or adopt Chinese thinking, customs, or language, nor assimilate into the Chinese culture.

The Yuan/Tang Dynasty, Mongolian Dynasty (1279-1368) had won concessions from the Song Dynasty of China and continued to consolidate its power with the belief that it had its beginning with the origin of the universe.

Korea once again was forced to use its countrymen (35,000), as well as timber and materials for the benefit of a larger power. Nine hundred (900) ships were constructed to carry out Kublai Khan's expansion policy to conquer Japan. His ships and soldiers were lost, not to the Japanese, but to strong storms and typhoons. Japan determined these were *divine winds* – kamikaze, and had saved their country. The idea arose after this *miracl*e that the country was invincible – divinely protected. These two costly Yuan disasters drained the treasury of Korea. Eventually with excessive taxation, crop failures and other excessive abuses, the Mongol people rebelled, until the dynasty was weakened and lost power.

This was near the adventurous time of Marco Polo (1260-1269 and 1271-1295), the Venetian merchant who was the guest of Kublai Khan in Beijing. His stories and book paved the way for establishing Xian, the beginning of the Silk Road, and trade with Arab countries and Europe. Stories from the Orient inspired Coleridge to write the poem "Kubla Khan" with the setting of Zanadu**,** being Kublai Khan's Mongolian capitol and summer home. Samuel Taylor Coleridge's poem is said to be considered the most beautiful poem in the English language.

Lee Song-gye (Yi Song-gye) founded the Joseon, Chosun Dynasty (1392-1910) and called itself Dae Joseon Guk, Great Joseon Nation or Great Han People-Nation, which is similar to Great Korean Empire. The Chosun or

Joseon was a great Dynasty because of advanced social conditions, art, technology, and the arrival of the Hangul Language.

The western world saw it could trade directly with China and the Far East, bypass the Arabs and make large profits. But first ports in Japan, China and Korea had to be opened. Spain was the first to come to the Orient in 1614, and again in 1626, with the Dutch arriving in 1624. American Admiral William Perry led the Great White Fleet to the Far East and pressured Japan into signing a Goodwill Treaty in 1854.

A competitive rush began to the Far East by Russia, Italy, Britain, Germany, France and the United States, with imperialist and colonial ideas. Once the ports were open there would be markets for the West's manufactured goods and products and access to much needed raw materials – iron and timber from Manchuria, silk and tea from China, as well as porcelain from Korea and China. The gold leaf/designed *tea paper* used to line the decorative metal tea containers was much prized by rich Europeans to wallpaper special rooms and areas in their homes. Europeans could not get enough of the exotic, opulent, hand painted porcelains, colorful silks, finely gold-embroidered fabrics, delicate china, anything Oriental, as depicted in opulent fashions in Gilbert and Sullivan's *Three Little Maids*, from the Mikado. Even the Pekingese lap dog – *the sacred lion dog* – became a status symbol. Merchants were dumbfounded by China and Korea's adamant stand to remain closed to trade when so much money was to be made.

Little did I know then that the Korean War I was fighting had its beginning with many earlier wars in Europe that began with the Koguryo - Koryo Dynasty (918-1392 AD), the **Seven Year War - IM JIN WAR** (1592-1598), **Opium Wars** (1840-1842), the **Bong-in yang-yo Incident – French War Ship Invasion** (1866), the **Shibnmiyango** – the **Western Disturbance of the Year Sinmi 1871, Week-end**

War in Korea, Marine Redoubt, The Korean Expedition of 1871, the **First Sino-Japanese War** (1894-1895), **Eulmi Incident and Ulsa Treaty** (1895-1910) and (1931-1937), **Donghak Struggle of 1894 - Gabo Donghak Revolution** (1894-1895), **Boxer Rebellion** (1900), **March 1st Movement** (1919), **Russo-Japanese War** (1904-1905), the **Mukden Incident** and **Second Sino-Japanese War** (1931-1937).

Japan, *the Land of the Rising Sun*, had organized marauders and pirates - *Wo-ku, Waco or Wu-co* - to attack, pillage and harass the villages along the southern coasts of Korea and China -Yellow Sea, and Taiwan, as early as 918 AD. The raids were often repulsed, preventing the Japanese from getting a toe-hold for expansion. These raids continued on and off for many years until 1592 AD, and the beginning of the **Seven Year War (IM JIN WAR),** when a wanton and unprovoked invasion by Toyotomi (Hashiba) Hideyoshi sent his forces into Korea.

He was teased and called *monkey-face*, or referred to as *Saru Kuanja* – the monkey servant, because of his head shape and appearance. His facial features belied his adroitness, intellect, political maneuvering, and acts of surprise. By 1592 AD he had brought the War Lords, *aimyo,* under his power and he was the *King of Japan*, but never Shogun-General because he was not of Minamota birth.

By alliances, bribes, diplomacy and forceful attack, he had now conquered all of Japan. He was in total control of the nation and needed something for his large army and housed samurai to do. The dream and ambition of this polydactyl, two-thumbed megalomaniac's dream was to conquer China. The route to China was through Korea.

He began to build a huge fleet of Kamikaze warships – divine *god-made wind* – and troop transports to carry the thousands of soldiers to quickly defeat China. The blitzkrieg in 1592 of 200,000 soldiers and 2,000 samurai warriors quickly overran Korean defenses, leaving behind the maimed, death, and devastation. China rushed a horde of troops to the border, while Korean guerillas harassed the Japanese army and supply lines.

The Japanese withdrew but not before they burned Seoul to the ground, destroyed ancient temples and landmarks, pillaged and foraged, devastated farms, burned towns and villages, disbursed population, plundered, and kidnapped skilled workers to take to Japan to help develop their craft. But worst of all, Korean heads, on Hideyoshi's orders, were decapitated for collection. Later, noses of men, women and children were pickled and sent to Japan. A recorded 38,000 ears were also taken. The mountain of pickled ears was shipped back to Hideyoshi at the port of Osaka, and buried in Kyoto in the **Mimizuka Shrine** or ***Mounds of Ears***. The horrid collection of noses that were substituted for heads at Chinju and Namwon, during the second invasion (1597-1598), is interred in a burial mound near **Hideyoshi's Great Buddha.** Only recently has the Korean government asked Japan to destroy this abusive monument and level the site, but to no avail.

This cruel, insane, senseless slaughter, merciless maiming and treatment by the samurai are recorded in the diary of a **Keinen** – Buddhist Monk, who was an eyewitness. The Monk's diary was held by Japan and unpublished until 1965. I suppose the cruel mindset and loathing of the Korean population was a carry over from the battles of **Buinroku (1592) and Keicho (1596),** when Toyotomi Kideyoshi sent his forces across the East Sea (Sea of Japan) to annex Korea.

Hideyoshi became ill and his illness made him greatly concerned about who would succeed him. His first son had died at an early age. He now favored his younger son for the throne. He exiled his nephew, who was next in line for the throne, with instructions to commit *seppuku,* ritual suicide. To assure his younger son's succession, he is reported to have had killed three children, and decapitated all ladies of rank, who might have any connection to the throne. They are buried in the **Tomb of Traitors.** The number dead is said to be thirty-one.

We know now that he was obsessed and unstable. He died of his illness in 1589, losing to China and Korea, because of the great feats of Korean Admiral Lee (Yi) Soon-shin's (Sun-shin) Turtle Ships in sinking one-half of his remaining fleet, not assessing China's overwhelming strength, and repeating the mistakes of the first invasion. For 300 years after Japan suffered its decisive land and sea defeats at the hand of Chinese and Korean forces, the peninsula enjoyed relative peace. Modern-day Korea would do well to heed the lessons learned from their great Admiral Yi by building a large, advanced naval force both above and below water to protect their peninsula from the Japanese and all possible expansionist encroachments.

To the Japanese, Hideyoshi (1582-1598) was and continues to be a great, brave hero - the strong unifier of the Japan's warring factions. He does need to be commended for abolishing all slavery. Slavery and forced labor were reinstated during the Japanese **Colonial Period (1910-1945),** especially during WWII. As mentioned, Korea's skilled celadon pottery artisans and their formulas had already been taken to Japan.

The Manchu of Manchuria (1627-1644) toppled the mighty Ming Dynasty, took over China and founded the Qing Dynasty, the Empire of Great Qing. The Chinese considered the Manchus primitive aliens, inferior, abhorrent and repugnant.

The Chinese would not become Manchu and the Manchu did not want to be Chinese. This rejection by the Chinese was met with a law of submission. The law was that every Chinese male was to shave the front of the head and grow the *queue*, ***bianzi*** – braided pig tail. This order antagonized the people even more. Korea fared a little better under the Manchus in that it only had to pay tribute as a vassal. Korea had paid tribute to Genghis Khan until his son Ogedei's death in 1241.

Early in the 6th century there arose a group of *pig-tailed robbers* called Suo Lu, with Lu meaning enemies or savages. The pigtale was the Manchu's utter form of humiliation and subjugation of the reticent Chinese. Also the Chinese dress became the *Tang Zhuang* clothing of the Manchu, required to be worn by every Chinese. Chinese fashion today, regarded as traditional Chinese dress, is actually of Manchu style and design. Previous dynasties had lost power and the will to fight the Manchu and invaders because of civic unrest, excessive abuse, over taxation, loss of revenue, and corruption, as did the Manchu later on.

Korea's case was different because its people were always willing to fight but they did not have modern weapons and a trained army. The blame for this is laid on the many destructive invasions that weakened the country, the Japanese incursions, and the Korean **Yang Ban (Yangban)** upper class, who were overly concerned with Confucian rituals, who quarreled over etiquette, and through corruption and over-taxation prepared the country for Japanese annexation.

Trade and the promotion of trade under Manchu rule had been unprecedented. Western ideas and Christianity had crept in thru China and Korea in the seventeenth century with the beginning of the industrial revolution, but the door was once more closing.

China was on the verge of greatness but she refused western ways and thinking and any new technology, and was unwilling to build a strong, well-equipped army. Instead she closed her borders to trade, and to anything the *uncivilized* West had to offer. China believed the country was so vast and its people so numerous that Western ships and troops could not reach China's interior - they would be swallowed up. The smugness can be seen in the reply to Great Britain upon its request to open a Chinese port. The Emperor's reply was that King George was welcome to pay *homage* to the Chinese Court. This infuriated the British and fortified their will to gain access to China trade.

The Opium War of 1838-1842 ensued with China burning British opium, and the British killing one man and destroying a temple at Kowloon. Great Britain declared War on China after the Empress Dowager Cixi had removed the British, and is said to have declared war on all eight nations trying to access Chinese ports. **The Treaty of Nanking** gave Great Britain both Hong Kong and Kowloon, unlimited access to ports, and the right to send British war ships up rivers.

Maritime trade by the end of the eighteenth century had developed colonies in India and Indonesia, opened ports in Japan, Korea and China, and saw Russia annex part of Manchuria. Competition was the driving force of European nations to gain most-favored nation status, monopolize trade, and access raw materials.

Overland and maritime trade brought Europe in contact with the East, exposed Asia to new technologies, new ideas and ways of thinking, including engineering, scientific developments, new food crops, herbal medicines, modern weapons, and western methods of warfare. The push for ports of trade and border expansion through mercantilism, mineralization, commercialism and colonization had a revolutionary effect on the Western world.

The **Second Opium War** in Canton (1856) – ***Arrow Incident*** – opened additional ports in Taiwan and the Pescadores, Islands – Tamsui, Keeling, Amping, Takao and Kaohsiung. The Portuguese were in Macao and the British had a ninety-nine year lease on Hong Kong and Kowloon.

The Empress Dowager, Cixi – Empress Xialqin Xian, T'su Hsi (1861-1908), the major concubine of Emperor Xian Feng, became the de facto ruler of China in 1861. She continued the closed-port, anti-Western policy, and witnessed the Sino-Japanese War (1894-1895) with Japan.

Korea, at the time, was caught between the reformists who wanted to align with Japan, modernize and open ports and the Confucian conservatives who favored the closed door policy and aligned with China for protection. As a result, Korea had neither generals, a strong army, modern weapons, nor navy with which to defend itself.

The Sino-Japanese War between Qing China and Japan (1894-1895 **Korea's Qing-Japan War**, **China's War of Jiawu**) began with the Chinese Emperor's request for troops (approximately 1,500) to suppress a Korean rebellion – Donghak Peasant Revolt.

Japan sent a force approximately three times larger – 4,000 soldiers and 500 marines to support the Korean reformists. The Japanese had entered Korea on the false pretense of quelling the ***Korean Problem*****, then** fabricated incidents to confront China and to declare war.

The war began at Pyongyang with Korea and China quickly losing to a formidable and well-equipped modern Japanese army. This victory over China led to the decision to send the Japanese First Army to invade the northeastern part of Manchuria. This brought Japan in conflict with Russia, who perceived Manchuria their sphere of influence, off limits to invasion, and a safe buffer between China and Japan.

The **Treaty of Shimonoseki** April 17, 1895, gave Japan virtual control in perpetuity over Korea in less than a month and led to the annexation of all Korea in 1910. China under the Manchus (Qing Dynasty) feared additional Japanese expansion and declared the island of Taiwan a Province of China.

Korea had to pay 200,000 Kuping (Gubing) Taels to China for losses incurred during the Sino-Japanese War. China was weak, having trouble with the French in Vietnam (1894), and was willing to give concessions and eager to settle with Japan. But to no avail. Japan's aggressive policy and might caused China to cede sovereignty over Taiwan and to recognize Japan's complete authority and independence in Korea as a Japanese province.

Japanese expansion:

1875 Ganghwa Do Island Incident - Korean-"Unyo-ho Sageon" or "Unyo" Incident.

1894-5 Japan defeats China over Korea – First Sino-Japanese War

1904-5 Japan defeats Russia over Manchuria – RUSSO-JAPANESE WAR

1905 Japanese navy defeats and sinks Russian navy at the Battle of Tsushima

1905 - 1910 Japan claims Korea with armed legation guards and later soldiers.

1920's - Japan expanded control to the islands in the Pacific including Formosa (Taiwan) to build an Empire and further the expansion of the later idea of the East Asia Company, Prosperity Sphere, and Sphere of Influence. Islands lost by Germany after WWI were left to Japanese expansion, including islands both north and south of the Equator in the Marianas and the Caroline Islands.

The Cairo Declaration 1943 and the Potsdam Conference in 1945 returned Taiwan (Formosa) to China. Generalissimo Chiang Kai-shek fled mainland China with his forces, took control of the Island in 1948, and later established the Republic of China (ROC) with Taipei, Taiwan, being the capitol.

The Empress Cixi (T"su Hsi) tried her best to keep China together against Japan, Britain, Russia, Italy,

Germany, France, Portugal, Austria, and European countries who entered the Far East for a sphere of influence and exclusive trade rights. She had to flee Beijing and returned later to give concession after concession by forced treaty. She died in 1908, but not before China realized she needed a strong central government to maintain her sovereignty.

The Boxer Rebellion in 1900, named after the *Righteous and Harmonious Fist* or *Plum Blossom Fist,* a secret society that practiced martial arts, advocated the overthrow of the Ch'iang imperial government and the expulsion of the *foreign devils.* A group estimated to be 20,000 surrounded the compound of foreigners located outside the Forbidden City walls. By the time US Sailors and Marines and international forces arrived at Beijing, *250 foreigners had been killed.*

The Boxer Protocol (1901) allowed foreign military to be stationed in the Chinese capital; the prosecution of officials who participated and aided and abetted the Boxers, and indemnity for losses to be paid to European countries. These countries wanted to divide up China like a piece of pie, carving up China for their own purposes, yet they saw the necessity to keep China intact.

John Hay, US Secretary of State, proposed all nations adopt an "Open Door" policy in China. All the nations agreed in principle to an open China. John Hay took that as definitive, and an intact China was made policy. It could be said China owes the United States a word of gratitude for intervening on its behalf, and preserving and protecting China from imperialism and colonization.

The Donghak Revolution 1894, or Peasant War of poor *white-clad* folk, was against the rich, oppressive landlords and over-taxation. It was an Eastern learning religious movement that combined with the Donghak – Gabo Donghak Revolution in a peasant protest against the Yangban ruling class, the corrupt Joseon (Chosen) government, a resistance to foreign governments, and resentment of Japanese occupation.

The Tanghak or Donghak religious movement's name was changed to Ch'ondogo (yo) or Cheondoyo, *Heavenly Way or Master of Heaven.* It was a nationalistic movement consisting of Confucian, Buddhist, Shamanistic, Daoist and Catholic. By 1880 Korea was awakening to Methodist and Presbyterian missionaries and other Protestant religions coming to its shores.

The Donghak Struggle and the Gabo Donghak Revolution (1894-1895) for independence, nationalism, autonomy, and elimination of class distinction, brought Korea into fierce conflict with Europeans, first with a Prussian ship Ernest J. Pert in 1866, and then came the USS General Sherman in 1871. Seven French ships in 1866 under the command of Admiral Pierre G. Roze were sent to retaliate for the execution of three French Jesuit Priests, and the massacre of approximately 10,000 Catholics for secretly proselytizing and meddling in government. The French had come for retribution and concession but were repulsed and withdrew, but not before doing considerable damage to forts and structures with a ship's cannon. The **Byong-in yang-yo Incident** at Ganghwa **(French Warship Invasion 1866),** led by Korean General Yan, Heon-su at night left one Korean soldier dead with sixty French killed.

The Seagate Stone placed at the approach to Joseon Territory (1392-1910) (Ganghwa, Island) gives this warning even today. The weathered stone overlooking the best approach to the island reads in paraphrased Chinese characters*: Foreigners, Foreign Ships strictly forbidden, do not pass.* The Hungul-Korean language, promulgated by King Sejong the Great in 1450 eventually replaced Chinese and has become today's national language.

In 1865 the US Navy gunship, Princess Royal, renamed the SS General Sherman, was owned by the British trading firm, Meadows and Co. With the ship's owner, W.

B. Preston on aboard, the General Sherman sailed for Korea in 1866 to open ports of trade and obtain concessions. Grounded and stranded near Pyongyang in the Tae Dong River, the ship was set afire with the ship's owner and crew massacred. Disrespect and unfriendly acts ashore as well as the injury or death to one Korean by the ship's officers and crew is said to be the reason and cause for the Korean attack. This action was named the **Ganghwa Incident 1866.**

Six months later in 1867, the USS Wachusett, a sloop of war and under the command of Captain Robert W. Schufeldt was sent to the aid of the stricken vessel and to investigate after she failed to return. Foul weather and fog turned the Wachusett back. The USS Shenandoah, under Captain John C. Febiger, later received an official Korean letter stating they all were dead. It is ironic that the USS Pueblo AGER-2 was moored in the same spot where the General Sherman was destroyed in the 19th century. In 1999 the Pueblo was moved to Nampo, a North Korean seaport 50 kilometers Southwest of Pyongyang, in the Taedong River, near the Ssuk Inlet. I understand the ship is a tourist attraction with approximately one-thousand visitors a day. North Korea holds an annual propaganda celebration on the date of the General Sherman's demise. The United States wants the vessel returned and North Korea has recently indicated a willingness to return the one hundred and seventeen foot long former AKL-44 Auxiliary Cargo Light, Army FP-344 Light Cargo Ship Army, currently the AGER-2 USS Pueblo. The Pueblo was commanded by Captain Lloyd Bucher, with a crew of eighty-two and captured on January 23, 1968, eleven miles north of Woman Harbor. One crew member was killed, the others imprisoned and tortured until released months later. The USS Tawakoni ATF-114 had plied these same coastal waters only sixteen years before the Pueblo capture.

In 1871 the United States government sent the USS Colorado (BB-45) under John Rodger and four other war ships into the Kwanghwa (Ganghwa) Strait to prevent brutal abuse and assure safe treatment for shipwrecked American bluejackets, and get an Amity Treaty with Corea, also for free trade and to see more about the General Sherman.

The Coreans (Koreans) were informed the US ships were only going to take soundings near their coast lines and adjacent islands. The lack of a Korean reply after four days was taken to mean the mappings and depth findings along their coasts were agreeable. One American ship nearing Ganghwa Do Island and Kwangseong Fortress was fired upon by a fortress cannon and forced to withdraw, but sustained no damage or causalities. A naval bombardment and significant conflict began with the assault landing of some 651-680 US Sailors and Marines attacking Kwanghwa Fortress, named **Fort McKee-the Citadel,** on Kwanghwa, Island near the mouth of the Han River. Several fortresses were destroyed with 3 Americans killed and 13 wounded. Korean known casualties numbered 243 killed, including General Eo Jae-yeon, Uh, Je-yeon, and twenty wounded at the battle of Gwangseongdo. The twenty wounded Koreans were captured and taken aboard the American ship for treatment with the idea of negotiating, but to no avail. The Koreans would not negotiate nor did they want back the twenty wounded. General Eo and his brave soldiers are recognized as heroes today even though they lost the battle of **Shinmiyango** – literarily the **Western Disturbance of the Year Sin Mi,** because Korean forces had thwarted the efforts of mighty United States and European nations to open any of their ports. A tomb of martyrdom has been built for General Eo Jae-yeon and the 350 nameless heroes of these battles.

Several names but no certain name has been given to our misunderstood, unintentional, yet retaliatory attack on Korea's Kwanghwa Do, Island. The Weekend War in Korea came to be known as the *Marine Redoubt* or the larger term – *The Korean Expedition of 1871*. Today better names for the incursion might be the *First Inchon Invasion, The Other*

Korean War, or The Korean War of 1871. Whatever name is given, it is a sad story that citizens of both countries had to die, and especially General Eo and Lieutenant Hugh McKee who was the first Bluejacket to die from spear wounds. He had a premonition of being killed just like his father, Colonel McKee, who was the first to die at Buena Vista in the war with Mexico. McKee was heard to say before the Kwanghwa landing, "There never was a McKee that went into battle that was not killed." Five years later all of Korea became a protectorate of Japan because Korea did not have a strong Navy or an Admiral Yi.

Good did come out of the Korean Expedition of 1871 with the signing of the **Korean-American Treaty of Amity and Commerce** of October 1880, and the **Treaty of Mutual Friendship** - ***The Jemulpo Treaty of 1882 and Defense Against Attack.*** Some of the provisions included: Koreans' ability to emigrate to the United States, *Most-Favored Nation* status, extra-territorial rights for American Citizens in Korea, and non-interference with Christian missionaries, including proselytizing. The treaty was in effect until 1910 when Japan annexed Korea.

The French began to occupy Indo China in 1857 and finished the conquest of Vietnam in 1883. Control was lost to the Japanese in 1940. The Potsdam Conference (1945) returned Vietnam, Laos and Cambodia to the French. Vietnamese leader, Ho Chi Minh, who had formed the Communist party in 1930, had returned to Vietnam and established the Viet Minh Guerrilla Army (Vietnamese Independent League). By 1950 fighting had broken out between French forces and the Viet Minh with the US assisting and supplying the French with three billion dollars in aid that included 80% of all supplies needed by the French. China had fallen to Communism in 1949 and was now aiding the Viet Minh, later the Viet Cong. The French were defeated at Dien Bien Phu in 1950 and withdrew all her forces under the Geneva Accord.

American involvement continued to increase until the Tonkin Gulf incident with the US Navy ship Maddox, causing Congress to pass the **Gulf of Tonkin Resolution**. The resolution was a Presidential Mandate to send troops to Southeast Asia (Indo China) to stop the spread of Communism. President Truman was determined to stop Communism on the Korea Peninsula and in the Far East in 1950. The Korean War was an inevitable consequence of the peninsula's warring pasts, and the aftermath of struggle between WWII Democratic and Communist nations.

The Great War - the war to end all wars – WWI – ended with Japan an ally to the West. In WWII Japan had sided with the Axis powers of Germany and Italy. The result of WWII left the United States the greatest power on earth at the time, and the Russian bear was next in power under Communist dictator, Joseph Stalin. Korea after WWII was to become a buffer between Communist USSR and the free world.

Early Korean history and the Korean War (1950-53) have profoundly shaped Korean history and literature, as well as documenting Korea's effort at self-determination and freedom. The Korea of tomorrow is admonished to learn from the past, to remain strong and vigilant, and keep its freedom with these two quotes:

"It shows you that if you don't want your nation to be kicked around, you've got to be strong. All the Korean Government did for its people was to demand all the grain they had and force them to work." - Kichung Kim, Professor of English and American Studies at San Jose State University.

"If the soldiers are committed to fight to the death, they will live, whereas if they seek to stay alive, they will die." – Admiral Yi Sun-sin, as quoted from Sun Tzu's, *Art of War.*

After the French and American ships left Korean ports and islands, the Japanese came next to Ganghwah Do with a strong enough force of ships and soldiers to take the island. Within five years of the forced Treaty of Kwangwha, Japan took over foreign and military affairs of Korea through the **Eulmi Incident of November 18, 1905,** and the forced **Protector (Eulsa) Treaty of 1905.** China and Japan have been a thorn in Korea's side for many centuries. China depleted Korea's wealth by what is known in China as ***"jimi"*** (cefeng), a yearly tribute in crops and money paid to the Emperor of China through duress and coercion. The **Jimi Fuzhou** was a Confucian philosophy system that was supposed to show a sign of respect, submission or allegiance to the *older* brother nation from the *younger/lesser* nation. China has always been the *first born,* allowing trade, giving gifts, requiring a *tithe,* and demanding respect from Korea, Japan, Manchuria, Southeast Asia, and even expecting tribute from European nations. It may be that the English slang word "*gimme"* as used in golf or as spoken *"it's a gimme"* – (give me), came from the Chinese word *"jimi."*

For thirty years Korea dealt with the Mongol Khan invasion and only paid tribute as Suzerainty. Korea is a country that has lost territory to China and Russia but never been totally conquered or divided. Japan may have annexed the country, and the United Nations may have divided the country at the 38th parallel, but in the hearts of her people North and South Korea are still one.

The Korean Queen Min (1851-1895) concurred and was adamant to keep the ports closed because her advisors said dealing with the West would contaminate the people. Confucian prestige, cliques in court, social unrest, crop failure, bad harvest, a small army and an antiquated navy were internal reasons for the Japanese to take the country over. Queen Myeong-seong earlier had believed that contact with the West was dangerous, and capitalism was immoral and hurtful to Korean society, and continued the boycott of European goods. She was later to pay a great price for her open port nationalistic policy. That for a time stymied

Japanese expansion. Confucian belief as quoted by Ogyu Sorai was about to come to an end. "Morality is nothing but necessary means for controlling the subjects of the empire."

A reform movement began in 1876 -1880. A precursor to the Donghak Revolution, was brought about by a booklet titled, ***Joseon Chaengnyak*** – Korean strategy to grow strong by acceptance of European institutions and technology. But it came too late.

Queen Min bravely resisted Japanese takeover of government, oppression, and loss of freedoms. She was assassinated early in the morning at age of forty-four (1895) by a Japanese intrusion into Gyeongbok Palace - but not before the assassins had killed three women they thought might be the Queen, and the Queen's royal guards.

The Queen was raped and her body burned with kerosene. Other accounts say she was dismembered and burned in a pine forest, raped then burned alive, or raped after she was dead then burned. Recent documents and eyewitness accounts reveal she was dragged from Kyungbok Palace, hacked to death with swords, and her body burned.

The attack was ordered by Japanese Minister to Korea, **Miura Goro** who was a retired Japanese Army Lieutenant-General. He and the assassins fled back to Japan from the Korean port of Inchon under Japanese protection. International opinion caused Mirua Goro and the assassins to be tried, but all would later be acquitted due to lack of evidence. Mirua Gora was later honored to serve in high positions in the Japanese government. Queen Min is the last Empress, the end of the Joseon Dynasty, and the only Empress to be enshrined with former Queens in the sacred **Jongmyo Shrine** in Seoul.

Japan continued to establish control over Korea by quartering Japanese troops in the capitol, asking for 500,000 Won for uprising and occupation costs, and forcing Korea into unfair unilateral treaties. Korea, weakened by years of war, was forced to give unconditional concessions and its impoverished people were deprived of their livelihood. She had no recourse other than to open her ports to the Japanese and Europeans.

The March First Independence Movement (1919), a non-violent movement in Pagoda Park at Seoul is known by every Korean as the **Samil-jul or Sam-il Movement,** (other references **- 3.1 Movement or Three One Movement).** The idea prevailed that Korean oppression would soon be lifted and the people would have freedom and independence. This idea was bolstered by the several peace conferences – **Hague Peace Conference 1907, Paris Peace Conference and treaties of 1919**, and later the **National Conference in Geneva 1922.**

Basically these conferences mandated international military disputes be settled by special treaties, peace conferences, and resolutions. The League of Nations was to adhere to the fourteen points of the **Paris Peace Conference,** four of which were: Freedom of the seas, Respect for post war boundaries, Disarmament of Germany, and the Creation of an international association for the settlement of international disputes.

The Korean Declaration of Independence was drafted by Historian/Writer Che Nam-seon and Poet/Buddhist Monk Manhae (also known as Han Yong-un), and was signed by 33 Nationalists at 2 pm, 1 March 1919. A copy was sent to the Japanese Governor General with their compliments:

> ***We herewith proclaim the independence of Korea and the liberty of the Korean people. We tell it to the world in witness of the equality of all nations and we pass it on to our posterity as their inherent right.***
>
> ***We make this proclamation, having back of us 5,000 years of history and 20,000,000 of a united***

loyal people. We take this step to insure our children for all time to come, personal liberty in accordance with the awakening consciousness of this new era.

This is the clear leading of God, the moving principle of the present age, the whole human race's just claim. It is something that cannot be stamped out, or stifled, or gagged, or suppressed by any means.

Materialistic Japan totally disregarded the new League of Nations by crushing the March First Movement. **History of the Korean Independence** by Park Eunsil gives these figures of Japanese suppression - 7,509 killed, 15,849 wounded and 46,303 arrested. Instead, at the Paris Peace Conference, Japan, being an ally during WWI, got German holdings in the Shantung Peninsula and several Pacific Islands.

The Russo-Japanese War (1904 -1905) began between rivalries of imperialistic ambitious Japan and *bear* Russia's determination to control Korea and Manchuria, Port Arthur, an extension of the Qing Railroad from Harbin, China into Manchuria, and the warm water ports needed for the Russian fleet, extending south from Vladivostok.

Japan gave Russia an ultimatum, a two-day notice that would have been ruled a *sneak attack,* and the breaking of international law, except the nations considered the ultimatum a warning. Japan's surprise attack on Pearl Harbor shows her preference for the *surprise – sneak attacks.*

Admiral Heihachiro Togo opened the war with a surprise torpedo attack against the Russian fleet at Port Arthur (aka Lushan – Lushunkou). The Japanese mine laying policy deployed tactile offensive harbor mines to restrict and curtail ship movement. Russia also deployed underwater offensive mines. Each country lost two large warships to these underwater mines. Later the United States, Japan, Russia and Korea would deploy both offensive and defensive mines – the United States mined Japanese ports in WWII.

Japan laid siege to the port, and with her modern, faster ships and her large caliber long range guns decimated the Russian fleet that was bottled up in harbor. With the victory at Port Arthur, Japanese ships confronted and defeated the remaining Russian fleet, and her soldiers attacked Manchuria. Even though Russia had a larger army, she acted to negotiate peace because of instability of the Russian Revolution of 1905. These two quick victories over China and Russia, the unopposed annexation of Korea in 1910, the occupation of Taiwan, and the mandated Pacific islands, gave rise to the remembrance of the divine wind ***Kamikaze*** defeat of Kublai Khan. Japanese imperialism and armed intervention began with the intrusion into China in 1937, and into Southeast Asia. Japan's confidence was bolstered by the realization that she, a non-Western power, had defeated Russia, a strong established European power, and now was one of the three most modern and powerful nations in the world – Japan, Germany and Italy.

Japan established the **Greater East Asia Company** and was readying to gain control over all of East Asia, first by attacking the Chinese in Manchuria on September 13, 1931, causing ***the Manchurian Incident, Mukden Incident or the Chinese 9.18 Incident.*** The Japanese Army had deliberately dynamited – *blown* – a section of Japan's South Manchurian Railway. The Chinese were blamed and a near-by garrison of Chinese soldiers was attacked to provoke a war. Japan's victories over Manchuria, Russia, China, and Korea provided for the slogan **Hakko ichiu,** ***Holy War 1930*** **(Seisen),** *eight corner under one roof or, the entire world under one roof.* Japan believed she was of divine origin, and had a mandate from heaven to establish a **Prosperity Sphere-a New Order in Asia –** and justly seize Manchurian resources for preparations of war.

The ***Shantung Incident*** **1928-1929** was another earlier provocation for war on the pretext of mass deaths of Japanese soldiers. The actual number killed had been thirteen. Japan sent in soldiers for *protection,* bombed the capitol of Tsinan, killing 18,000 Chinese citizens, and then withdrew from the League of Nations. The *third claw* nation was unstoppable and ready for expansionist rule over China and all of Asia and the Pacific Rim.

Korea's Provisional Government had been in Shanghai waiting to return to Korea and set up a free government. Provisional Governor and Director Syngman Rhee was waiting in the United States. The Provisional Government of Korea declared war on Japan and Germany in 1945. Syngman Rhee (Lee Seung-man), had graduated from The George Washington University and Harvard University with a PhD. He was installed as the first president of the Republic of Korea, May 10, 1948, and led throughout the Korean War (1950-'53), and presided as President during the years 1948 – 1960.

U.S. President Woodrow Wilson at the Paris Peace Conference in 1919 proclaimed an end of colonial rule and against Japanese totalitarian rule with his proclamation, **"A free, open-minded, and absolute impartial adjustment of all colonial claims, based upon a strict observance of principles that in determining all such questions of sovereignty have equal weight with the equitable claims of the government whose title is to be determined."**

The brutality and atrocities committed by Imperialist Japanese leaders and forces in Japan's sordid rise to power, and their merciless behavior during WWII, must be known and remembered along with Germany's extermination of the Jews.

Japanese police wasted little time in cruelly squashing Korean *freedom* marches they considered uprisings by brutal force. Racism was practiced all over Korea and even with Koreans living in Japan. Koreans were even blamed for the damage of the 1923 earthquake. Christians who were singing hymns were fired into and killed or wounded. Other Christians were tied to a cross for a slow death – *so they can go to Heaven.* Photo evidence shows several men being executed in this heathen manner.

Yu Kwan-soon, ***Jean d'arc,*** was a Christian and caused the Japanese much trouble by being open in her protest, opposition to foreign rule, and her strong desire for independence. She was arrested and unmercifully tortured for twenty months by alternately being frozen then thawed, and even worse, the unmentionable forcing and bloating the body with cold water. She died a martyr October 20, 1920.

Beheading, as we have seen earlier, was the choice method of Japanese punishment and killing. The worst atrocity occurred after a peace march by the village of **Jeam-ri** one month after the March First Movement. Leaders and participators in the Jeam-ri march were rounded up, place inside a church, and fired upon – massacred. The church was then set afire with some alive still inside. Those who were able to jump from windows or run out the doors were either sliced with swords or shot. Sixteen villages were burned, 326 houses and five churches destroyed with 1,600 left homeless, plus thousands of other crimes perpetrated against a courageous but helpless people. There was one Japanese policeman for every 722 Koreans at one time.

Land was bought (confiscated) from Korean farmers at only 17% of its value. 98,000 of these farmers and families had to be resettled. 70-75% of the farmers were in debt to the Japanese at 15-35% usury interest. 48-50% of rice production was going to Japan. Korean farmers were forced to raise sheep for wool, plant cotton, and fell trees that would all go to Japan. Rents were raised by 50-80%, until the farmers had no choice but to walk away from their farms and family.

Japanese government and wealthy merchants siphoned off raw materials, mineral wealth, fisheries and anything of value. The Royal Lands were confiscated and added to the tax rolls. The older Korean continues to harbor a hatred for the Japanese, and to a lesser degree by Korea's youth.

Korea suffered from reduction of capital, and 200,000 to 300,000 books were burned. Korean History was reinterpreted. Koreans were forced to adopt Japanese names and to speak only Japanese in elementary/intermediate schools and businesses. Schools and universities were reduced in number. Academic standards were lowered until only 1.8% of the population was educated. Koreans were to convert to **Shintoism** – native Japanese religion. Hundreds of churches, temples, shrines, schools and homes were destroyed. Between 1868 and WWI, Japan displaced 4 million Koreans and Chinese to Manchuria to work in coal mines and industry to maximize production for the mother country and help build up her army and navy.

Korean men and youth were drafted into the Japanese Army or taken to Japan as slave labor in defense factories during WWII. Girls, as young as 13-14, and women were conscripted as Comfort Women for 2,000 brothels beginning in the early 1930's, and more so after the rape of 20,000-80,000 women, sacking and killing of an estimated 200,000 Chinese – the **Nanjin Massacre of 1937-1938,** known as the brutal ***Rape of Nanking*** by Japanese soldiers. Evidence shows that many civilians were disemboweled, defaced by having their ears and nose cut off, and some without mercy crucified as was done in Korea. The Internal Military Tribunal of the Far East, (equivalent to the Nuremberg Trails) tried Emperor Hirohito, who had made all major military decisions, and his uncle Prince Asaka, who issued the order to *kill the (Chinese) Captives,* a main cause of the Rape of Nanking. Both were found guilty but never sentenced.

Eighty percent of those forced to be ***Comfort Women Serving in the War*****, Jugun-ianfu, ('ianfu' means Comfort**

Women) for the Japanese Imperial Army and Navy came from Korea, with the others coming from Taiwan, Burma, China, Philippines, and Dutch Indonesia. Japan had received bad press from the free nations after the Nanjing Massacre, and thought the Comfort Stations would reduce the number of reported rapes in areas of Japanese occupation and influence.

In 1992 Japan admitted to the planned practice of using 130,000 to 200,000 foreign as well as Japanese women as sex slaves, but did not, have not, will not, apologize for the forced rape and abuse of these many thousands of women. A token payment of $2,272 was made to each of a few women whose lives had been broken, tarnished, and in most cases left childless, unable to marry or bear children. The few women and girls who had not died from disease or infection were embarrassed and shunned upon returning to their cities or home towns. Many were left stranded after the war, never to return home.

Japan has tried to use this payment amount to persuade the world that it has fulfilled its obligations to all the Comfort Women. I believe the Japanese government is waiting for them all to die off, and then there will be no more problem. Today there are probably fewer than ninety still living to bring charges against their captors.

My brother-in-law, Harold Brawner, had served with a Navy Construction Battalion (CBs) at Guadalcanal during WWII. I found upon his death a Japanese soldier's translated *onion skin paper* diary that told of Comfort Women aboard his Army supply ships - the **Kodogama Maru and Ryoyo Maru or Ryiokoama Maru,** and ports where the crew had access to Comfort Stations: twice at Palao, at Rafael, New Britton – Port Moresby for both Army and Navy, Singapore, Malaya Peninsula aboard ship, and again on July 19th to August 6th, September 15th, and September 21st.

I was in Korea and turned the yellowed diary over to the Director of the **"Sharing House Museum"** (Women

Museum) in Seoul, Korea. (SharingHouse@gmail.com). **The Korean Council for the Women Drafted for Military Sexual Slavery by Japan** and other like organizations, the 121 Organization's (Blog Roll 121) drafted a resolution for Japan to apologize. (The organization has over 200 member organizations protecting women's rights and fair treatment.) Japanese women are rising to the cause of women's justice with Japan's new ***Women's Active Museum on War and Peace,*** in Tokyo. The museum contains a portrait gallery and hundreds of testimonials and records of Comfort Women. The Japanese had wanted the Korean girls and women ignorant, subservient and without an identity, actually considered no more than cargo when transported by ship.

They couldn't run Away;
They hardly had time
To put their clothes on.
If they were sick or tired
To say no, they were beaten.

By: Troy Germaine Taylor
– Pacific Rim Magazine

We will not die without a fight.
Japan created us through violence...and we want the whole world to learn about our plight...

Kang Duk Kyong,
survivor of Japanese military sexual slavery.

The atrocities and exploitation of land that began in 1905 increased and did not stop until the end of WWII. August 15, 1945, is celebrated in Korea as **Korean Liberation Day.** A pavilion of the Dead and a Memorial Tower to the 1 March Movement have been erected. Each year at 1400 hours (2 pm), Koreans gather at the memorial site for solemn prayer for those who sacrificed, suffered and died. A special thanks is given for their abundant freedom, remembering the horrible years of cruel oppression under Japanese occupation and rule.

The Treaty of Portsmouth (September 5, 1905) ending the **Sino-Russian War** was mediated by President Theodore (Teddy) Roosevelt. It left each participant with resentment. The Manchurian Incident was one cause of WWII. Another was the United States in 1941 placing an oil embargo that cut off the oil for Japan's war machine. The need for oil was the reason Japan decided to invade oil-rich Indonesia.

Japan had ended the Sino-Russian War because of financial troubles at home, and expected a monetary indemnity. She received none. Japan had won the war and expected control of all the Sakhalin Islands. She was given half of the islands. Manchuria was evacuated by both Japan and Russia. Japan left the conference table feeling cheated, treated like a defeated power, insulted, and disrespected. Russia was bitter because her expansionist policies in Asia had been stymied.

Japan was emerging as a pre-eminent power to be reckoned with. She needed oil and raw materials and trade. The West had isolated Japan and stopped trade mainly because of her anger, arrogance, and lust for power, bigotry, superior attitude and brutal conquest in Asia. Years of conquest and Japanese early history had taught Japanese leaders that her troops were the best and unstoppable and her people racially superior. The United States in 1941 placed an oil embargo and froze assets because Japan had reverted to its former isolationist policies and begun an imperialist scheme to seize oil in mineral rich Southeast Asia, French Indo China, and the Dutch East Indies.

Axis Japan aligned with Nazi Germany and Fascist Italy for world conquest. World War II and war in the Pacific was inevitable. **Pearl Harbor was a sneak attack at 0753**:**7seconds on December 7, 1941,** with the delayed Japanese diplomatic statement – ***It is important to reach an***

agreement. Admiral Yamamoto said, ***"I fear all we have done is to awaken a sleeping giant and fill him with a terrible resolve."*** Germany and Italy declared war on the United States three days later.

Eighteen United States warships were sunk or damaged that quite early Sunday morning: eight battleships, three light cruisers, three destroyers, two tugs, and two cargo vessels, with a loss of 2,896 military personnel. The island's hospital was also bombed. Japan had defeated the mighty Russian fleet and knew if she was to win the war with the United States she would have to sink the American fleet and seize the Hawaiian Islands, which she planned to do.

The sunken USS Arizona BB 39 battleship became, and continues to be, the resting place for 1,177 sailors. World War II was the continuation of WWI – the Great War, ***the war to end all wars***, and the precursor of the rise of Communism - the beginning of the ***Cold War*** with Russia – and the growth of Communism in China and North Korea. The start of the Korean War was only five years away.

August 15, 1945, the Allied Powers had unconditionally defeated the *tripartite* with their leaders dead: Hitler and his new wife, Eva Braun by suicide on April 22, 1945, Benito Mussolini (Il Duce) and Mistress Clara Petacci by gunshot. Mussolini was publically hung upside down and spat upon in April 1945, General Tojo would later be hung - November 8, 1948. And Emperor Hirohito, Showa-tenno – *His Majesty the Son of Heaven* – had lost his *glory* and *divinity*. The despots of WWII were either all dead or had *lost face*. Korea was now free of Japanese rule, but sadly divided at the 38th parallel.

The brutal, inhuman, and sadistic Bataan Death March saw 11,000 American prisoners-soldiers die or be killed, and another 16,000 died later in prison. The American people could not help but to fight and get revenge for such cruelty. The nation was united in an unstoppable flow of anger and patriotism. Japan was to find that the

American *mixed blooded-mixed race* were not cowards, nor *to be treated like dogs.* The clarion call of the older American can still be heard, ***"Remember Pearl Harbor."***

Hitler's view was Aryan supremacy of the Master Race. Japan's was divine purpose with Royal superior undefeatable troops of a homogenous people, and Fascist dictator Bonito (IL DUCE) Mussolini's was the restoration of the Roman Empire. All three nations were left in rubble, with economies shattered, untold numbers of their people killed or wounded or without food or shelter. What agony and waste! There are no good wars, but I believe the world should know there are *just* and *necessary* wars. Otherwise, the United States and the world would be speaking German or Japanese.

Joseph Stalin installed Kim Il Sung to form the totalitarian - dictatorial **Democratic People's Republic of Korea (DPRK)** on September 8-1948. Kim Il Sung would soon develop an economic and diplomatic policy of *self-reliance* to thwart Russian and Chinese domination and influence. North Korea was armed with Soviet weapons, and sought and received Stalin's permission three times to invade the South and unify Korea. The Soviet Union did not want any problem with the West and warned Kim Il Sung, a Major in the Soviet Army, he would have to go it alone with military advisors, mine technicians and limited air cover. North Korean troops crossed the 38th Parallel capturing Seoul in four days.

It is fair to say Syngman Rhee had wanted to invade the North and unify Korea. But the United States feared what he would do if he were given arms, planes and heavy equipment. The Soviets on the other hand had furnished tanks and heavy artillery to the North because Communism was on a world conquest. Russia had what she wanted in minerals, hydro-electric power, raw materials and warm water ports. If Kim Il Sung wanted to invade South Korea, it was fine with Stalin. In September 1949 Stalin's permission was asked and finally given. Later with North Korean forces losing, Kim Il Sung asked Chairman Mao Tse Tung of China to send troops.

The Korean War was actually a civil war because Korea had always been undivided. The West saw and feared the comparison of a divided Berlin to a divided Korea. If South Korea fell to Communism, then partitioned Berlin could fall to Communism. Communism had to be stopped everywhere and anywhere. The United States entered the war because it feared inaction in Korea would be construed as appeasement of Communist aggression. Seoul fell on June 27, 1950, and General MacArthur was made Commander in Chief (CinC) of Far East Command. The UN's Secretary – General Trygve Lie said the invasion *was* "war against the UN."

China under Mao Tse Tung (Mao Zedong) was afraid that the United States and United Nations forces would cross the Yalu River into Manchuria and destabilize Communist China, and the UN's action would be a threat to his government, power and legitimacy. Chairman Mao notified Stalin on October 2, 1950 of his intentions to fight the US and UN forces in Korea by saying: "We are going to dispatch Chinese troops to Korea under the name of Volunteer Force to fight the US imperialist and Syngman Rhee's forces, side by side with our comrades, the North Korean forces. The reason we are sending Chinese troops to Korea is that, if the US occupies the Korean Peninsula, the Korean Revolutionary forces would be completely removed, and it would result in a situation unfavorable to China."

General MacArthur strongly but unwisely pursued the sizeable retreating enemy with a token force of US, ROK and some UN troops. Should he have gathered together an overwhelming number of United States, United Nations and Republic of Korean forces, I believe Chairman Mao Tse Tung would have reconsidered entering the war. I believe China's breaking point was MacArthur's continuous strong rhetoric and threat of escalating the war. General MacArthur assured President Truman that China would not enter the war and any North Korean resistance would soon be quelled. China did enter the war, a war that reduced Korea to rubble with 80% of the country's industrial, public facilities and transportation infrastructure destroyed, and 75% of government buildings and 50% of all housing destroyed. One very important aspect of the war was that it began an accelerated arms race between the East and the West. It spurred Japan's post-war industrial recovery, and was a precursor to the United States' decision to remain in Japan, and keep 37,000 American troops in Korea. I do believe MacArthur's policy statements and his wanting to bomb, cross over the Yalu River, and move American troops into Manchuria influenced Mao Tse Tung to enter the war.

MacArthur's *stepping stone policy* in the Pacific, the taking of each and every island as he moved towards the Philippines to carry out his promise of "I shall return," caused the unnecessary sacrifice of many servicemen's lives in WWII. Many islands with stranded Japanese soldiers without supplies could have been bypassed. Perhaps MacArthur's ego would not let him. This is the sentiment I heard expressed by servicemen that fought in the Pacific and read in a commentary at the time of MacArthur's removal as General over forces in Korea.

For better or worse, good or bad, the sleeping dragons of Asia are awake and growing prosperously and militarily. General MacArthur I surmise is the Korean people's Korean War Liberation Hero, the one who brought freedom to South Korea. He is well spoken of, not a disparaging word I heard, and I saw that his Korean War Memorial statue is the largest and tallest. But should not the statue of President Harry S. Truman be larger, and in a place of more prominence? Aside from the early contributions of the late pompous *prima donna,* General MacArthur, who said earlier and later that China would not come into the war, I see President Truman and his Truman Doctrine the real hero – the liberator and sustainer of South Korea. It was Truman who said the Communists are not going to take all of Korea. He caused a convening of the United Nations Security Council to take an affirmative vote to aid the United States effort to thwart Kim Il Sung's ambition to make all of Korea a Communist state.

There was talk and the question of could we, should we use the atomic bomb to bring the war to a quick end? And what if it did not bring the war to an end? The bomb was a weapon designed for total destruction. How could it be used in a limited war? Korea was our country's first limited war. Russia at the time had the bomb but not the delivery capability.

President Truman insisted upon Voluntary Repatriation of Prisoners after the Korean War. Truman had become our President at the end of WWII and was aware of the Yalta Agreement between President Roosevelt, Churchill, and Stalin to *the involuntary forced repatriation of prisoners*, and their dreadful fates. This tragedy of repatriated prisoners after WWII resulted in suicides, executions by firing squads, hangings, torture and gulag Siberian imprisonment. The repatriation agreement was known as *Operation Keelhaul,* with the actual transfer of WWII prisoners, and known as *East Wind.* I suggest a plaque of gratitude by the Korean Government and its people is called for, remembering President Truman's brave and courageous stance against *involuntary forced repatriation.*

The adamant holdout of the Chinese Red Army and North Korean People's Army leaders for involuntary repatriation is thought to have prolonged the war for two years. In spite of disgruntled members of Congress and the public, former U.S. Army Captain President Harry S. Truman – Commander-in-Chief Truman – being the stubborn man from Missouri, a man of high principles and resolve, undoubtedly saved the lives of thousands of prisoners held by the United States and United Nations forces.

American Commander Clarence Hill (June), The American Legion Magazine, "We defeated the North Korean Military and held off a vastly larger Chinese Army."

China, North Korea and South Korea War Names, and South Korea Holidays and Memorial Days:

China: Hanguo Zhanzheung or Hanzhan – *The War to Resist American and Aid Korea*

South Korea: Hanguk Jeonjaeng – *6.25 War or the Korean War* or Yugio Sabyeon – *Korean Civil War – "Restoration of Light Day" Gwangbokjoel*

North Korea: Joguk Haebang Jeonjaeng – *Fatherland Liberation War Homeland* or *Motherland Liberation War* – Choguk Hae Bangui Nall "*Liberation of Fatherland*" – also *The Korean War*

United States: *A Police Action, The Korean Conflict, The Korean War – The Forgotten War, The Unknown War or Forgotten Victory.*

South Korea: Hyun Chong Il – *Memorial Day* Chogukhaebangui nal or Gwangbokjeol – *Liberation Day* (from Japan)

United Nations Day – October 24

UN Rememberance Day – UN Memorial Cemetery, Busan, Korea, November 11

Korean Armistice Day – *National Korean War Veterans Day July 27*

Gwangbokjeol – *Liberation Day* or *Liberation Day from Japan, August 15, 1945*

Japan WWII: Shuusen-Kinenbi – *the Day of Mourning of War Dead and Praying for Peace*, or *Memorial Day for the End of the War*

There is a strong cultural link between Baekje (Paekche) and Japan's upper classes. Early Japanese records show a Korean bloodline in Japanese Royalty by the words of an early Japanese Emperor – "I, on my part feel a certain kinship with Korea given the fact it is recorded in The Chronicles of Japan that the mother of Emperor Kamumu was of the line of King Muryeong of Paekche, and I believe it was fortunate to see such culture and skills transmitted from Korea to Japan."

Korean royalty was recognized in Japan until just before the Japanese Constitution, 1947. Princess Yi Pang Ja married Korea's Crown Prince Yi Un in 1920. She died in Seoul, Korea, in Chang Duk Palace – the Secret Garden Palace in 1989. Korea has long been Japan's benefactor, but no more. The four-clawed Korean Dragon has awakened and once again the **Tiger of Tan'gun,** the father of Kobuksun – the early Korean nation – prevails.

Chapter 15

Sea Power and Navy Humor

The Navy played a major role in bringing the Korean War to a final end, and prevented China from invading Taiwan (Formosa). Documents released from the archives of Moscow and Beijing clearly show that the Navy's rapid show of force of the aircraft carrier – Valley Forge CV-45, the cruiser Rochester CA-124, eight destroyers and three submarines of the 7th fleet kept Communist China from carrying out its plan to launch an amphibious force across the Taiwan Strait (Formosa Strait) to invade the island of Taiwan during the Korean War. The Nav Op T-45 (Navy Operation T-45) also laid siege at Wonsan, North Korea, the longest siege in history – 28 months, a total of 861 days. The Navy had complete control of the waters surrounding the Korean peninsula after October 1950 until the end of the war in 1953.

President Truman wanted the war to wind down, and the Soviet Union was encouraging North Korea to settle at Panmunjom. Joseph Stalin had died in March 1953. Chairman Mao Ze Dong, (Mao Tze' Tung) was ready because he was thwarted at every turn by sea power and air power with staggering losses of men and equipment that caused China a financial burden.

Chairman Mao was dealing with China's financial problems, with Russia pressing for payment for war materials, and his officers coming from the field with various but credible reasons for the war going so badly. Some of these reasons were: extreme cold weather, inadequate clothing, supply lines too long and not adequate, a lack of ammunition, old ammunition, old weapons, lack of heavy guns and tanks, lack of or no air cover except the MiGs flown by Russian and North Korean pilots. *MiG Alley* between Pyongyang and the Yalu River was to see the first battles between jet aircraft and the first use of helicopters in war.

Continuous bombing and strafing by Navy, Marine and Air Force planes, siege of ports, and the constant bombardment of coastal supply lines by auxiliary ships, destroyers and large Navy ships, was a major cause of ending the war. The bravery and sacrifice of UN Forces, US soldiers and US Marines at - ***Bloody Ridge, Chosin (Choson) Reservoir, Hamhung, Heart Break Ridge, Hwa Chan Reservoir, Iron Triangle, Punch Bowl, Old Baldy, Pusan Perimeter, Finger Ridge, Pork Chop Hill,*** **and the** ***Battle for the Hill,*** were the seesaw sacrificial battles for securing South Korea's freedom.

Korea was a place of death and destruction with nearly as many of our men lost in three years as were lost in Vietnam in ten years. One million seven hundred and eighty-nine thousand (1,789,000) of our men and women served in the Korean War. The numbers lost in the war vary between available sources, but the sources indicate the United States had in excess of 54,000 killed in action (KIA), more than 100,000 wounded and something between 6,600 and 8,800 missing in action (MIA). In addition there were between 7,100 and 7,250 prisoners of war (POWs), with over 2,800 dying in prison camps – all in three years. Fifty-four percent (54%) of the casualties occurred between June 1950, and mid-year 1951. Navy personnel that served in Korea numbered 265,000. 475 were killed; 4,043 died of disease or injury; and 1,576 were wounded.

In addition to the American casualties, North Korea saw 200,000 soldiers dead with 1,000,000 civilians killed. China had 145,000 soldiers dead with 260,000 wounded. The Soviet Union's known losses were 315 killed, some were fighter pilots. The numbers vary, but even using the most conservative estimates prove there was a Korean War, *a war not to be forgotten.*

"Nasty little war. Men asked to die for a tie." - Unknown

Each soldier and paratrooper, sailor, Marine, airman, UDT man, Navy Seal, member of special forces and MASH doctor and nurse fought the war in his or her own way with honor, courage, dignity, and with dogged determination and sacrifice on the testing ground between Communism and Democracy. The Veterans of the Korean War returned home without fanfare or acknowledgment. There was neither a complaint, whine nor whimper. ***They had fought in an unknown war that was not a war in a land unknown and came home unnoticed to a history that was forgotten.*** Men of my era served against Communism in Korea in direct response to the treatment accorded the veterans of WWII.

World War II had ended in 1945 and the Korean War began in the early morning, only five years later on June 25, 1950. I believe the main reason the Korean Veteran was overlooked and not appreciated was because the wars came so close together. People on the homefront did not want to be bothered after experiencing WWII. They were through with war and wanted peace; neither did most Americans know where Korea was nor much about the Far East. Today, the long and controversial Vietnam War and Desert Storm overshadow the Korean War. The wars in Iraq and

Afghanistan that our country is fighting now fade the memory of the American people even more. The average age of the Korean Veteran is eighty years, soon to be gone. The men who fought in Korea were the younger brothers and sisters of WWII veterans born in the same depressive 1920's and 1930's, a part of our nation's ***Greatest Generation,*** and deserve acknowledgement, remembrance and gratitude for their patriotic service. We must acknowledge and remember the Korean War, the first undeclared war, which has not ended – only a stalemate and cease fire at the 38th parallel. The Forgotten War remains a conflict in the minds of most Americans, maybe a substitute for WWII.

North Korea – Democratic Republic of Korea (DPRK) – referred to the Korean War as the **June 25 Incident or Fatherland Liberation War.** China – Peoples Republic of China (PRC) referenced the war as **The Resisting American War to Aid Korea or** the **War of Chosun.** Nearly 3,000,000 soldiers and civilians were killed on both sides and 700,000 were made homeless. United States and United Nations soldier, sailor, airman and Marine losses neared, and in some cases exceeded, the losses of the long war in Vietnam. The Korean War was a short war of three years but an extremely bloody war.

"The willingness with which our young people are likely to serve in any war, no matter how justified, shall be directly proportional as to how they perceive the veterans of earlier wars were treated and appreciated by their nation." – George Washington

Countries that participated directly in the war were: **The Netherlands, New Zealand, Canada, Australia, Great Britain, Ethiopia, Greece, Turkey, Columbia, the United States, the Republic of Korea, Luxembourg, the Philippines, Thailand, and France.**

Countries that did not participate directly in the war but did furnish aid were **Denmark, India, and Norway. Sweden** provided medical units**. Italy**, not a member of the

UN, provided a hospital. A total of 41 countries sent equipment and supplies.

The purpose of the Truman Doctrine of 1948 was to contain the Soviet Union and the spread of Communism. A mutual defense assistance program was given to South Korea to preserve the nation's sovereignty, but it came too little and too late.

Out of this tragedy with great sacrifice, tenacity, determination and love of their country, came South Korea's ***Miracle of the Han*** (River), which began in the middle 1980's. Their great effort allowed the country and its people to rise from the ashes of war. "***Beauty for ashes"***, (Isaiah 61-3KJV). The greatest evidence of South Korea's growing economy is the ***63 Building*** overlooking and reflecting in the Han River. The sixty-three story shiny gold building is the pride and a glowing example of the nation's success - the rise from poverty to prominence.

United States and Allied Forces made it possible for the people of South Korea to lay the foundation and build anew, a very modern nation based on democratic principles of free enterprise, free elections, self-determination, and freedom of religion.

Humor has always been a part of war for the release of tensions and pent up emotions. So it was aboard the USS Tawakoni ATF -114 and USS Castor AKS-1. The tales and antics of many crew members long gone are as fresh in my memory as if yesterday. Bear with me as I try my best to tell a few ***ending sea stories*** of young Navy men who fought for our freedom, the freedom of South Korea, and ultimately the freedom of the world. I will begin with a true tale of my good buddy from Omaha, Nebraska, whom I referred to as an *Omahuyon.*

Carson and I were up on the foc's'le talking one day as we came into port. I said, "Carson, look over yonder" at something. He said, "Yonder? You mean over there." I said, "No, I mean, over yonder." He said, "You mean, over there.

There is no such word as *yonder*." The exchange became more heated until I saw I was not going to win, and Carson's face was becoming red. I conceded the word *yonder* might not be a word, and *over there* did sound much better. My late wife, who was from Oklahoma, and I had an impasse for forty-two years over the words *pond* and *tank* that never was resolved. A pond in Oklahoma and a tank in Texas are the same – a *POND* for watering cattle.

Carson and I almost got into it again one Sunday afternoon down in the crew's compartment. There was no library or books to read on a tugboat except the Blue Jacket's Manual. Entertainment on our tug was limited to poker, dice, Monopoly, cribbage, and a record player with a few records. I had selected Artie Shaw's "Stardust" by Carmichael-Parish to play first. He had selected the obverse side, and wanted to hear, "Begin the Beguine" by Porter.

Again we bickered back and forth until we reached a compromise with the understanding that ***Stardust*** was the better of the two, and was to be played first. We were shipmates, and had he insisted stringently I would have capitulated, because he was my buddy, my very good shipmate.

Memetz was a potato peeler – *scullery worker* – who forgot to get his dirty clothes to the laundry on the designated wash day. He needed a clean pair of dungarees and had the great idea of letting his dungarees trail aft - let the ocean water do the washing. He knotted a line to his work pants and threw them over the fantail (stern). He forgot they were *washing,* and they *washed* all night. The next morning when he pulled in the line there was nothing left but the waist band and some stringed short frayed fibers. I thought, "In his forgetfulness, he lost his pants." His countenance fell. I did have a little compassion for him when I saw his bewildered look and sad eyes of dejection.

Soon after we made port in Japan nothing would do until Danford could have a tailor make him a dress uniform with wide flared bell bottoms and dragons embroidered on both the cuffs and underneath the jumper collar. I remember him saying, "I may not be regulation, but I sure am sharp." Inspection day came and here was Danford lined up at attention in his skin tight tailor made Japanese dress blues. The Captain came down the line, stopped, and said, "Unbutton your cuff. Now turn it back." There was the most beautiful, bright gold dragon stitched to the underside of the cuff. The Captain admonished the wayward sailor and said to his aide, "See that this man is in a regulation uniform before he goes ashore. And have him shine his shoes!"

Danford continued to wear his uniform ashore while in Japan, but not that day. When he was transferred he gave the uniform to me. I wore it ashore only once. The bell bottoms were too flared, the legs were too narrow, and the material did not feel as soft, warm and heavy as my regulation uniform. But I too was not very regulation, but *I sure was sharp*!

The engineering department had the propensity to raid my bread locker and take sugar and raisins, for *raisin jack,* and apples for *apple jack*, or any fruit that would make alcohol. They brewed the concoction in a water cask taken from one of the life boats.

One muggy and dreary night at sea I walked past the ladder leading down to the engine room. The sweet, pungent smell of ***apricot brandy*** wafted through the opening and quickly caught my attention. Halfway down the ladder I saw the cask with the plug out. The libation was being poured for the brave. I too was willing to try just a swig of this intriguing high alcohol content *orangey* mess. My warning to the *snipes was* to go easy on the powerful stuff, but it was not heeded. By 2300 hours the engine watch was either drunk or half-drunk, stumbling up and down the ladder. I cringed at the thought of their noise and boisterous talk attracting the attention of the engineering officer and him seeing their inebriated condition. The mid-watch relieved them early and all was well. The next morning I never saw a bunch of men so pale, sick and hungover. My problem of dried fruit or apricots being taken from the bread locker was over for the last time.

Late one night in Japan three of us engaged a bicycle petty cab to take us to the boat landing. Heavy Commissary Chief Sully from Ft. Worth, Texas needed a ride too, but all the petty cabs were taken. Sully hesitated but finally agreed with our coaxing to ride with us. As we seated ourselves, the bicycle wheels began to bend, about to collapse from the excess weight. The petty cab owner saw the pending disaster and began to berate us in loud Japanese and waved excitedly for us to all get out. A single petty cab was quickly found for Chief Sully. We reboarded our cab with laughter and mischievous grins of "well done".

I believe the closest that some members of the crew came to being caught with liquor aboard was one afternoon in San Diego. A large wooden lawn chair was spotted in the water and was being fished out by a deck hand. This was an unusual sight and attracted several onlookers. One crew member brought out a pint of whisky to share with the *salvaging party.* The bottle was being passed around when the Captain walked up. While his attention was directed to the chair, crew members lined up along the gunnel and passed the bottle behind them, one to the other, until the Captain left, none the wiser. The very comfortable *anybody's* chair added a homey touch to the fantail and was greatly enjoyed until it had to be jettisoned in Korea to make way for buoys and equipment.

Crossing the International Date Line had become routine to us but not to a new inquisitive seaman apprentice. We were due to cross the Date Line early that evening. He was instructed to show up with the boat hook, a bronze tipped 8' long pole. His duty was to keep *the dateline* out of our screw. At the appointed time he mustered on the fantail with his pole ready to protect the ship's screw from entanglement. With the word of command, "Now!", and hearty encouragement, he plunged his pole up and down, swung it back and forth, fishing the dark waters for the elusive International Date Line. The quartermaster soon determined that we had successfully crossed over the underwater hazard and with a ***well done*** the young man proudly, though a little confused, left to go stow his boat hook.

Chief Bos'n Cain was the ship's Supply Officer and always gave me a touch of home with his expertise in rolling a Bull Durham brand cigarette. Even on a windy deck, with his back to the wind he would take out his sack of tobacco, shake just the right amount into the gummed cigarette paper, roll it up tight, and with a lick and a twist at the end express a look of satisfaction. With his trusty Zippo lighter he would light his favorite smoke. There in the corner of his mouth the cigarette burned a bright red due to the wind. I marveled at the Chief Bos'n's dexterity and judgment of rolling and smoking his cigarette in the wind, I never did see a hole burned in his clothes. I had seen this *roll your own* done a thousand times back home during WWII because Lucky, Camel, Chesterfield, Kool, Old Gold, Pall Mall and the Viceroy filter tipped and r*eady roll* cigarettes were not to be had. A common sight was the pull string sacks of Bull Durham, Duke's Mixture, pouched Bugler tobacco, and cans of Prince Albert. Men would chew Brown Mule, Tinsley, Day's Work or Beech Nut chewing tobacco. Honest and Garrett dipping snuff was mostly for women in the 20's and up until the early 50's.

Because of Chief Bos'n Cain's good nature I was saved from a Captain's Mast and maybe loss of my Good Conduct Medal. I had just made Second Class Storekeeper – SK2, and was now allowed to visit the NCO – Non-Commissioned Officers club. I was aching to go ashore to celebrate my advancement with my good buddies, but I had the duty. My watch was from 2000 to 2400 hours. Alan, a quartermaster had the 0800 to 1200 hours watch. After much talk and explanation, he was confused, knew it was not quite right, but agreed to be my stand-by and take my watch, and I would take his the next morning. We were both in the duty section and I knew I could not have a stand-by in the duty section. But I had to go ashore. The NCO Club was so much nicer with waitresses and mixed drinks, even champagne. For a country boy a long way from home, cold, sparkly champagne in such a nice place, good music, a tropical setting with matching paintings on the walls was the height of luxury. I had had about all the good time I could take for one night. The next morning I was still woozy and sick of champagne and mixed drinks as I made my way to quarter deck to begin my four-hour watch. I looked up and there was the Supply Officer coming toward me in a deliberate mood. He said, "Mac, how come you went ashore last night?" I told him I had a stand-by. Without his usual grin and soft demeanor he said, "You know you can't have a stand-by from the duty section." I was about to try and explain, when he said, "Last night the Captain wanted the Plan of the Day. You, your Storekeeper Striker-trainee, and the Yeoman were all ashore and no one to type the Plan of Day." Before I could speak he said, "Don't let it happen again." I said, "Aye, aye, Sir." I felt I had betrayed his trust and caused him trouble with the Captain. I was sorry.

I left the Far East for the last time and returned to the States aboard the USS Castor AKS-1, after being gone for nearly four years. The colorful homeward bound pennant, blue and white streamers, a tribute to our service and sacrifice was flying briskly as we approached the Golden Gate Bridge. I brought up the half pint of foul tasting Japanese *Suntory Whiskey* I had been saving for the occasion.

Just as the ship went under the bridge, right there on the open deck, port side mid-ship, I broke out the bottle, cracked the seal, and grimaced a big swig of *celebration.* The bottle was passed around until empty, and *deep-sixed,* as we cleared the bridge. My eyes truly moistened and my heart was full of pride and elation. I might have doubted whether I was a man or not when I enlisted, but after months of adventure, adversity, and combat, I came to know the meaning of ***this man's Navy***.

My honorable discharge was the 26th of August, 1952 with the Presidential Election only little over two months away. On Election Day, I went down to the Cleburne Courthouse to cast my vote. There was a lady of some renown who I had known before I enlisted. She was handing out the ballots and recognized me, but had no idea. She was oblivious to the Korean War.

I walked up to the folding table all covered with printed ballots and said, "I would like to vote." She asked with what I deemed a hostile *snotty* attitude, "Are you registered?" I told her I had just returned from Korea, and was only recently discharged from the Navy. I explained in my calmest voice that I had not registered and did not know I had to register, having been overseas so long. She told me in an emphatic manner, **"You cannot vote."** Those were fighting words. I had fought for her freedom and the right to vote, and now I was being denied that right. I appealed to her better nature and judgment that if anyone should be allowed to vote it should be me. She maintained her adamant attitude. It was at that moment that I told her emphatically, **"I am going to vote or turn this table upside down in your face."** She quickly moved back from the table with an astonished look of disdain and utter surprise. Without a word she reluctantly laid a ballot and pencil on the table. I voted. Whether my vote counted or not I do not know. It might have gone in the trash, but I voted. I understand this wrong has been righted with overseas military personnel being allowed to cast absentee ballots. Yet these ballots are not counted unless the election is very close. Strange, I and thousands like me were trained in the use of hand guns and rifles, big gun and little guns to fight a foreign power to keep our freedom and the right to vote, and then come home from war, and we're told we cannot vote or have the right to own a gun - to protect ourselves from those at home who would try to take our right to vote away. Veterans have been trained in gun safety, fought, died, and were wounded for our freedom. They should be encouraged to have and have the right to *bear arms*, with no questions asked, that they might continue to protect our freedoms.

"Democracy is two wolves and a lamb voting on what to have for lunch. Liberty is a well armed lamb contesting the vote." –Benjamin Franklin

It was not so much that I could not vote, I was used to rules and regulations, but here ignorance and lack of gratitude for the sacrifice of servicemen killed and wounded, and the thousands who served that she might have the privilege to distribute ballots for the President of the United States. But I should not have been surprised. My own family's response when I walked in unannounced after my four years in the Navy was, **"Well, I see you're back."**

World War I was the war to end all wars. World War II was a ***real*** war. The United States has experienced eighty-five wars in the last 235 years. Veterans of our many limited wars in the last sixty years have come home with little notice, even been accosted and ridiculed. Those of us who have served under severe circumstances view with a bit of pity and disgust those who take freedom for granted – they, not knowing how fragile and tenuous, how quickly their freedom can be lost.

I believe my ex-Navy brother understood, but we did not talk about our wartime service. We told a few tales, some humorous sea stories. He was a little curious to where I had been, what islands I had been to, and some of what I had done - but not really, because it would have stirred up his recurring bad memories. I felt sad and sorry for my brother Everett, and two sisters, Opal and Esther. Like so many during the Korean War their world was so small; they never knew, never put forth the effort to know the Korean War was a real war. They never knew, realized or accepted the fact that I had faced immediate danger and loss of life like my older brother Dewey. It hurt then, and at times still hurts, after 60 years.

Six or seven times I have returned to South Korea, once on a Korean Government sponsored ***Revisit Program*** for veterans in 1983. We saw military personnel on the street who snapped to attention and saluted when our bus decorated with Korean characters noting we were veterans approached. Often in our hotel we heard these words, **"Thank you for my freedom."**

Today many of the Korean teachers who come to study at Oklahoma City University or University of Central Oklahoma to get their master's degree express their gratitude for having a free country and personal freedom. A look of dread crosses their face when they remember their fellow countrymen and relatives isolated in North Korea, and what they have to endure.

I was in Kona, Hawaii, volunteering at the University of the Nations a few years ago, when I met several young international campus workers – Mission Builders and DSTS students. One young educated Korean who learned I had been in the Korean War came up to me with an unappreciative attitude and with a smirk asked, **"Why did you free only half of our country? You had a powerful army, the guns and weapons, you were the richest country in the world, and you could have done it."** I was hurt. I began to explain a little, but he was not interested, a waste of time to try and talk to him right then.

A few weeks later I said to him, "Tonight I want to talk to you." He came to my apartment after dinner and we had a frank talk. I thought he would be the messenger to take back to his countrymen the reasons why all his country was not free and joined together. I had to begin with WWII. Russia had come into the war just before WWII ended.

Because Russia had contributed a little toward defeating Japan she was given the divided area north of the 38th parallel, a British idea, to repatriate all Japanese forces back to Japan. The Korean Peninsula was free from Japanese dominance and influence for the first time in thirty-five years (1910-1945). The Allies agreed that Korea would be one, and free elections would be held the following year. Russia reneged. Joseph Stalin installed guerilla commander Kim Il Sung, who had been trained in Moscow during WWII, and was now a Major in the Russian Army, was to head a puppet government. Free elections were held in the South with Sigmund (Sigman) Rhee, a graduate of George Washington University, Harvard and Princeton, elected as president.

The United States after WWII had pulled all her troops out of Korea expecting never to return. The country was left devastated after so many wars and Japanese occupation. The South Korean Army and Police Force were ill-equipped, ill-trained, with a small Navy, and ripe for invasion and takeover. Not to say that the South had not given thought of invading the North, and had sought arms from the United States, but were refused.

Kim Il Sung, asked Stalin four times if he could invade the South. Stalin finally consented, and shortly thereafter on June 25, 1950, in early morning hours, Communist forces crossed the 38th parallel. Within a week, the Northern invading army had driven to the Naktong River, near Dae-gu (Tae-gu) and Busan (Pusan) – the southern-most tip of the peninsula.

The President of the United States, Harry S. Truman, said this will not stand. The freedom of the South Korean people would not be given over to Communist expansion. Truman sent US troops from Japan and Okinawa under the United Nations mandate. A vote was brought before the UN Security Council to oppose the invasion. Russia, one of the six permanent members with veto power, was absent when the vote was taken. The UN resolution was to send troops, ships and equipment to thwart Kim Il Sung's forces. A total of sixteen United Nations joined together.

General MacArthur made a bold move, took a calculated risk, and landed an American force at Inchon, Korea in September 1950. Soon the peninsula was divided. Communist soldiers in the south were cut off, killed, captured, or in retreat. There was talk of VK Day – Victory of Korea Day, like VE and VJ Day.

But MacArthur was mistaken about the Red Chinese coming into the war. By the middle of November 1950, a huge army crossed over from Manchuria and soon had overrun US, ROK and some UN forces. An emergency evacuation had to be made at Wonsan and Hungnam on the East Sea, and Inchon on the West Sea. The Red Army pushed all the way to Seoul, the Korean Capitol. The city changed hands three times. US troops retook Seoul though seesaw battles that lasted into the summer of 1953. A ***ceasefire*** was finally agreed to – not a peace treaty.

I told him I did not hear any words of gratitude or appreciation for the thousands of men killed, in military hospitals, or at home carrying wounds of war. I suggested instead of peace demonstrations, the young people should concern themselves and find ways to thank the veterans, the United States and other countries for their freedom and prosperity. Then I asked the question, "Had you rather the US not have intervened and all of Korea be a Communist State, and you live under today's Communist Government of Il's son, Kim Jong Il?" I challenged him with these words: "We gave half of your country freedom; now it is up to you to defend it and keep it free. Or you can select to have peace at any price, become weak, and again lose your freedom, with little food, with torture and no religious liberty as before." His hesitant answer was a sheepish, "No." Then I explained the bigger picture of why his country was not all one.

Chairman, Mao Tse Tung entered the war because of MacArthur's strong language and perceived threats to cross the Yalu River. There was fear that the US and UN forces would cross into Manchuria. He felt his power and hold on China would be weakened should all of Korea and Manchuria become free with a democratic government. He had to protect himself and his regime by having Manchuria a buffer zone.

I explained China was a country of 1.3 billion people. Yes, we were strong, had many big guns, ships, planes and weaponry, but not enough to win against so great a number. We just did not have the men, bombs and ammunition to keep killing thousands of Chinese reinforcements. We fought to a standstill at the 38th parallel with us winning 500 square miles more than the Communists. A Demilitarized Zone (DMZ) was established that is 2½ miles or 4km wide, encompassing 1,500 square miles or 3,880 square kilometers with a 155 mile-long buffer zone, a No Man's Land of land mines, between North and South Korea.

I, and thousands like me, had no regrets about serving his country. Maybe it was idealism, or we fought for a great cause to stop Communism, or that someone had to do it. It was not for glory, a show of strength or conquest. What was paramount to us was the safety of our ship and crew, a strong desire to finish the job, leave the area, and an early return home. He rose to leave, paused a moment, turned and said, **"I do have gratitude, and thank you for my freedom."** A Korean businessman visiting our country and learning I had fought for his country bowed and expressed his gratitude with this poignant remark, **"Thank you for saving half my country."** The forgotten war has not been forgotten in the forgotten land that is no longer known as the Hermit Kingdom.

The southern half of Korea is free; the northern half with its capitol at Pyongyang under former dictator Kim Jong Il, now under his son, Kim Jong Un, and the Communist

Party. The country is divided for the very first time in history. But to the Koreans their country is still one, because the people are one of the most homogenous of all peoples, and reverence their country mightily. My recent visit to Seoul allowed me to observe the people, new skyscrapers dotting the skyline, super highways, a high speed rail system, the new modern airport at Inchon, a high standard of living under a democratic government, and a special sight - fully fed, healthy children playing and laughing in a modern Korea that I and all who served can be proud of.

Korean War Memorial, Washington D.C*:*

Our nation honors her sons and daughters who answered the call to defend a country they never knew and a people they never met.

In the granite memorial wall a simple message inlaid in silver reads***:***

Freedom is not free.

I am last reminded of a quote embedded in the granite floor of the U. S. Naval Academy Annapolis, Maryland, by former President John F. Kennedy, on August 1, 1963:

Any man who may be asked in this century what he did to make his life worthwhile can respond with a good deal of pride and satisfaction, "I served in the U. S. Navy."

Addendum

Confucius' Temple – Duke's wedding

The Temple last was used by "The First Family under Heaven" with a Duke's wedding in 1935. After 1949, Confucius and his teachings fell out of favor with the Communist Party even until now. Confucius' teachings are once again on the rise and accepted in modern China.

The damage by the Red Guard during the Cultural Revolution (1966-1968) which was led by Jiang Qing and the Gang of Four has mostly been repaired and restored, but as a lesser temple.

Turtle Ship

The Kobukson - Kobukseon – Kobuksun – Geobukseon Turtle Ship was designed by and for the Royal Korean Navy in the Joseon Dynasty by Korea's noted Admiral Yi Sun-sin to thwart an intimate invasion by Toyo Hideyoshi's fleet from Japan – circa 1592-1598.

Hideyoshi's plan was to take Korea, conquer China and move into India. Twice his huge naval force attempted to invade Korea only to be utterly destroyed twenty-three times by the Turtle Ship. The result was that Japan withdrew and there was a 300-year peace.

The Turtle Ships varied in size from 100-200 feet (33-37 meters) and were a ***Dreadnaught*** for their size. There were five types of retractable long and short cannons.

The bow was a ***smoke dragon*** dragon's head that generated and emitted acrid sulfuric and saltpeter smoke, at times poisonous smoke. The *fearful dragon face* had a large protruding beam to ram into the enemy ship. The sight of these low powerful ships spouting smoke and fire had a psychological warfare effect. The smoke downwind allowed for coordination, maneuverability and a surprise attack that brought fear and anguish to the Japanese soldiers and sailors. Many Turtle Ships concealed gun ports which allowed the crew to fire arrows into the ship's rigging port and starboard. Ship's complement was the Captain, 50 to 60 fighting men, and 70 oarsmen. Oarsmen were used in shifts. All oars were used for swiftness in battle and speed for ramming. Japanese ships were made of light wood for speed and troop transport. There was little protection against Korea's various sizes and modern long range cannons.

Japan's style of fighting at sea was to come alongside firing arrows with limited use of their light cannons. The thick deckboards of the Turtle Ship sustained little or no damage. The Japanese boarding party would grapple a Turtle Ship and try to overwhelm the Ship's crew with sheer numbers. The Turtle Ship had a surprise for the boarding party. The deck was covered with iron plating and very sharp retractable spikes concealed under straw or matting to puncture the feet of the enemy. Japan's two invasions and seven-year conquest of Korea are known as the **Injin War**, so named for the Japanese Injin Year. After his first massive defeat at sea, Hideyoshi's next attack was one of retaliation. Admiral Yi Sun-sin **(Samdo Sugun Tongiesa – Naval Commander** of three **Province, Duke of Loyalty and Warfare-Hwachas**) defeated and decimated Japan's Navy at the battles of **Dang Po, Dang Han Po, Yul Po, Hansan Do** and **Angol Po**, and died fighting after being wounded in the shoulder. His great effort and leadership ended the Japanese incursion. Japan's **japanocentral order of imperialism** was in direct conflict with China's tributary system.

China viewed itself as having a ***Mandate from Heaven.*** Korea was middle brother and Japan little brother. These two views made Japan and China common enemies and caused conflict over trade. Today with China's ***sleeping***

dragon of commerce awaking, it is arousing concern of all ***dragons*** of Asia, especially Japan, as seen in the world's daily news.

Mines and Torpedoes

David Bushnell first applied the name mine-***torpedo*** to an underwater powder keg with a Trigger, that was used against British ships in 1776. The first attempt failed against a copper-bottom British ship. Later, against the frigate HMS Cerberus the charge sunk a schooner anchored astern. Robert Fulton, who launched the sub Nautilus floated an explosive device called a *torpedo.* The explosive would be towed underwater beneath the enemy vessel or dragged in contact with the ship's bottom. During and until end of the Civil War a torpedo was a 35' spar with a 60 pound charge set off 6 feet below the waterline.

Most familiar today is the horned mine often shown in the movies. The mine horn contains a vial of sulfuric acid. When the metal horn breaks the acid is allowed to come in contact with a lead-acid battery which becomes energized. An electric charge then detonates the explosives.

Admiral David Farragut's famous words, **"Damm the torpedoes, full speed ahead,"** were said after the USS Tecumseh was sunk by a contact (torpedo) mine. Fear of an underwater explosion and ship sinking had halted him and the fleet until this time.

The Torpedo, Torpedo Ray – Torpedo Macneilli is a bottom dwelling fish approximately 18 inches long, and a most feared electric fish, a ray, capable of discharging a strong and often severe sudden shock. Torpedo Rays [L Torpedo-inis], from Torpere are known to be stiff, numb or torpid species of the Elasmo branch of fishes.

Dialogue in Ben Johnson's play evidences the fear of the Torpedo Ray:

Thos: *They write where one Cornelius Son hath made the Hollanders an invisible eel to swim the Haven at Dunkirk, and sink all the shipping there...*

Pennyboy: *But how's it done?*

Cymbal: *I'll show you, Sir. It is an automa, runs underwater, with snug nose, and has a nimble tail made like an augur, with which tail she wiggles betwixt the coasts of a ship and sinks it straight.*

Pennyboy*: a most brave device to murder their flat bottoms.*

The first vessel sunk by a self-propelled torpedo was the Turkish steamer, Intibah (1877). It was fired upon from a torpedo boat from the tender Velikiy Knyaz Konstantine by commanded by Stephan Osipovich Makarov – Russo-Turkish War 1877-'78. An interchangeable distinction would later make standard a different designation between the torpedo and the mine. Japan lost the battleship Hatsuse and Yashima to Russian mines laid by the Russian minelayer Amur during the Russo-Japanese War (1904) lost her battleship Petropavolvsk and fleet commander, Admiral Makaroff and most of the crew to a Japanese mine in 1904.

The 1st self-propelled mines of WWI that traveled underwater were fired by the Ottoman sub ABDULHAMID (1886) using compressed air. Soon improved versions with a heavier charge, greater stability and speeds up to 24-30 knots came to be known as the ***Devil's Device***. Mines from the famous Turkish Minelayer NUSRET (NUSRAT) of the Ottoman Empire Navy during the Gallipoli Campaign during the First World War sank HMS (Her Majesty's Ship) the battleship **Irresistible**, **HMS Ocean,** and the French battleship Bouvet in 1915, in the Dardanelles. The HMS Inflexible was badly damaged.

The mine ship NUSRET is preserved at Mersin – a province in southern Turkey. A replica can be seen at Canakkale by the shore of the narrows of the Dardanelles – along with WWI mines and types of mines.

The Russian submarine Krab was the first to be designated as a minelayer. The USS Argonaut (SS-166) became a mine-laying submarine. European ports and harbors were mined with various types of mines, and United States aircraft of WWII were the first to be designated a minelayers.

The United States dropped thousands of mines in Japanese harbors contributing to loss of ships and Japanese shipping. This action of war contributed to Japan's early surrender. Japan's mine-eradicating abilities learned by sweeping these mines from her ports after WWII was used in the waters along the Korean Peninsula to detect and destroy many Russian mines during the Korean War. Ship defensive methods against mines include degaussing, flashing, whipping and for larger ship – deperming. Many more and modern methods are deployed today to defend against mines.

Ship's Log: COMFORT STATIONS

Ship's Log of two Japanese ships – *taken from a Japanese Soldier's Diary found on Guadalcanal in WWII listing Comfort Stations.*
Lae – Second largest city in Papua New Guinea, located on Huon Gulf at mouth of Markham River – N.E. New Guinea.
Saidor –Papua New Guinea – near Mot River
Cape Gloucester – Glocschter (Tuluvu) New Britain
Biak Island, City – Kota Biak (Bosnik Beach). A small island located in Cenderawasih Bay on Northern Coast of New Guinea three islands: Biak, Supiopi and Nuemfoor (Numfor)
Morotai, Island – in Halmahera Group of Eastern Indonesian Maluku (Morty-Moluccas, Islands) – a part of Maluku Provence. Tacloban City and Luzon, Cebu and Mindanao are northerly with the largest island of Leyte being most northerly.
Lingayen Gulf (Lingayyen Gulf), Philippines. City Balikpapan located on eastern coast of the island of Borneo in east Kalimantan.
Aitap New Guinea located in N.E. New Guinea and Culebra Island.
Hollandia or Jayapura City – Paupan New City – New Guinea
Kota Baru and Sukarnopura – city in Malaysia – capital Kelantan

Comfort Women of WWII: *Countries-Islands-Army Cargo Ships*

Kaiman Island, Japan
Malaya Peninsula
Bay of Siam, Thailand
Kozman or Kozan, Japan
Shinabunsol, Japan

Shinabunso, Japan
Kote, Japan: Chinese People
Yancho – Arono Strait – Japan
Lalay – Thomas Bay – Philippines
Malaya – Shingoro – Malaysia
Saigon, South Vietnam
Indo China Sea – Thailand, Vietnam, Cambodia (Indo China)
Celebes, Indonesia-Sulawesi, Is
Macasar or Makassar Strait, Indonesia
Nagasaki, Japan
Hiroshima, Japan – Dad's home – a few hours by railway

Ship name(s): Ryoyo Maru or Ryiokoama Maru

Davo or Davao, Philippines – 0020' N Lat., 144 or 14 degrees 17' W Longitude and 45' S Latitude, 147 degrees 50 minutes E. Longitude
Pala or Palao, Philippines: Consoling Women
Davola – Philippines – Mindanao
Rafael, New Britton – Port Moresby: Consoling Girls – Army and Navy
New Guinea – Paw Paw – Buna: Shintaisan Barracks Ciruwa Malaysia
Ujina – Yokosuka, Japan
Hiroshima: Niroshima Camp
Ship Kodogama Maru: Consoling Women sent ashore
Singapore – Malaya Peninsula: Women sent ashore
Sumatra – Nagang Indonesia
Java – Surabaya Indonesia
Palau – Konor Pacific Ocean
Pattani – Thailand or Malay Peninsula
Port Nia: Japanese –Thailand
Port of Kotoo, Kuala Lumpur, Malaysia
Yellow Sea
Hiroshima, Japan

Taiwan
Rabaul East New Britain
Comfort Women aboard ship – July 8th – Palao: Women sent ashore
Consoling Stations: Army and Navy – August 6th
September 15th: Women on Ship
September 21st: Access to Consoling Group

QUOTES – MOTTOES – MEMORIALS

"I have not begun to fight." John Paul Jones, September 23, 1779

"All that is necessary for the triumph of evil is for good men to do nothing." Edmund Burk

"Uncommon valor was a common virtue." Tribute by Admirable Chester Nimitz.

"The safest place in Korea was right behind a platoon of marines and Lord how they could fight." Maj. Gen. Frank Love – U.S. Army

"Panic sweeps my men when they are facing American Marines." Captured North Korean Major.

"If we allow the U.S. to occupy all of Korea – we must be prepared for the U.S. to declare war with China." Chairman Mao – Mao Tse-tung (Mao Zedong).

"We have now done so much for so long with so little, we are now capable of doing anything with nothing." Source unknown

"A ship is called a she because it costs so much to keep her in paint and powder." Fleet Admiral Chester Nimitz

"Our nation honors her sons and daughters who answered the call to defend a country they never knew and a people they never met." -Unknown

"In a granite wall a simple message inlaid in silver, "Freedom is not free" Korean War Memorial, Washington, DC

"To the strong and ready valor of these men of the United States who in the Navy, the Merchant Marine and other paths of Activity upon the waters of the world have given life and still offer it in the performance of the heroic deeds this monument is dedicated by a grateful people."

"War is an ugly thing, but not the ugliest of things: the decayed and degraded state of moral and patriotic feeling which is much worse a man who has nothing for which he is willing to fight: nothing he cares for more about than his own personal safety; is a miserable creature who has no chance of being free, unless made and kept so by the exertions of better men than himself." Author Unknown
Navy-Marine Memorial, Columbia Island, Washington, D.C.

Korean War Veterans Associations Mission:

Defend our nation
Care for our veterans
Perpetuate our legacy
Remember our missing and fallen
Maintain our memorial
Support a free Korea

Navy Hymn

Eternal Father, strong to save,
Whose arm has bound the restless wave,
Who bids the mighty ocean deep
Its own appointed limits keep;
O hear us when we cry to thee, for those in peril on the sea.

"Navy Hymn" –
Eternal Father Strong to Save

Memorial to the United States Marines and Honor to all forces who served in the Korea War: Navy, Marines, Coast Guard, Seabees, Air Force, UDT and Special Forces.

"In honor and memory of the men of the United States Marine Corps who have given their lives to their country since 10 November 1775." The Marine Corps War Memorial – near Rosslyn, Virginia

"They died that their country might live."
Peace Monument – Washington D.C.

Motto: "Peace through strength." – Ronald Reagan

Motto: "Can Do" – United States Seabees WWII and Korea

Motto: "In peace and war." – US Merchant Marine

Korean War Music in Japan and Korea 1950-1953

It's Magic – Doris Day
I Can Dream, Can't I – The Andrews Sisters
"China Night" – **Shnnoyoru or Shin Noyo Ru,** by S. Yamaguchi
"Arirang" – Korean Folk Song – Eastern Love Song
"Arirang" was made the official marching song of the US Army's 7th Division in Korea as of May 1956, in recognition of the Division's service in the Korean War. The "New Arirang March", an American arrangement later became the Division's official song.

ALLIANCES:

WW I The Great War: (1914-1918) – Allies (Triple Entante): United States, Britain, France (Japan and other countries)
Central Powers: German Empire, Austro-Hungarian Empire, Ottoman Empire and The Kingdom of Bulgaria

WWII (1939-1945)
Allies: United States, Britain, France and Russia

Axis Powers – Germany, Italy and Japan

Korean War Alliances: (1950-1953) United Nations: United States, Australia, Belgium, Canada, Colombia, Ethiopia, France, Greece, Luxembourg, Netherlands, New Zealand, Philippines, South Africa, Thailand, Turkey, Britain, South Korea

Nations that Assisted: Denmark, Italy, Norway, India, Sweden

SOURCES AND REFERENCES

Fact Sheet – Naval Operations during the Korean War
Navy "Primary Roll – Help UNC United Nations Command to avert disaster in the Far East."
7th Fleet helped President Harry S. Truman oppose the Communist challenge in Asia.
U.S. Naval Operations in the Korean War – The Battle Turns at Inchon; Blockading the Coastlines – www.korea50.army.mil/history/factssheets/navy.html
Your Navy – Navy training courses edition of 1946, U. S. Government Printing Office, Washington D.C. 1946
DANFS-USS Bushnell AS-2 Submarine tender
Logistics and Support Activities in Japan 1951-1953 – Ships in Japanese Waters – Groups of Ships.
The Sea War in Korea US Naval Institute, 1957 Chartered Merchantmen
Military Sea transport Service and Merchant Ship, Participation in Hungnam Korea Redeployment.
History of United states naval Operations. James A. Field, Jr. www.history.navymil/books/field/abbrev.htm
The Sinking of the USS Sarsi, The Sea War in Korea – Sailors and Naval Combating 20th Century at War at Sea. Ronald H. Spector, Pg. 325, Penquin Books
Sarsi. www.texramp.net/~n5kgn/hist.html
Pirate. www.hazegray.org/danfs/mine/am275htm
Partridge. www.koreanwar.org/htm/units/navy/uss_partridge.htm
Pledge. www.hazegray.org/danfs/mine/am277.htm
Revised U.S. Military Korean War Statistics, The Commemorator, Spring 2001
Korean War-Wonsan Mine Clearance, October –November 1950. Photo #:80-G-423625. Opening of Wonsan, October 1950
Veterans of the Korean War P 347.7 (KW)

WWW.Haze Gray.Org/DANFS – Dictionary of American Fighting Ships
The World Book Encyclopedia Vol. 11, J-K, c1978, page 303
U.S. Navy Ships: Sunk and Damaged in Action during the Korean Conflict
WWW.History.Navy Mil
Haze Gray: DANFS Ship Description
Hyperwar – NavSource Photos
Naval Historical Center
Log Book of the USS Tawakoni-AFT-114
Personal Diary 1948-1952
War Diaries of Rock (ROK) Navy Amphibious Group 3
National Archives The Navy Historical Center
Japan's value in the Korean War – Issues Surrounding the Dispatch of Mine Sweepers. Dr. Yoichi Hirama (Radm.Ret.) Professor of naval History National Defense AOL Sea Search.com
The Korean War, June 1950 – July27, 1953 – Introductory Overview and Special images.
On Line Library of Selected Images: Events – The Korean War, 1950-1953, The Hungnam Evacuation, December 1950
www.History,Nav.Mil/Photos/Events/KoreaWar/50CH
www.homeofheros.comwallofhonor/korean1871/3htm-67k
Maritime Digital Archive
Maritime Digital Encyclopedia.
Your Navy Pages 16-17, 129, 229. Navy Training Courses, Edition of 1946, United States Printing Office, Washington, 1946
Your Navy British Small Wars
Mine Sweeping in Wonsan Harbor, 1950-1952 by Burle Gilliland Captain Navy Reserve, Retired.
www.britainssmallwars.com/korea/sea.hotml-waratsea
United Nations Command – www.korea.army.mil/unc.htm
Dictionary of Naval Fighting Ships Vol 1, Part A, NavHist.

United States Department of Commerce – Maritime Administration 193 @ Hungnam-Chosen Peninsula.
“Military Sea Transportation Service in Korean War”: The first Shots – by: Salvatore R. Merrcogliana
Korea Service 1950-1953 – www.history.navy.mil/faqas-23htm
DANSF – Mineron 3.
The Sea War in North Korea
America War in Korea
History of Mine Warfare Vessel Classifications.
Members.aol.com/_ht_a/fredricxxx/history.htm
U. S. Navy Ships: Sunk or Damaged in Action during the Korean Conflict. www.korean-war.com/USNavy/usnavyshipssunk.html
The Naval Historical Center, Washington, D.C., korea50.army.mil/history/factsheet/Navy/html
The Korean War, June 50 – July 53 – Introductory Overview and Special Image Section
A GI’s Combat Chronology 1950-53
Mine Warfare Korea
Mine War news Vol. 13, #3
Scramble in Mine Warfare
The Sea War in Korea
1950: The Baptism by Fire
Aircraft Carriers of United States.com
Mine Warfare WW II
NAFTS.Org –National Association of Fleet Tug Sailors.
Navy Auxiliary Fleet Tug Ships
Towline@NAFTS.com
Janes Fighting Ships
Russian Mines, Magnetic-Contact
Mine Warfare during the Korean War and Its Aftermath, 1950-1961
Korean War [article]-World Book On Line Americas Edition

"Korean War" World Book On Line.www.AOLSAVC. WorldBook.AOL.Com/wBOL, WB Page NA/AR/Co 304360, December 19, 2001
Tank Landing Ship – History Index
Decater, Jr. Captain – James, The Remains of War – Jin Taro Ishida, The Baron Lion Press
History of U.S. Naval Operations: Korea by: James a. Field, Jr., Chap 10: The Second Six Months.
Members.aol.com/-ht-a/fredR/cxxx/history.htm.history of Mine warefare-Adm. Sherman
Korean American Amity and Commerce Treaty
Ocean Highways 7/a0th of Troop Movement By Water – International Archives Vol LC 15.
www.globalsecurity/org/militaryu/systems/ship/auxiliary/htm
World Book Encyclopedia Vol. 11, J-K, C1978, pp. 303s and 82h.
Online Library of Selected Images –Picture Data. Photo#: 80-G-423913. Hungnam Evacuations, December 1950
Enid Victory – MATS – Military Sea TransService& Merchant Ships Participating in Hungnam, Korea Redeployment
Military Sea Transport Service – MATS
7th Fleet "Best of The Net". Underway Replenishment Transport Ship Log.
www.history.mil/photos/events/koreanwar/log-sup/log-sup.html
NRCC Fleet Support Navy Ships
Floating Supply Depot for Fleet-UnRep-underway Replenishment
Yoichi Hirama on Japan's Value in the Korean War Issues Surrounding the Dispatch of Mine Sweepers – www.glocometorJP/OKAZA/INST/OZAKI/Eng.html
Navy Art Collection Branch – Remembering the forgotten War: Korea, 1950-1953 - www.history.navy.mil/branches/org6-7.htm
www.JanesOceania.com/MicronesiaYap

www.geo.kya.com;travelimages/midronesia.htm
www.coinmail.com/csma/art012.htm
www.money.org
The isle of stone money. Complied by Tim Engle and Francine Orr – Google
www.FM/yap.htm (Jeannie Wilson)
www.kcstrar.com/projects/micronesia
www.yapdiver.com/history-of-yaphtm
Webster's New Collegiate Dictionary, Second Edition. G & C Merriam Company Publishers. Springfield, Mass USA 1951
www.diskshovel.com/commanchetwo.html
www.Britians-smallwars.com/carriers/triumph.html
www.History-Navy.mil/photw/events/kowar/unroks.htm
www.c.s.u.of.edu/~midlink/new.bald.home.html
www.DickShovel.com/commanchetwo.htm
The Commentator, spring 2001, pg. 5 and 6
Homeofheros.com/wallofhonor18711/3-assault.htm
http://members.tripod.com/beastroker/mckeansubhistory2.htm
www.texasescapes.com/CentralTexasTownsNorth/CleburneTexas/...
www.ok.state.edu/osuorgs/ksa/021KKorea/Historyhtm
www.campus.northpark.edu/history/webchon/china.html
http://members.AOL.com/USregistry/allwars.htm
http://en.wikipedia.org/wiki/Korean_War_Veterans_Memorial
www.koreanhistoryproject.org/ket/C12/E1203htm-31k
www.umich.edu/-urecord/9899/feb22_9m/imjinhtm
Imjin War diaries are memorial of invasion for Koreans
Gendercide Watch – Case Study The Nanjing Massacre 1937-1938, pg 284
www.gendercide.org/case_Nanking.html-28K
US Forces Information MASTER Kong by Fergus M. Bordewich
Book – "Travelers" Tales of China pp81-82 & 86

Distributed by Publishers Group West
Edited by Sean O'Rielly and James O'Rielly
Cold War International History Project
Http://en.wikipedia.org/wiki/marchlstmovement
Dictionary of Indian Tribes of the Americas, Vol III, Second Copyright 1965, American Indian Publishers, Inc, 177 F Riverside Ave, New Port Beach, CA 92663 Pg 952.
INDIANS OF OKLAHONA, Oklahoma, Tribes A-Z, pp 311-313, 315, Reservations in Oklahoma Treaty 1837-1856, Somerset Publishing, Inc. St. Clair Shores, Michigan 48080
Encyclopedia of Native American Tribes/Carl Waldman; Illustrations by Molly Brum -
Rev. Ed. 1999, pp 261 & 262, Check Mark Books, An Imprint on Facts on File, Inc. 11 Penn Plaza, New York, NY 10001
Dictionary of Indian tribes of the Americas, American Indian Publishers Inc. Pg. 52 Wichita Vol.III
Caddoan Indians XIII Wichita, Waco, Kechai, University of Oklahoma Press
University of Oklahoma Press
CADDOAN INDIANS X111 Whichita, Waco & Kechai
INDIANS PLACES – NAMES BY John Rydjord pg. 158 Oklahoma Press, Oklahoma City, OK
Red River –Wichita Confederacy Whichita Name frequently used for the Tawakonies or Tawakonis
OKLAHOMA TRIBES A TO Z pp.311, 312,313,314,315 Reservation in Oklahoma 1837 & 1856
Sand Hills – Wichita Group of the Middle Brazos & Trinity Rivers in Texas
Waco & Palestine Wichita Dialect
Tawakoni means "River Bend among Red" ("River Bend among Men") Sand Hills+ Wichita Group–Middle Brazos & Trinity Rivers in Texas Wichita Dialect
DICTIONARY OF INDIAN TRIBES OF THE AMERICAS American Indian Publishers, Inc. Pg. 52 Wichita Vol. III

Nebraska – (Arkansas River into Kansas and along Red River to Brazos
Tawakoni + Pre-eminent, "Wichita, Waco, Tawakoni & Kichai – Applied name "tattooed Faces", Tattooed Pawanees or Painted People pp l66 & 167
Encyclopedia of Native American tribes/Carl Waldman; Illustrations by Molly Braum –Rev. Ed.1999 PP. 261 & 262
Check Mark Books
An imprint of Facts on File, Inc. 11 Penn Plaza, New York, NY 10001
Tawakoni known as Plains Indians – Sometimes Prairie Indians.
Conical grass houses covered with dry material. Circle pg. 261
Hold title to small tract of land in OK, near Wichita Mountain – Ft Sill l850
Celebrations at Anadarko and Pawnee, OK
INDIANS OF OKLAHONA 1999
Somerest Publishers, Inc. P>O> Box 160, St Clair Shores, Mich 48080
Oklahoma Tribes A to Z PP. 311, 312, 313, 15.
Reservations l837 & 1856
Middle of l8th & 19th century – Canadian River, OK 1719
Dictionary of Indian Tribes of the Americans Vol. III, Second Copy6right 1965
American Indian Publishers, Inc pg 952
177 F Riverside Ave, Newport Beach, CA 92663
Name applied: Tattooed faces, tattooed Pawnees or painted people pp 166 & 167
Witchita Tribe refer to themselves as Kitikiti'shor or Kirikirish+group-Caddoian Language. Wichita – pre-eminent or paramount among men.
Reside in Southern Plains – 1855-1859 Tawakoni on Resv. On Brazos in TXTribes of Witchita Confederacy – Wichita, Iscani, Taovayas, Tawakoni and Waco

Encounter Coronado in 1541 – did not like Spaniards
Friendly with France.
Pani Pique – (Fr.) Tattooed Pawanee Yr. 1541, Pique (Fr.) Pricked
The Korean War At Sixty – by William Stueck – The American Legion Magazine
MASTER KONG by Fergus M. Bordewich Book – Travelers' Tales CHINA pp81-82 & 86. Distributed by: Publishers Group West. Edited by Sean O'Reilly, and James O' Reilly and Larry Habeggar
The American Legion Magazine June 2010
www.vfw.org
The Bulletin – The Official Newsletter of Oklahoma Chapter #89 – Korean War Veterans Association – Issue #02-10, 15 April 2010
Operation Keelhaul – Wikipedia
Lake Tawakoni – Trails.com
www.okazaki-inst.jp/hinep.hirama
Korean War US Pacific Fleet Operations. Commander US Pacific Fleet Evacuation reports
Japanese-Invasion-of~Korea-1592-1598 Overview
www.longsentryi.kcom/articles/TTT/Japanese=wii-motor-vehicles-truck.htm
http://11F.Rumi.TheCarl.ounge.net/zerothreaded.?1D2148046
HistoryNavy.milKoreaServiceMedalinCombatZone
Itcamebooks/Hermansen/51htm.43K
The first Battle of WWII
Cold Ware International History Project
Science New on Line
Discovery Magazine 1994
Naval Mine – Wikipedia, the Free encyclopedia – En.wikipedia.org/wiki/naval-mine
www.google.com/search?hl
http.//en.wikipedia.org/wiki/Mersin-Province
General O. P. Smith Letter, dated Dec. 19, 1950

http.//enwikipedia.org/wiki/anabasis-(Xenophon)
www.marzone.com/dog2=7hist-1'.htm
Minesweepership
http.//en.wikipedia.org/wiki/Minsweper_%28ship$%29
http.//en/Wikipedia.org/wili/istMarinediv(United States)
www.mike.com/marinecorpskorea/marines.htm
Brief History of the Marine Corps during the Korean War
www.times.org/2007/1/cp.history/8pdf
Gen. Ward and Chennault & China Post 1, A Pictorial History of China Post 1
www.sourceserver12com/pipermail/koreaweb.ws/1990september/001220.htm
Wikipedia.org/Davy-Jones-Locker/History
World of Quotes - www.worldofquotes.come/author/Navy-quotes/1index/html
H-1 Helicopter Squadron
Korean War UIS Pacific Operations – Commander US Pacific fleet Interim
Evacuation Reports
Korean War Veterans Association: Music you will remember

Made in the USA
San Bernardino, CA
26 April 2014